FRUITS & NUTS

Design and Typesetting: Alice Leroy
Editorial Collaboration: Estérelle Payany

Project Coordinator, FERRANDI Paris: Audrey Janet
Chefs, FERRANDI Paris: Marc Alès (Meilleur Ouvrier de France 2000),
Georges Benard, and Carlos Cerqueira
Students, FERRANDI Paris: Noura Abou-Zeid, Laëtitia Collardey,
Amine El Makoudi, Liangya Lin, Margot Masson, Laurine Petiteau,
and Zihan Zeng

Editor: Clélia Ozier-Lafontaine

English Edition
Editorial Director: Kate Mascaro
Editor: Helen Adedotun
Translation from the French: Ansley Evans
Copyediting: Wendy Sweetser
Proofreading: Nicole Foster
Indexing: JMS/Chris Bell

Production: Christelle Lemonnier
Color Separation: IGS-CP L'Isle d'Espagnac
Printed in Slovenia by Florjancic

Simultaneously published in French as
Fruits: Recettes et Techniques d'une École d'Excellence
© Flammarion, S.A., Paris, 2021

English-language edition
© Flammarion, S.A., Paris, 2021

21 22 23 3 2 1
ISBN: 978-2-08-024852-7
Legal Deposit: 10/2021

FERRANDI
PARIS

FRUITS & NUTS

RECIPES AND TECHNIQUES FROM
THE FERRANDI SCHOOL OF CULINARY ARTS

Photography by Rina Nurra

Flammarion

PREFACE

For over one hundred years, **FERRANDI Paris** has taught all of the culinary disciplines to students from around the world. After our three previous books published by Flammarion—a comprehensive guide to the art of French pâtisserie, as well as volumes focused on chocolate making and cooking with vegetables—it is time to explore the infinite variety of fruits and nuts, and discover how they can be used in both sweet and savory dishes.

Orchards, groves, and plantations around the globe produce a vast range of fruits and nuts—from apples, pears, and strawberries, to kiwifruits, lychees, and tamarillos—with an array of shapes, tastes, and delicious aromas. Synonymous with pleasure since the Middle Ages, fruits not only lend their unique flavors to memorable desserts, but they also enhance numerous savory dishes with their contrasting notes. Thanks to this incredible diversity, fruits and nuts constitute an infinite source of inspiration for chefs and pâtissiers.

Both traditional skills and creative innovation lie at the heart of **FERRANDI Paris's** teaching philosophy. We maintain a balance between the two through strong ties to the professional world, making our school a leading institution in this field. That is why this book not only provides delicious recipes in which fruits and nuts are given pride of place, but also demonstrates fundamental techniques and shares expert advice. Anyone who wishes to explore the inspiring world of fruits, whether it be at home or in a professional kitchen, will find this book invaluable.

I extend my warmest thanks to those members of **FERRANDI Paris** who have made this volume a reality, particularly Audrey Janet, who coordinated the project, as well as Marc Alès (Meilleur Ouvrier de France 2000), Georges Benard, and Carlos Cerqueira, pâtissiers at the school, who generously shared their expertise and adeptly combined technical skills and creativity to demonstrate the rich culinary potential of the orchard world. The recipes for your delectation in this book are truly the fruits of their labor.

Bruno de Monte
Director of FERRANDI Paris

CONTENTS

INTRODUCTION

A Portrait of **FERRANDI Paris**

In over one hundred years of history, **FERRANDI Paris** has earned an international reputation as one of the premier culinary and hospitality schools in France. Since its inception, the school—hailed "the Harvard of gastronomy" by the press—has trained generations of groundbreaking chefs and entrepreneurs who have left their mark in the industry around the world. Whether at its historic campus in the Saint-Germain-des-Prés neighborhood in Paris, its campus in Bordeaux, or its soon-to-open sites in Rennes or Dijon, this institution is dedicated to world-class teaching with the aim of training future leaders in the culinary and pastry arts, hotel and restaurant management, and hospitality entrepreneurship.

Founded in 1920 by the Paris Île-de-France Regional Chamber of Commerce and Industry, **FERRANDI Paris** is the only school in France to offer the full range of degree and certification programs in the culinary and hospitality arts, from vocational training to the master's degree level, in addition to international programs. The school takes pride in its 98 percent exam pass rate, which is the highest in France for degrees and certifications in the sector. No matter the level, a **FERRANDI Paris** education is rigorous and combines mastering the basics with an emphasis on innovation, management and entrepreneurial skills, and hands-on experience in a professional environment.

Strong Ties to the Professional World

A space for discovery, inspiration, and exchange—where the culinary arts mingle with science, technology, and innovation—**FERRANDI Paris** brings together the biggest names in the sector to discuss and shape the future of the hospitality industry and push the

boundaries of culinary creativity. The school trains 2,200 apprentices and students each year, in addition to three hundred international students of over thirty nationalities and two thousand adults who come to the school to perfect their skills or change careers. The hundred instructors at the school are all highly qualified: several have received prominent culinary awards and distinctions, such as the "Meilleurs Ouvriers de France" title (Best Craftsmen in France), and all have at least ten years of work experience in the culinary field in prestigious establishments in France and abroad. To give students maximum opportunities and the chance to connect with other fields and the greater global community, the school has formed collaborative partnerships with several other institutions. In France, partner schools include the

ESCP Europe Business School, AgroParis Tech, and the Institut Français de la Mode; abroad, the school collaborates with Johnson and Wales University in the United States, the ITHQ tourism and hotel management school in Canada, the Hong Kong Polytechnic University, and the Institute for Tourism Studies in China, among others. Since theory and practice go hand in hand, and because **FERRANDI Paris** strives for excellence in teaching, students also have the chance to participate in a number of official events through partnerships with several chief culinary associations in France, including Maîtres Cuisiniers de France, Société des Meilleurs Ouvriers de France, Euro-Toques, and more. In addition, the school offers numerous prestigious professional competitions and prizes, giving students many opportunities to demonstrate their skills and knowledge. A dedicated ambassador of French culture, **FERRANDI Paris** draws students from around the world every year and is a member of the French Interministerial Tourism Council; the Strategic Committee of Atout France (the French tourism development agency); and the Conférence des Formations d'Excellence au Tourisme (CFET), a group of institutions in France offering top-quality training in tourism-related fields.

Extensive Savoir Faire

FERRANDI Paris's expertise, combining practice and close collaboration with professionals in the field, has been shared in three previous volumes—one devoted to French pâtisserie, another to the specialized art of chocolate making, and a third to the diverse world of vegetables—intended for both professional chefs and amateur cooks. Following the success of these three books—*Pâtisserie* received a Gourmand World Cookbook award—**FERRANDI Paris** has now turned its attention to fruits and nuts.

Fruits and Nuts—An Inspiring World of Flavors

With an immeasurable variety of shapes, colors, and flavors, fruits—whether grown on home soil (apples, pears, or strawberries) or further afield (bananas or pineapples)—offer a veritable feast for the senses. They provide an infinite palette of tastes and textures, as evidenced in time-honored preparations such as jams, tarts, and cakes, as well as in new recipes inspired by dishes from around the world, such as mochi, granitas, and pavlovas. In this book, the **FERRANDI Paris** chefs share their inspiration and invite you to explore the incredible culinary possibilities of fruits and nuts in recipes that are guaranteed to surprise and delight in equal measure.

FRUITS AND NUTS: THE ESSENTIALS

What is a fruit?

Unlike the word "vegetable," the word "fruit" is a technical botanical term. Scientifically speaking, a fruit is an organ in flowering plants that develops from the ovary after the ovules have been fertilized and turn into seeds. Fruits serve to spread the seeds or attract seed dispersers, and they have evolved to appeal to animal senses with traits like bright colors and sweetness. In the kitchen, this sweetness is the main defining characteristic of the edible parts of plants that we call fruits. Fruits can take many forms, including drupes (mangos, cherries, peaches, etc.); berries (such as blueberries, grapes, tomatoes, and even avocados); pomes (apples, pears, quince, etc.); pods (peas, legumes, peanuts); capsules; and achenes. Botanical fruits are not always considered fruits from a culinary standpoint: the real "fruits" on strawberries, for instance, are the many tiny seeds covering the plump flesh that we eat. Certain plant parts that we consider to be vegetables are technically fruits, such as tomatoes, zucchini, and squash, while some plants that we treat as fruits are actually vegetables, such as rhubarb, which is a leaf stalk. There are also plenty of exceptions to the rule that vegetables are for savory dishes and fruits for sweet ones: melon can be served as a starter or dessert, while citrus stars in a number of sweet-savory salads and dishes like duck à l'orange. Botanical and culinary perspectives are not always the same. In this book, we explore fruits from a culinary point of view.

Different types of fruits

Fruits are usually classified according to their appearance and texture. This makes it possible to group them together by how they are used, which makes most sense in the kitchen. In this book, fruits have been classified into the following categories: citrus fruits (oranges, lemons, grapefruit, etc.); stone fruits (cherries, plums, peaches, etc.); seed-containing fruits (apples, quinces, pears, grapes, etc.); berries and rhubarb (strawberries, blackberries, rhubarb, which is traditionally paired with berries, etc.); tropical fruits (pineapples, mangos, bananas, etc.); and nuts and dried fruits (pistachios, hazelnuts, dried cranberries, dried figs, etc.). Alternatively, they could have been classified according to their composition, such as fruits with a high water content (grapes, peaches, melons, pears, etc.); fruits rich in fats (coconuts, almonds, etc.); or pectin-rich fruits (quinces, citrus fruits, strawberries, etc.). Some fruits belong in multiple categories, such as the kiwifruit. Classified as a seed-containing fruit in this book, the kiwifruit is, botanically speaking, a berry but is also often grouped together with tropical fruits.

Different farming and gardening methods

Organic or conventional? Integrated, permaculture, or intensive? In greenhouses or open fields? There are many ways to grow fruits and there is much debate as to the best way to feed the planet. For cooks and pastry chefs, the most important factors to consider are:

• **Seasonality:** Fruits are at their most flavorful when they are in season and do not require heating or artificial ripening, which can be energy intensive.

• **Freshness:** Buying locally produced vegetables that have traveled as short a distance as possible is the easiest way to guarantee freshness. Depending on where you live, minimal transport can be more difficult to guarantee for tropical fruits.

• **Flavor:** Flavor will depend on the variety and can vary according to how the fruit is grown. As a general rule, fruits that are harvested ripe and in season will taste the best.

• **The root-to-stem potential:** So that fruits can be used in their entirety, including peel, cores, and other less "noble" parts, it is preferable to use produce from organic or integrated producers. Ensure that they are thoroughly washed.

Selecting fruits at their best

As a general rule, the fresher the fruit, the better it will taste. Signs of freshness include a vibrant color, no blemishes, and a texture that is neither too firm nor too soft. Some varieties continue to ripen after they have been picked (see below), so keep an eye on them to enjoy them as soon as they have reached their peak. Shininess and luster are not synonymous with freshness: when plums and grapes are covered with a thin, powdery film, known as "bloom," it is an indication they have been picked recently. Nuts keep longer in their shells, which protect them from turning rancid. Ground, sliced, chopped, or slivered nuts such as hazelnuts and almonds keep for less time and are best purchased vacuum-sealed and recently processed.

Preparation

It is essential to wash and dry fruits thoroughly to remove dirt and any pesticide residues or surface bacteria. To limit vitamin loss and prevent waterlogging, avoid soaking fruits in water for long periods of time. Particularly fragile fruits such as berries and hydroponically grown varieties only need to be gently cleaned with a damp cloth or a soft-bristled brush. Peeled and cut fruits should be kept in the refrigerator and consumed quickly to avoid nutrient loss and discoloration. **Note:** many fruits (such as apples, bananas, peaches, pears, and apricots) turn brown quickly once they have been peeled and cut. To avoid this natural oxidation process, it is best to prepare these fruits just prior to using, to coat them with lemon juice (or vinegar or another citrus juice, depending on the recipe), or to

poach them in simple syrup. Cutting fruits into equal-sized pieces (see cutting techniques pp. 52–70) allows for even cooking, but keep in mind that smaller or thinner cuts expose fruits to more air, resulting in greater vitamin and mineral loss.

Cooking

Although the vast majority of fruits can be eaten both raw and cooked, some tough-fleshed fruits such as quinces must be cooked to make them more palatable. In the case of fruits such as peaches, apricots, apples, and pears, certain varieties have a better flavor and firmer texture that make them more suited to cooking or preservation methods such as canning or candying. Long cooking times diminish the nutritional value of fruits, which lose some of their vitamins as they cook. Short cooking times are best to preserve their flavor and nutritional value. Poaching, roasting, candying, and stewing, along with other techniques, are all explained in this book (see cooking techniques pp. 74–122).

Zero waste

Respecting our fruits means using every part of them rather than throwing the trimmings away. Although we tend to eat only certain parts of a fruit, what is left can be used advantageously in other recipes.

• **Apples and pears:** Cores and peel can be turned into a jelly that is perfect for glazing fruit tarts.
• **Apricots:** Break the pits open to remove the slightly bitter almond-like kernels inside, as these can be eaten in moderation. The kernels contain a small amount of amygdalin, which our metabolism converts into hydrocyanic acid, also known as the dangerous poison cyanide. However, an adult would need to consume at least thirty of these kernels in one hour to become intoxicated, so the European Food Safety Authority recommends that adults only consume three apricot kernels at a time and children only one half-kernel at a time. Besides eating them on their own, apricot kernels can also be used for flavor: slip a few into apricot jam or compote, use a small amount in cookies calling for almonds, such as financiers or amaretti, or infuse them in cream for making panna cotta or ice cream with mild bitter almond notes.
• **Strawberries:** The green stem and leafy crown tend to get thrown away, which is a shame. If they are organic, you can use them to make refreshing strawberry-flavored water. Place the stems and crowns in cold water and let infuse for 24 hours in the refrigerator, then strain and serve well chilled.

• **Mangos:** Mango flesh clings to the pit, so a little fruit always remains. The pits can be left to infuse in warm cream to make panna cotta or whipped cream with a hint of mango flavor.

• **Pineapples:** The thoroughly cleaned skin of organically produced pineapples can be used to flavor a simple syrup. Heat ½ cup (3½ oz./100 g) sugar and 1 cup (250 ml) water in a saucepan until the sugar dissolves. Add the peel of 1 pineapple and bring to a simmer. Let simmer for 10 minutes, then strain through a fine-mesh sieve, pressing down on the pineapple peel to extract maximum flavor. Store in a sealed jar in the refrigerator.

• **Citrus fruits:** All citrus zests can be candied, dried, or ground into fragrant powders.

Fruits that are less attractive or a little past their prime can be transformed into compote, roasted in the oven, or used in smoothies or coulis. Finally, any fruit trimmings you cannot use can be composted, with the exception of citrus scraps due to their acidity.

Storing fresh fruits

All fruits are made up of living cells and must be stored properly to keep them fresh for as long as possible. Temperature has a significant impact on storage time, and some fruits are more fragile than others. Apples and citrus fruits keep for a long time at cool room temperature, while berries have a shorter life and need to be stored in the refrigerator.

Climacteric and non-climacteric fruits

Fruits that can be picked green and continue to ripen at room temperature are known as climacteric fruits. This category includes apricots, avocados, bananas, quinces, figs, passion fruit, guavas, kiwifruits, mangos, peaches, nectarines, apples, pears, plums, and tomatoes. Climacteric fruits emit ethylene, a colorless, odorless gas that plays a key role in the ripening process. In contrast, other fruits (i.e., non-climacteric) must be picked ripe, such as citrus fruits and berries. These fruits are sensitive to ethylene and they spoil more quickly. Conclusion: do not mix bananas, apples, and oranges in your fruit bowl, or the oranges will quickly soften or even turn moldy. By keeping non-climacteric fruits separate, you can keep them fresh for longer. You can also take advantage of climacteric fruits to speed up the ripening process of other climacteric fruits: place the fruit you would like to ripen, such as an avocado, in a paper bag with a high ethylene-producing fruit like a banana or apple. When your fruit is just ripe (tender to the touch and fragrant),

store it in the refrigerator and use it quickly. To enjoy the full range of flavors and aromas, it is best to remove the fruit from the refrigerator 1 hour before serving it. Once fruits are cut, they begin to brown and lose vitamins, so keep them in the refrigerator in an airtight container for a maximum of 24 hours; to limit browning, coat the fruit with a little lemon juice. Nuts and dried fruits are best kept in airtight containers in a cool, dry place away from direct light, such as a dark cupboard. Once the original packaging has been opened, ground almonds and hazelnuts should be stored in an airtight container in the refrigerator, where they will not turn rancid as quickly.

Long-term storage solutions

While refrigeration temporarily slows the ripening process, other methods have been perfected over the centuries that enable us to enjoy fruits throughout the year:

• **Drying:** used for over 5,000 years, this is the oldest known means of preserving fruit. Grapes, figs, apricots, and dates are among the most common dried fruits. Fruits can be dried in an oven, in the open air, or in food dehydrators. They can then be rehydrated in water or a liquid of your choice, or added directly to your recipe, according to the desired texture.

• **Sugar preservation:** another ancient method for preserving fruit that is used to make jams, fruit jellies, and syrups, among other preparations.

• **Canning:** involves heating fruit compotes or fruits in syrup to between 230°F–250°F (110°C–120°C) to kill harmful microbes and then sealing them in an airtight steel container. The intensive heat treatment can result in fruits losing color, flavor, nutrients, and texture.

• **Freezing (0°F/-18°C):** to ensure minimal browning, first blanch fruits in boiling water, cool them quickly, and then freeze in airtight containers or bags. Alternatively, toss them in sugar or lemon juice before freezing to slow the browning process, which does not alter the flavor. Freezing affects the texture of fruits, which are often mushy and tend to lose juice after defrosting.

Fruit and Nut Seasons around the World

This table provides general guidelines as to the standard harvesting seasons of the fruits and nuts listed. However, the exact range depends on the latitude and climate where you live, as well as other factors. In many cases, there may be early or late varieties available. Although many fruits are available fresh year-round in supermarkets, outside their local cultivation season they are likely to have been transported from other parts of the world. Those harvested at peak ripeness and sold close to where they are grown yield superior nutrients and flavor. Whenever possible, let local farmers' markets be your guide.

SPRING

- Apples
- Apricots
- Bananas
- Blueberries
- Cape gooseberries
- Cherries
- Coconuts
- Dates
- Guavas
- Kiwifruits
- Lemons
- Limes
- Lychees
- Mandarin oranges
- Mangos
- Melons
- Nectarines
- Oranges
- Papayas
- Passion fruit
- Peaches
- Pears
- Pineapple
- Pistachios
- Plums
- Rhubarb
- Star fruit (carambola)
- Strawberries

SUMMER

- Almonds
- Apples
- Apricots
- Avocados
- Bananas
- Blackberries
- Black currants
- Blueberries
- Cape gooseberries
- Cherries
- Coconuts
- Dates
- Figs
- Fraises des Bois
- Grapefruit
- Grapes
- Hazelnuts
- Lemons
- Limes
- Lingonberries
- Lychees
- Mangos
- Mangosteens
- Melons
- Mirabelle plums
- Nectarines
- Oranges
- Papayas
- Passion fruit
- Peaches
- Peanuts
- Pears
- Pineapple
- Pine nuts
- Pistachios
- Plums
- Raspberries
- Red currants
- Rhubarb
- Star fruit (carambola)
- Strawberries
- Watermelons

FALL

- Almonds
- Apples
- Avocados
- Bananas
- Blackberries
- Blood oranges
- Blueberries
- Cape gooseberries
- Chestnuts
- Clementines
- Citrons
- Coconuts
- Dates
- Figs
- Grapefruit
- Grapes
- Hazelnuts
- Kiwifruits
- Kumquats
- Lemons
- Limes
- Lingonberries
- Lychees
- Mandarin oranges
- Mangos
- Mangosteens
- Medlars
- Melons
- Mirabelle plums
- Nectarines
- Oranges
- Papayas
- Passion fruit
- Peaches
- Pears
- Persimmons (kakis)
- Plums
- Pomegranates
- Prickly pear (Barbary figs)
- Pumpkins
- Quinces
- Raspberries
- Rhubarb
- Star fruit (carambola)
- Strawberries
- Walnuts
- Watermelons

WINTER

- Apples
- Avocados
- Bananas
- Blood oranges
- Chestnuts
- Clementines
- Coconuts
- Dates
- Grapefruit
- Guavas
- Kiwifruits
- Kumquats
- Lemons
- Limes
- Lychees
- Mandarin oranges
- Medlars
- Oranges
- Papayas
- Passion fruit
- Peanuts
- Pears
- Persimmons (kakis)
- Pine nuts
- Plums
- Pomegranates
- Prickly pear (Barbary figs)
- Quinces
- Rhubarb
- Star fruit (carambola)
- Strawberries
- Walnuts

EQUIPMENT

UTENSILS

1. Cake, pastry, and confectionery rings and frames
2. *Candissoire* (candying pan)
3. Stainless steel cooling rack
4. Piston funnel
5. Flexible silicone molds

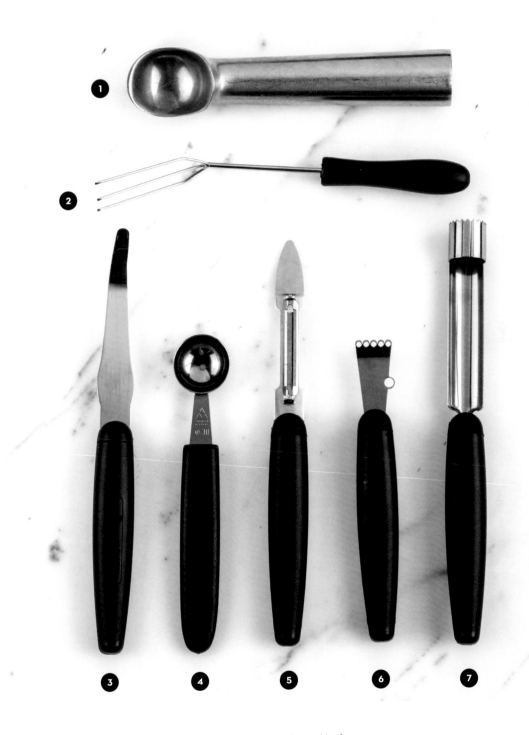

1. Ice cream scoop
2. Chocolate dipping fork
3. Grapefruit knife
4. Melon baller
5. Peeler

6. Zester with a channel knife
7. Apple corer

1. Refractometer
2. Digital instant-read thermometer
3. Bird's beak paring knife
4. Paring knife
5. Microplane grater
6. Serrated knife
7. Chef's knife
8. Palette knife
9. Scraper
10. Offset spatula
11. Flexible spatula
12. Exoglass or heatproof spatula
13. Whisk
14. Skimmer
15. Fine-mesh sieve or strainer
16. China cap or conical sieve or strainer

1

2

3

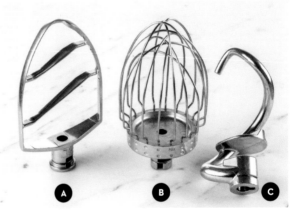

A   B   C

ELECTRICAL APPLIANCES

1. Immersion blender

2. Stand mixer
   Stand mixer attachments: paddle beater (A),
   whisk (B), and dough hook (C)

3. Food processor

TECHNIQUES

PREPARATION

Peeling Pineapples

This technique allows the pineapple "eyes" (the dark spots under the skin) to be removed while retaining the maximum amount of flesh.

Ingredients
Pineapple

Equipment
Chef's knife
Paring knife

1 • Using kitchen scissors, snip off the smaller leaves around the base of the pineapple crown. All of the leaves can be removed, if desired.

2 • Using the chef's knife, cut off the base of the pineapple.

3 • Stand the pineapple upright and cut away the tough skin in strips, working from top to bottom and following the natural curve of the fruit.

4 • Use the paring knife to remove the eyes.
Follow the natural diagonal pattern of the eyes,
working from right to left and top to bottom.

5 • Insert the knife above the first diagonal row
(just above an eye). Cut into the flesh at an angle
and, following the line to the end, cut around the
pineapple in a spiral.

6 • Return to the top and insert the knife just below
the first eye, at an angle. Cut to the end, making
a V-shaped groove. Carefully lift out the cut flesh
to remove one row of eyes.

7 • Repeat until all the eyes have been removed.

Blanching Almonds

This is a technique to easily remove the skin from nuts such as almonds, hazelnuts, or pistachios. It can also be used to peel certain fruits, such as peaches, plums, or tomatoes, without damaging their delicate flesh.

Ingredients
Almonds

Cooking time
2–3 minutes

Equipment
Skimmer

1 • Place the almonds in a saucepan of boiling water.

2 • Leave them to boil for 2-3 minutes.

3 • Remove the almonds with the skimmer and plunge them into a bowl of cold water to stop them cooking.

4 • Drain the almonds and place onto paper towel.

5 • When the almonds are cool enough to handle, rub each one between your fingers to remove the skin.

Skinning Hazelnuts

Ingredients
Hazelnuts

Cooking time
15 minutes

Equipment
Silicone baking mat
on a baking sheet
Clean towel

1 • Preheat the oven to 350°F (180°C/Gas Mark 4).
Spread out the hazelnuts in an even layer on the
silicone mat and roast for 15 minutes. Stir halfway
and keep a close eye on them.

2 • When their skins begin to crackle, remove them from the oven and slide them onto the clean towel.

3 • Gather the towel around the nuts. Holding it closed, press down on top of it and roll it vigorously over the work surface to create friction between the nuts, so they separate from their skins.

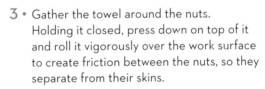

CHEFS' NOTES

Watch the hazelnuts closely toward the end of the roasting time, as they will color and burn very quickly.

4 • Open the towel and transfer the hazelnuts to a bowl, rubbing them gently between your hands to remove any remaining pieces of skin.

Peeling Peaches

Ingredients
Peaches

Equipment
Paring knife
Skimmer

Cooking time
20 seconds

1 • Using the paring knife, score a cross on the base of each peach.

2 • Plunge the peaches into a saucepan of boiling water for 20 seconds.

3 • Using the skimmer, remove the peaches and plunge them into a bowl of ice water to stop them cooking.

4 • Carefully remove the peel using the paring knife,
pulling it away in sections from the cross cut at the
base of each peach toward the stem.

Peeling Chestnuts

Ingredients
Chestnuts

Soaking time
15 minutes

Cooking time
5 minutes

Equipment
Skimmer (or slotted spoon)
Paring knife
Silicone baking mat on
a baking sheet

1 • Soak the chestnuts in a bowl of cold water for
15 minutes, to soften their shells. Drain them using
the skimmer. Preheat the oven to 480°F (250°C/
Gas Mark 9).

2 • Using the paring knife, slit the shell on the flat side
of each chestnut and place on the silicone baking
mat. Place in the oven for 5 minutes.

3 • When the chestnuts are cool enough to handle,
peel away the outer shell and the inner brown
membrane, using the tip of the paring knife.

Removing Melon Seeds

Ingredients
Melon

Equipment
Chef's knife

CHEFS' NOTES

For an eye-catching presentation, you can also cut the melon in half using a crown cut (see technique p. 70).

1 • Trim off the top and bottom of the melon.

2 • Cut the melon in half crosswise using the chef's knife.

3 • Using a spoon, scrape out all the seeds and threads from the center of each half, leaving the flesh.

Opening Coconuts

Ingredients

Coconut

Equipment

Chef's knife

Fine-mesh sieve

1 • Hold the coconut firmly in one hand over a large bowl.

2 • Using the blunt edge of the chef's knife, tap the "equator" line running round the center of the coconut firmly two or three times, until the shell cracks open.

3 • Insert the tip of the knife into the crack to open the coconut, collecting the water inside in the bowl.

4 • The coconut water can be strained through a fine-mesh sieve. To remove the coconut meat from the shell, pry it loose with a paring knife.

Juicing Citrus Fruits By Hand

Ingredients

Citrus fruits,
preferably organic

Equipment

Paring knife
Fine-mesh sieve

1 • Wash and dry the fruit. Roll each fruit on the work surface, pressing down lightly with your hand, to make extracting the juice easier.

2 • Cut the fruit in half crosswise using the paring knife.

3 • Place the fine-mesh sieve over a bowl to catch the pulp and seeds. Squeeze the halved fruit over the bowl, using a fork to help release the juice.

4 • Using a spatula, press down on the pulp in the sieve to extract as much juice as possible.

Preparing a Fresh Fruit Coulis

Ingredients

1 lb. 2 oz. (500 g) raspberries
(or other soft fruit of your
choice)

¼ cup (1¾ oz./50 g) sugar

Scant ½ cup (100 ml) water

Juice of ½ lemon

Equipment

Fine-mesh sieve

Immersion blender

1 • Wash the raspberries by placing them in the sieve
and running cold water over them.

CHEFS' NOTES

Making a coulis is a good way
to use up fruits that are just past
their peak of freshness.

2 • Place the raspberries in a high-sided container
and add the sugar, water, and lemon juice.

Preparing a Fresh Fruit Coulis (continued)

3 • Process to a puree using the immersion blender.

4 • Place the sieve over a bowl and push the pureed fruit through it to remove the seeds.

5 • Press down on any pulp left in the sieve with the back of a ladle, to help the juice pass through the sieve.

Preparing a Sorbet

Ingredients

1 sheet (2 g) gold-strength gelatin, 200 Bloom
(or 1 g stabilizer)

Scant ¼ cup (55 ml) cold water

½ cup (3⅓ oz./95 g) superfine sugar

1 tbsp (15 ml) lemon juice

10½ oz. (300 g) raspberries

Cooking time

20 minutes

Maturing time

12 hours

Storage

Up to 2 weeks in the freezer

Equipment

Immersion blender
Refractometer
Fine-mesh sieve
Ice cream maker

1 • Soak the gelatin in the cold water in a bowl until softened. Remove it and squeeze excess water back into the bowl. Pour the soaking water into a saucepan, add the sugar, and heat until the sugar dissolves. Bring to a boil, then remove from the heat.

CHEFS' NOTES

The optimal sugar concentration for sorbet bases is 27–30 percent. If too sweet, the sorbet will not freeze properly; if there is insufficient sugar, it will be hard and icy. Depending on the fruit, more or less sugar is needed to reach this ideal range. Check the sugar concentration of the starting fruit puree or juice with a refractometer and add sugar until the desired concentration is reached.

2 • Add the lemon juice, then stir in the gelatin until melted. Let cool. When the syrup is almost cold, pour it over the raspberries in a bowl.

Preparing a Sorbet (continued)

3 • Process to a puree using the immersion blender. Measure the sugar content of the sorbet mixture using the refractometer—it should read 27–30° Brix.

4 • Strain the mixture through the fine-mesh sieve into a bowl. Cover and chill for 12 hours to mature the flavors.

5 • Pour the mixture into the ice cream maker.

6 • Churn according to the manufacturer's instructions. Transfer to an airtight container and freeze.

Preparing Brandied Cherries

Ingredients

10½ oz. (300 g) tart cherries (preferably Montmorency)

⅔ cup (4½ oz./130 g) sugar

½ cup (130 ml) kirsch (40% alcohol), or other brandy

Steeping time

1–2 months

Storage

Up to 1 year in the refrigerator once opened (make sure a clean spoon is used each time to serve the cherries)

Equipment

Kitchen scissors

Clean glass jar with an airtight lid

1 • Wash and dry the cherries. Cut off the upper half of the stems using the scissors (this will boost the flavor).

2 • Place the cherries in the jar and pour the sugar over them.

3 • Pour in the kirsch.

4 • Seal the jar tightly and store in a cool, dry place for a minimum of 1–2 months. Turn the jar over once a week.

CUTTING

Slicing

Ingredients
Apples, pears, oranges,
lemons, limes, etc.

Equipment
Chef's knife

1 • Using the chef's knife, cut the fruit crosswise
into equally sized slices.

CHEFS' NOTES

You can also use a mandoline
to slice fruit. However, the fruit must be firm
(apples, pears, quinces, etc.).

2 • You can make the slices as thick or as thin as you
wish, depending on how they will be used.

Julienne Cut

Ingredients
Apples

Equipment
Chef's knife

1 • Using the chef's knife, cut the apples into equal slices about 1/16 in. (2 mm) thick.

2 • Stack several slices on top of one another and cut crosswise into matchsticks about 1/16 in. (2 mm) wide. If not using immediately, toss the apple matchsticks in lemon juice to prevent them from discoloring.

Mirepoix Cut

Use this technique to cut fruit into evenly sized large dice for dishes such as fruit salads.

Ingredients
Mangos, pears, melons, peaches, etc.

Equipment
Chef's knife

1 • Peel and cut the fruit into slices about ½ in. (1 cm) thick.

2 • Cut the slices into ½-in. (1-cm) dice.

Preparing Fruit Balls

Ingredients
Melons, papayas, kiwifruits, pitayas etc.

Equipment
Melon baller

Press the melon baller into the flesh of the fruit and twist with your wrist to scoop out a small round ball of fruit.

CHEFS' NOTES

These attractive fruit balls will add an elegant touch to plated desserts or give an original twist to fruit salads. They can also be used for fruit skewers.

Cutting Mangos

Ingredients
Mangos

Equipment
Chef's knife
Paring knife

1 • Using the chef's knife, cut off the base of the mango to make it flat.

2 • Stand the mango upright and cut lengthwise through the flesh on one side, along the pit. Repeat on the other side.

3 • Cut the skin off the central part of the mango surrounding the pit.

4 • Remove as much flesh as you can from the pit using the paring knife.

5 • Cut the flesh off in sections, following the curve of the pit.

6 • Cut the two mango halves into quarters.

7 • Peel the quarters.

Cutting Pineapples (Method 1)

Before starting, the pineapple must first be prepared following the technique on p.28.

Ingredients
Pineapple

Equipment
Chef's knife

1 • Cut the peeled pineapple in half lengthwise.

2 • Cut the pineapple halves lengthwise into quarters.

3 • Remove the core (although edible, it is often quite hard).

4 • You can then cut the pineapple quarters lengthwise into equally sized slices.

5 • Alternatively, slice the quarters crosswise.

Cutting Pineapples (Method 2)

This method is quicker and easier than the preceding technique.
However, a little more pineapple flesh is lost in the process.

Ingredients
Pineapple

Equipment
Chef's knife
Grapefruit knife

1 • Using the chef's knife, cut off about two-thirds of the crown. Cut the pineapple in half lengthwise.

2 • Using the grapefruit knife, cut into the flesh about ½ in. (1 cm) from the skin. Following the natural curve of the fruit, work the knife under the flesh so it can be removed in one piece.

3 • Repeat with the other pineapple half.

4 • Cut each half in two lengthwise and, using the chef's knife, remove the core.

5 • Cut the flesh into slices as required. The fruit can be served in the hollowed-out skins, if desired.

Cutting and Seeding Pomegranates

This technique allows the pomegranate seeds to be removed without damaging them.

Ingredients
Pomegranate

Equipment
Paring knife

1 • Using the tip of the paring knife, cut out a "hat" by scoring the skin around the bottom of the pomegranate.

2 • Remove the hat, using the knife if necessary.

3 • Cut several vertical slits through the skin, following the natural sections of the fruit.

4 • Remove the central core that was attached to the calyx.

5 • Pull the fruit apart with your hands, separating it into its natural sections.

6 • Hold each section over a bowl. Using your fingers, gently separate the seeds from the membrane, letting them drop into the bowl.

Canelling

This decorative cut is mainly used for citrus and other firm fruits.

Ingredients
Oranges, lemons, limes, kumquats, etc., untreated

Equipment
Chef's knife
Channel (canelle) knife

1 • Slice off the top and bottom of the fruit.

2 • Using the channel knife, remove vertical strips of zest, cutting at regular intervals around the fruit.

3 • For a stylish presentation, cut the fruit in half lengthwise and remove any seeds.

4 • Cut each half crosswise into thin slices, as required.

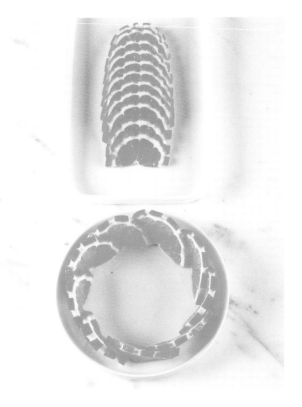

Cutting Citrus Zest into Thin Strips

Ingredients

Citrus fruits, untreated

Equipment

Vegetable brush
Vegetable peeler
Paring knife
Chef's knife

1 • Clean the fruit in warm water using the vegetable brush.

CHEFS' NOTES

• When using the zest of citrus fruits, it is best to select untreated, preferably organic fruits.

• Make sure you remove all the white pith, as it is very bitter.

2 • Cut off both ends of the fruit. Using the peeler, remove the zest in wide strips.

3 • Lay each strip flat, zest side down, and cut away the pith (white part) using the paring knife.

4 • Overlap the strips of zest on a chopping board.

5 • Using the chef's knife, slice them into long, thin strips about 1/16 in. (1–2 mm) wide.

Peeling and Segmenting Citrus Fruits

Ingredients
Citrus fruits

Equipment
Chef's knife
Paring knife

1 • Cut off the top and bottom of the fruit and stand it upright. Using the chef's knife, cut away the peel (zest, pith, and membrane), following the natural curve of the fruit, to expose the flesh.

2 • Cut off any remaining pith using the paring knife.

3 • Holding the fruit in one hand, cut between each membrane to release the segments. Do this over a bowl to catch the juice.

4 • Squeeze the membrane with your hand to extract the remaining juice, if needed.

Preparing a Fruit Crown (*Historier*)

This technique is used to cut fruits such as melons in a decorative way.

Ingredients

Melon, citrus fruits, kiwifruits, etc.

Equipment

Paring knife

1 • Using the paring knife, lightly score a line crosswise around the center of the fruit, as a reference point for cutting.

2 • Place the tip of the knife on this line and push the blade into the fruit at an angle, cutting all the way to the center.

3 • Remove the blade and repeat, inserting the knife at the opposite angle to form a "v." Continue cutting around the fruit to obtain a zigzag pattern.

4 • Once the fruit has been cut all the way round, pull the two halves apart. If preparing a fruit such as melon, use a spoon to scrape out the seeds and membrane from the center of each half.

COOKING

Blanching Citrus Fruits

Ingredients
Citrus fruits

Cooking time
5 minutes

Equipment
Round wire rack the same size
as the inside of the saucepan
Skimmer

1 • Place the fruit in a large saucepan of water.

2 • Place the rack over the fruit to keep them
submerged in the water.

3 • Bring the water to a boil, then let boil for
5 minutes. Remove the rack, taking care not
to burn yourself.

4 • Drain the fruit using the skimmer and plunge into
a bowl of ice water to stop them cooking.

Poaching Pears

Ingredients

3 pears, preferably Conference
Juice of ½ lemon
4 cups (1 L) water
8 oz. (225 g) raspberries
1 cup (7 oz./200 g) sugar
1 vanilla bean, split lengthwise
and seeds scraped

Equipment

Chef's knife
Vegetable brush
Small square food-grade
stainless steel mesh
Large oven-safe saucepan
Immersion blender
Fine-mesh sieve

Cooking time

45 minutes

1 • Preheat the oven to 175°F (80°C/Gas on lowest
setting). Wash and peel the pears, without
removing the stems. Slice off the bases so they
are flat.

2 • Fill a bowl with cold water, add the lemon juice,
and submerge the pears to prevent them from
browning. Scrub the pears with the vegetable
brush to encourage them to soak up the poaching
liquid.

3 • Gently rub the stainless steel mesh over the pears
to remove any bumps and ridges.

CHEFS' NOTES

Smoothing the surface of the pears with stainless steel mesh is not essential,
but it gives them a regular, more attractive finish.

4 • The surface of each pear should be perfectly smooth.

Poaching Pears (continued)

5 • Pour the 4 cups (1 L) water into the saucepan and add the raspberries, sugar, and vanilla bean and seeds. Mix with the immersion blender, then strain through the fine-mesh sieve.

6 • Pour back into the saucepan and bring to a boil. Remove from the heat and add the pears.

7 • Cover the pears with a disk of parchment paper with a small hole cut out of the center, folding up the edges so it fits neatly inside the pan. Transfer the pan to the oven for about 45 minutes.

8 • Remove from the oven and let the pears cool in the syrup. Drain, then strain the poaching liquid through the fine-mesh sieve into a pitcher.

9 • Stand the pears upright on a serving dish and pour
  the syrup over them.

Roasting Pineapples

Ingredients

1 vanilla bean

3 tbsp (1¾ oz./50 g) butter, diced

2 tbsp (1½ oz./40 g) honey

2 tbsp (30 ml) rum

Juice of 1 orange

1 pineapple, preferably Victoria

Cooking time

30 minutes

Equipment

Paring knife

1 • Preheat the oven to 350°F (180°C/Gas Mark 4). Split the vanilla bean lengthwise and scrape out the seeds using the paring knife.

2 • Place the vanilla bean and seeds in a saucepan with the butter. Heat gently until the butter has melted.

3 • Warm the honey, rum, and orange juice together in a separate saucepan over low heat.

Roasting Pineapples (continued)

4 • Peel the pineapple (see technique p. 28) and wrap
  aluminum foil around the crown to protect it
  in the oven.

5 • Place the pineapple in a roasting pan and brush the flesh generously with the vanilla butter.

6 • Cut the vanilla bean into small pieces and push them into the pineapple. Pour over the warm honey and rum mixture.

7 • Roast the pineapple for 30 minutes, spooning the pan juices over it every 5 minutes.

CHEFS' NOTES

Be sure to baste the pineapple generously with the pan juices while it is roasting, as this will make it more tender and enhance its flavor.

Candying Kumquats

Makes 1 lb. 2 oz. (500 g)

Ingredients
1 lb. 2 oz. (500 g) kumquats
4 cups (1 L) water
2¾ lb. (1.26 kg) sugar, divided
Scant ½ cup (5 oz./150 g)
glucose syrup

Candying time
7 days

Cooking time
15 minutes

Storage
Up to 3 months
in the refrigerator

Equipment
Toothpick
Instant-read thermometer
Candissoire
(candying pan with a lid)
Skimmer

1 • Wash the kumquats and remove the stems. Pierce both ends of each kumquat with the toothpick.

2 • Make a syrup by heating the water with 2⅔ cups (1 lb. 2 oz./500 g) of the sugar and the glucose syrup in a saucepan until the sugar dissolves. Bring to a boil.

3 • Add the kumquats to the syrup and cook at 185°F (85°C) for 15 minutes.

4 • Using the skimmer, transfer the kumquats to the candissoire. Pour over the syrup to cover the fruit. Put the lid on the candissoire and let the kumquats soak overnight at room temperature.

↺

Candying Kumquats (continued)

5 • The next day, lift out the rack with the kumquats on it and pour the syrup into a saucepan. Return the rack with the fruit to the candissoire.

6 • Add a scant ½ cup (3¼ oz./90 g) sugar to the syrup, then heat until the sugar dissolves and the temperature reaches 185°F (85°C). Pour over the kumquats, close the candissoire, and let soak overnight.

7 • Repeat steps 5 and 6 three more times, over 3 days. On the sixth day, add 1 cup (7 oz./200 g) sugar to the syrup in the saucepan, heat until it dissolves, then bring to a boil. Pour over the fruit in the candissoire and let soak overnight.

8 • The next day, repeat once more using the remaining 1 cup (7 oz./200 g) sugar.

9 • The kumquats are now candied and can be stored
in their syrup, in the refrigerator.

Glazing Chestnuts

Makes 10½ oz. (300 g)

Ingredients

10½ oz. (300 g) candied chestnuts in syrup (*marrons confits au sirop*), homemade or store-bought

½ cup (120 ml) syrup from the candied chestnuts, plus more as needed

Generous ½ tsp (3 ml) rum

1½ cups (7 oz./200 g) confectioners' sugar

Drying time

12 hours

Cooking time

5 minutes

Storage

Up to 1 month in a cool place away from light

Equipment

Silicone baking mat on a cookie sheet

Dipping fork

Candy wrappers (optional)

1 • Place the chestnuts on a wire rack and let them dry out for 12 hours. Preheat the oven to 400°F (210°C/Gas Mark 6). Warm the chestnut syrup and rum in a bowl set over a saucepan of barely simmering water (bain-marie).

2 • Add the confectioners' sugar and stir until smooth.

3 • The glaze should be relatively thick but fluid. If necessary, add a little more syrup to obtain the right consistency.

Glazing Chestnuts (continued)

4 • Set the rack with the chestnuts on the silicone baking mat and place in the oven for 1 minute to warm them. Leave the oven switched on.

5 • Using the dipping fork, dip each chestnut in the glaze until completely coated.

6 • Return the chestnuts to the rack to allow the excess glaze to drip off. When they have all been coated, return them to the oven for about 40 seconds to set the glaze (the sugar on the baking mat should begin to form into granules).

7 • Let the chestnuts cool to room temperature, then wrap each one in a candy wrapper, if desired.

Frying Pineapple Fritters

Ingredients

1 pineapple

1 cup plus 2 tbsp (5¼ oz./150 g) flour

2 tbsp (25 g) sugar

2 tsp (7.5 g) baking powder

Seeds of 1 vanilla bean

Scant ½ teaspoon (2 g) salt

1 egg

¾ cup (180 ml) whole milk, divided

1 tsp (5 ml) rum

Grape-seed oil for deep-frying

Confectioners' or vanilla sugar for dusting

Cooking time

4 minutes per batch

Equipment

Chef's knife

2¾-in. (7-cm) round cookie cutter, or one slightly smaller than the pineapple slices

Paring knife

1¼-in. (3-cm) round cookie cutter

Instant-read thermometer

Fine-mesh sieve

1 • Cut the pineapple crosswise into ½-in. (1-cm) slices, without peeling it. Using the larger cutter and paring knife, remove the skin to make even-sized rounds.

2 • Use the smaller cutter to remove the core.

3 • Combine the flour, sugar, baking powder, vanilla seeds, and salt in a mixing bowl. Make a well in the center and add the egg.

Frying Pineapple Fritters (continued)

4 • Add two-thirds of the milk and whisk to combine. Gradually whisk in the remaining milk and the rum until smooth.

5 • Heat about 2 in. (5 cm) oil in a deep pan until the temperature reaches 347°F–355°F (175°C-180°C). Using tongs or a fork, dip the pineapple slices one at a time into the batter.

6 • Slowly and carefully lower them into the hot oil. Fry for 2 minutes on each side.

7 • Drain the fritters on a plate lined with paper towel.

8 • Dust with confectioners' sugar or vanilla sugar and serve immediately.

Making an Apple Compote

Makes 1 cup (250 ml)

Ingredients
1 lb. 2 oz. (500 g) apples
½ tbsp (8 g) butter
1 vanilla bean, split lengthwise
and seeds scraped
1 cinnamon stick
2 tbsp (25 g) sugar
Water as needed

Cooking time
35 minutes

Equipment
Vegetable peeler
Paring knife

1 • Wash and peel the apples. Cut each one into six wedges and remove the cores using the paring knife.

CHEFS' NOTES

You can coat the apple pieces
with lemon juice once they are cut
to prevent them from browning.

2 • Cut the apples into approximately ¾-in. (2-cm) dice.

3 • Melt the butter in a large saucepan. Add the vanilla bean, seeds, and cinnamon stick.

4 • Add the apples and sugar, and stir gently until the apples are coated. Pour in a little water.

5 • Cover the apples with a disk of parchment paper with a small hole cut out of the center. Let steam over low heat for 30 minutes, stirring occasionally (add a little more water as needed if the pan becomes dry).

6 • Remove the vanilla bean and cinnamon stick. Transfer the compote to a bowl and let cool.

Making Strawberry Jam

Makes 3 × 9-oz. (250-g) jars

Ingredients

1 lb. 2 oz. (500 g) strawberries

1 vanilla bean, split lengthwise

2 cups (14 oz./400 g) sugar, divided

⅝ tsp (2.5 g) medium rapid set pectin

Scant ½ tsp (2 g) tartaric acid dissolved in ½ tsp (2 ml) water, or ½ tsp (2 ml) lemon juice

Resting time

6–12 hours

Cooking time

Varies according to the time needed to reach the required temperature

Storage

Up to 3 months at room temperature and 1 year if pasteurized in sterilized jars

Equipment

Paring knife

3 × 9-oz. (250-g) jars, sterilized and warmed (see Chefs' Notes)

Skimmer

Instant-read thermometer

1 • Wash, hull, and halve the strawberries. Place them in a bowl.

2 • Scrape the vanilla seeds into the strawberries. Cut the vanilla bean into four pieces lengthwise and add to the bowl.

3 • Add 2 cups minus 2 tbsp (360 g) of the sugar and stir until the strawberries are coated.

To sterilize, put the jars and lids in a pan of boiling water and keep them immersed for 20 minutes, separating the jars with clean dishcloths. Alternatively, place on a baking sheet and heat in a 300°F (150°C/Gas Mark 2) oven for 20 minutes. The jars should be kept warm until filled, or they could crack.

4 • Press plastic wrap over the surface of the strawberries and let them sit for 6–12 hours in a cool place to release their juices.

Making Strawberry Jam (continued)

5 • Transfer the berries and their juices to a saucepan. Bring to a boil, immediately skimming off any foam that rises to the surface.

6 • Combine the remaining sugar and the pectin in a bowl. Add to the berries and cook until the temperature reaches about 223°F (106°C)

7 • At the end of the cooking time, stir in the tartaric acid or lemon juice.

8 • Divide the jam between the warm jars, screw the lids on tightly, and turn the jars upside down so the jam is automatically pasteurized. When cold, turn the jars upright and store in a cool, dry place, away from direct light.

Making Citrus Marmalade

Makes 3 × 9-oz. (250-g) jars

Ingredients

9 oz. (250 g) oranges
(or other citrus fruit)

Scant 2½ cups (1 lb. 1 oz./475 g)
sugar, divided

Scant ½ cup (100 ml) water

2 cups (500 ml) orange juice
(from about 6 oranges)

4 tsp (20 ml) lemon juice

⅝ tsp (2.5 g) medium rapid set
pectin

Cooking time

Varies according to the time
needed to reach the required
temperature

Storage

Up to 3 months at room
temperature and 1 year if
pasteurized in sterilized jars

Equipment

Chef's knife

Instant-read thermometer

Skimmer

Refractometer

Immersion blender

3 × 9-oz. (250-g) jars,
sterilized and warmed
(see Chefs' Notes p. 97)

1 • Slice off the top and bottom of the oranges
and cut them in half.

2 • Cut each half into equally sized pieces.
Place in a saucepan of cold water. Bring to a full
boil and blanch for about 10 minutes, then drain.
Repeat this process three more times, using fresh
water each time.

3 • In a separate saucepan, heat ½ cup
(3½ oz./100 g) of the sugar with ½ cup (100 ml)
water until the sugar dissolves and
the temperature reaches 176°F (80°C).
Add the blanched oranges and cook for about
1 hour, maintaining this temperature.

↪

Making Citrus Marmalade (continued)

4 • In another large saucepan, heat the orange juice, lemon juice, and 1¾ cups (12½ oz./350 g) of the sugar until the sugar dissolves. Bring to a boil.

5 • Add the oranges and syrup to the juice mixture. Combine the remaining sugar and pectin in a small bowl and stir in.

6 • Bring to a boil, immediately skimming off any foam that rises to the surface.

7 • Continue to cook at about 223°F (106°C) until the refractometer reads around 63° Brix.

8 • Process with the immersion blender. Divide between the warm jars. Screw the lids on tightly and turn the jars upside down so the marmalade is automatically pasteurized. When cold, turn the jars upright. Store in a cool, dry place, away from direct light.

Making Quince Jelly

Makes 3 × 9-oz. (250-g) jars

Ingredients

2¼ lb. (1 kg) quinces

Sugar as needed

Scant ½ tsp (2 g) tartaric acid dissolved in ½ tsp (2 ml) water, or a scant ½ tsp (2 ml) lemon juice

Cooking time

Varies according to the time needed to reach the required temperature

Storage

Up to 3 months at room temperature and 1 year if pasteurized in sterilized jars

Equipment

Vegetable brush

Vegetable peeler

Chef's knife

Food-safe muslin bag

Fine-mesh sieve

Digital scale

Skimmer

Instant-read thermometer

Refractometer

3 × 9-oz. (250-g) jars, sterilized and warmed (see Chefs' Notes p. 97)

1 • Wash, scrub, and peel the quinces, reserving the peel.

CHEFS' NOTES

Using a muslin bag is not essential, but it makes it easier to squeeze out the juice.

2 • Cut the fruit into quarters, remove the cores and seeds, and set both aside. Cut the fruit into equally sized pieces.

3 • Place the fruit in a large saucepan.
Tie up the peel, cores, and seeds in the muslin
bag and add to the pan.

4 • Cover with water and bring to a boil. Reduce the
heat to low and let simmer for 45 minutes–1 hour,
until the fruit is tender.

5 • Lift out the muslin bag and place it in the
fine-mesh sieve placed over a bowl. Press down
on it with a ladle to squeeze out as much liquid
as possible.

6 • Remove the bag and place the fruit in the sieve.
Press down on the fruit with the ladle to extract
as much juice as possible. Discard the fruit pulp,
or save it for another recipe, such as making
quince fruit jellies.

↪

Making Quince Jelly (continued)

7 • Weigh the quince juice and add the same quantity of sugar to it.

8 • Heat until the sugar dissolves, then bring to a boil. Let simmer for about 1 hour, immediately skimming off any foam that rises to the surface.

9 • Continue cooking until the temperature reaches 223°F–224°F (106°C–107°C).

10 • Test the density with the refractometer: it should read around 70° Brix. Stir in the dissolved tartaric acid or lemon juice. Divide between the warm jars and screw the lids on tightly. Turn the jars upside down so the jelly is automatically pasteurized. When cold, turn the jars upright. Store in a cool, dry place, away from direct light.

Making Mango Chutney

Makes 1 × 10½-oz. (300-g) jar

Ingredients

Scant 1 cup (225 ml) white vinegar

4 oz. (110 g) onion

¼ oz. (8 g) fresh ginger

1 small clove (2.5 g) garlic

8 oz. (225 g) mango flesh

Scant ½ cup (2¾ oz./75 g) turbinado sugar

⅔ cup (150 ml) veal, chicken, or vegetable stock

Scant 2 tbsp (15 g) raisins

½ tsp (2 g) pectin NH

Cooking time

About 45 minutes, but varies according to the time needed to reach the required consistency

Storage

Up to 3 months at room temperature and 1 year in a sterilized jar

Equipment

Chef's knife

10½-oz. (300-g) jar, sterilized and warmed (see Chefs' Notes p. 97)

1 • Bring the vinegar to a boil in a large saucepan and boil until reduced by one-quarter.

CHEFS' NOTES

Served as a condiment, sweet-and-sour chutneys make excellent accompaniments to pâtés, cheeses, and fish.

2 • Peel the onion and ginger and chop into approximately ⅛-in. (3-mm) dice using the chef's knife. Peel and crush the garlic. Peel the mango and cut it into dice slightly larger than the onions (just over ⅛ in./4 mm).

↪

Making Mango Chutney (continued)

3 • Add the sugar, onions, and garlic to the vinegar and cook, stirring regularly, until nearly all the vinegar has evaporated.

4 • Pour in the stock and cook until reduced by half.

5 • Add the mango, ginger, raisins, and pectin. Stir to combine.

6 • Let simmer, stirring occasionally, until a thick consistency is obtained. Transfer to the jar, screw the lid on tightly, and let cool.

Making Passion Fruit and Apricot Fruit Jellies

Makes 1 × 8-in. (20-cm) square (to be cut into individual jellies)

Ingredients

9 oz. (250 g) passion fruit puree

9 oz. (250 g) apricot puree

2⅔ cup (1 lb. 2 oz./510 g) sugar, divided

2½ tsp (10 g) yellow pectin

Scant ⅓ cup (3½ oz./100 g) glucose syrup

¾ tsp (4 g) tartaric acid dissolved in 1 tsp (4 ml) water, or use ¾ tsp (4 ml) lemon juice

Coating

Granulated sugar

Cooking time

30 minutes

Drying time

12 hours

Storage

Up to 2 weeks, well covered with plastic wrap or in cellophane candy wrappers

Equipment

Instant-read thermometer

Refractometer

8-in. (20-cm) stainless steel confectionery frame

Silicone baking mat on a cookie sheet

Chef's knife

1 • Combine the fruit purees in a large saucepan and heat until the temperature reaches 113°F (45°C). Stir together ¼ cup (1¾ oz./50 g) of the sugar and the pectin in a bowl. Whisk into the hot purees until dissolved.

2 • Bring to a boil, then add the glucose syrup and half the remaining sugar in two amounts, keeping the mixture at a boil.

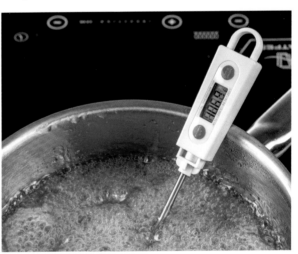

3 • Cook for about 3 minutes, whisking constantly. Add the remaining sugar in two amounts, maintaining the boil. Cook until the temperature reaches 223°F– 225°F (106°C–107°C). Test the density with the refractometer: it should read 73-74° Brix.

CHEFS' NOTES

Fruit jellies can be frozen. To freeze, do not coat in granulated sugar;
simply dust with cornstarch and cover with plastic wrap, keeping it flat.
Once thawed, moisten the jelly with a little water and coat with the sugar as below.

4 • Remove from the heat and whisk in the dissolved tartaric acid or lemon juice.

5 • Place the confectionery frame on the silicone baking mat and pour the fruit mixture into it. Let cool to room temperature.

6 • When the jelly has cooled, remove the frame. Spread granulated sugar over a rimmed baking sheet and coat the jelly with it on both sides.

7 • Cut into pieces of the desired size and let dry for 12 hours on a rack before wrapping.

Making Gianduja Paste

Makes 1¾ lb. (770 g)

Ingredients

1¾ cups (10½ oz./300 g)
skinned hazelnuts
(see technique p. 32)

6¼ oz. (180 g) milk chocolate,
40% cacao, chopped

1½ oz. (40 g) cocoa butter
chips

Scant 2 cups (9 oz./250 g)
confectioners' sugar

Cooking time

30 minutes

Storage

Up to 2 weeks in an airtight
container

Equipment

Food processor

Rimmed baking sheet lined
with parchment paper

Marble slab (optional)

Instant-read thermometer

Scraper

1 • Preheat the oven to 275°F (140°C/Gas Mark 1).
Spread out the hazelnuts on the baking sheet
and roast them in the oven for 30 minutes.

2 • Melt the chocolate and cocoa butter in a bowl
over a saucepan of barely simmering water
(bain-marie).

3 • Place the roasted hazelnuts in the bowl of the
food processor, add the confectioners' sugar,
and pulse until finely ground.

4 • Continue processing to a smooth paste.

5 • Add the melted chocolate and pulse to blend. Pour the mixture over the marble slab (if using), so it cools quickly to 79°F (26°C).

6 • Spread the mixture out using an offset spatula and scraper, pushing it back toward the center to speed up the cooling process. Store in an airtight container in a cool, dry place.

Making Almond and Hazelnut Praline Paste

Makes 10 oz. (275 g)

Ingredients

½ cup (3 oz./85 g) blanched almonds (see technique p. 30)

½ cup (3 oz./85 g) skinned hazelnuts (see technique p. 32)

½ cup (3½ oz./100 g) sugar

2 tbsp (30 ml) water

Seeds of 1 vanilla bean

1 pinch *fleur de sel*

Cooking time

45 minutes

Storage

Up to 2 weeks in an airtight container

Equipment

Silicone baking mat on a cookie sheet

Food processor

1 • Preheat the oven to 275°F (140°C/Gas Mark 1). Spread out the almonds and hazelnuts on the silicone baking mat and roast them in the oven for 30 minutes.

2 • As soon as the nuts are ready, heat the sugar and water in a saucepan until the sugar dissolves. Bring to a boil. Let boil for 2–3 minutes, then add the warm nuts.

3 • Cook, stirring with a spatula, until the syrup crystallizes and has a sandy appearance. Add the vanilla seeds.

Take care not to roast the nuts or cook the caramel for too long,
as if they darken too much the praline will have a bitter flavor.

4 • Increase the heat and continue stirring until the sugar dissolves, coats the nuts, and turns a light golden caramel color.

5 • Turn the nuts out onto the silicone baking mat and sprinkle with the *fleur de sel*. Let cool to room temperature.

6 • Break the caramelized nuts roughly into large chunks and place in the bowl of the food processor. Process to a smooth paste; do this in stages to avoid overheating the mixture.

7 • The paste is ready when it is smooth and a little runny. Transfer to an airtight container and store in a cool, dry place.

Making Chocolate Hazelnut Spread

Makes 2 × 8-oz. (230-g) jars

Ingredients

1 quantity (9¾ oz./275 g) almond and hazelnut praline paste (see technique p. 116)

7 oz. (200 g) gianduja paste (see technique p. 114)

1¼ oz. (35 g) hazelnut butter

1¾ oz. (50 g) *pâte à glacer blonde* (blond glazing paste)

2¾ tsp (12.5 g) refined coconut oil

Scant ¼ cup (25 g) powdered milk

Scant 2 tbsp (12.5 g) unsweetened cocoa powder

Storage

Up to 2 weeks in an airtight container in a cool, dry place

Equipment

Food processor

2 × 8-oz. (230-g) jars

1 • Place the almond and hazelnut praline paste, gianduja paste, hazelnut butter, *pâte à glacer*, and coconut oil in the bowl of the food processor.

2 • Process until smooth. Add the powdered milk and cocoa powder and process again until smooth and glossy. Divide between the jars, seal, and store in a cool, dry place.

Making Chestnut Spread

(*Crème de Marrons*)

Makes 1 lb. (450 g)

Ingredients
9 oz. (250 g) peeled chestnuts
(see technique p. 36)
1 cup (7 oz./200 g) sugar
Scant ⅓ cup (70 ml) water
1 vanilla bean

Equipment
Small round wire rack that fits
inside a large saucepan
Food processor
Instant-read thermometer
Fine-mesh sieve (optional)

1 • Pour enough water into a large saucepan to cover
the base in a shallow layer. Place the rack inside
(only the legs should be in the water). Place the
chestnuts on the rack in a single layer.

CHEFS' NOTES

• For a darker chestnut spread,
roughly chop the steamed chestnuts and add
to the sugar syrup in the saucepan. Cook over
low heat, stirring regularly, for about 15 minutes,
to allow the chestnuts to absorb the syrup
and swell. Transfer to the food processor
and process to a smooth paste.

• If the spread is too thick, thin it out
with a simple syrup made with equal quantities
of sugar and water.

2 • Cover the saucepan with heat-resistant plastic
wrap. Bring the water to a gentle simmer and
steam the chestnuts for about 30 minutes.
The chestnuts are cooked when they can be
easily pierced with a wooden toothpick.

Making Chestnut Spread

(*Crème de Marrons*) (continued)

3 • In a separate saucepan, heat the sugar and scant ⅓ cup (70 ml) water until the sugar dissolves. Bring to a boil. Stir in the vanilla seeds and cook until the temperature of the syrup reaches 234°F (112°C).

4 • Place the chestnuts in the bowl of the food processor and begin to process.

5 • Pour in the hot syrup in a thin stream and continue processing to obtain a paste.

6 • For a very smooth spread, press the mixture through a fine-mesh sieve.

Drying Citrus Slices and Coconut Shavings

Ingredients

Citrus fruits, untreated

1 coconut

4 cups (1 L) coconut water, water, or a combination of the two

1 cup (7 oz./200 g) sugar

Drying time

12 hours

Equipment

Chef's knife

2 wire racks covered with parchment paper

Paring knife

Vegetable peeler

Skimmer

1 • To prepare the citrus slices, preheat the oven to 160°F (70°C/Gas on lowest setting). Using the chef's knife, cut the fruit crosswise into very thin slices (1/16 –1/8 in./2-3 mm). Spread out the slices in a single layer on one wire rack. Dry in the oven for 12 hours. Store in an airtight container when cool.

2 • To prepare the coconut shavings, preheat the oven to 160°F (70°C/Gas on lowest setting). Open the coconut (see technique p. 38), reserving the water. Insert the paring knife between the shell and the coconut meat to remove the meat.

3 • Make coconut shavings using the vegetable peeler.

4 • Heat the coconut water and sugar in a saucepan until the sugar dissolves. Bring to a boil, add the coconut shavings, and cook for 1 minute.
Drain with the skimmer and place on the other wire rack. Dry in the oven for 12 hours.
Store in an airtight container when cool.

RECIPES

CITRUS FRUITS

HESPERIDIUM LEMON AND LIME TART

Tarte au citron Hespéride

**Makes 2 tarts,
each serving 3**

Active time

4 hours

Cooking time

3½ hours

Freezing time

Overnight

Chilling time

30 minutes

Storage

Up to 2 days
in the refrigerator

Equipment

Instant-read thermometer

Immersion blender

2 × 2½-in. (6-cm) baking
rings, ¾ in. (2 cm) deep

Silicone mold with ¾-in.
(2.2-cm) round cavities,
¾ in. (2 cm) deep

Silicone mold with 1¼-in.
(3.2-cm) round cavities,
1⅛ in. (2.8 cm) deep

Pastry bag with coupler
+ Saint-Honoré and small
plain tips

Silicone mold with 1½-in.
(4-cm) round cavities, 1½-
in. (3.6 cm) deep

Stand mixer + paddle
beater and whisk

2 × 6-in. (16-cm) baking
rings, ¾ in. (2 cm) deep

4-cup (1-L) whipping
siphon + 2 N₂O gas
cartridges

Paper cup

2 food-safe acetate sheets

Velvet spray gun

Ingredients

Lime cream

⅔ cup (5 oz./150 g) lightly
beaten egg (3 eggs)

¾ cup (5 oz./150 g)
superfine sugar

Scant ½ cup (105 ml) lime
juice

2 sticks (8¼ oz./235 g)
butter, diced

Finely grated zest
of ½ lime

A few drops natural
green food coloring

Swiss meringue

Scant ½ cup
(3½ oz./100 g) egg
white (about 3 whites)

1 cup (7 oz./200 g)
superfine sugar

Lemon mousse

4½ sheets (9 g)
gold-strength gelatin,
200 Bloom

2½ tsp (12 ml) hot
water

3½ tbsp (50 ml) lemon
juice

5 oz. (145 g) lime cream
(see left)

4 oz. (110 g) Swiss
meringue (see above)

Scant ½ cup (110 ml)
heavy cream, minimum
35% fat

**Genoise almond
sponge**

5¾ oz. (165 g) almond
paste, 50% almonds,
chopped

Scant ½ cup
(3½ oz./100 g) lightly
beaten egg (2 eggs),
at room temperature

3 tbsp (1½ oz./40 g)
butter, softened

Finely grated zest
of ½ lemon

2½ tbsp (25 g)
all-purpose flour

¾ tsp (3 g) baking
powder

Lemon shortbread

1½ sticks (6 oz./175 g)
butter

⅓ cup (1¾ oz./50 g)
confectioners' sugar

2½ tbsp (1½ oz./40 g)
egg yolk (about 2 yolks)

Scant ⅓ cup (1 oz./30 g)
almond flour

1⅔ cups (7 oz./190 g)
all-purpose flour

¼ tsp (1 g) baking powder

¼ tsp (1 g) salt

Zest of ½ lemon

Siphon sponge

3 tbsp (2 oz./50 g) egg
yolk (about 2½ yolks)

Scant ¼ cup
(1½ oz./45 g) superfine
sugar

2 tsp (10 ml) lemon juice

2 tsp (10 ml) water

2½ tbsp (25 g) all-
purpose flour

3¼ tsp (15 g) egg white
(about ½ white)

1 tbsp (14 g) butter,
melted and cooled

Cooking spray or
neutral oil for greasing

Yellow marzipan collar

2¾ oz. (80 g) marzipan,
33% almonds

A few drops natural
yellow food coloring

**White chocolate
velvet spray**

2¾ oz. (80 g) white
chocolate, chopped

2¾ oz. (80 g) cocoa
butter, chopped

Neutral glaze

3½ oz. (100 g)
neutral glaze

1 tbsp (15 ml)
water

2 tsp (10 g)
glucose syrup

To assemble

Dried lemon
and lime slices
(see technique p. 122)

A few tiny basil
leaves

1 finger lime
(optional)

PREPARING THE LIME CREAM (1 DAY AHEAD)

Cook the eggs, sugar, and lime juice over a bain-marie, whisking from time to time. Let cool to 122°F (50°C). Add the butter and process with the immersion blender until smooth. Weigh out 5 oz. (145 g) to make the lemon mousse. Pour some of the cream into the 2½-in. (6-cm) baking rings to fill. Stir the lime zest and green food coloring into the remaining cream and fill 12 cavities of the ¾-in. (2.2-cm) mold and 6 cavities of the 1¼-in. (3.2-cm) mold. Freeze the rings and molds overnight. Chill the remaining lime cream until assembling.

PREPARING THE SWISS MERINGUE (1 DAY AHEAD)

Preheat the oven to 160°F (70°C/Gas on lowest setting). Whisk the egg whites and sugar continuously over a bain-marie until the temperature reaches 113°F (45°C). Remove from the heat and whisk on high speed until the meringue has cooled completely. Weigh out 4 oz. (110 g) for the lemon mousse and spoon half the remaining meringue into the pastry bag. Fit the Saint-Honoré tip and pipe out petals, 1¼ in. (3 cm) long, onto a lined baking sheet. Change to the small plain tip, spoon the remaining meringue into the pastry bag, and pipe out meringue kisses, ½ in. (1 cm) in diameter, around the petals. Bake for 3 hours until dry but not colored. When cool, store in an airtight container.

PREPARING THE LEMON MOUSSE (1 DAY AHEAD)

Soak the gelatin in a bowl of cold water until softened. Place the hot water in a mixing bowl, squeeze the gelatin to remove excess water, and stir it into the hot water until dissolved. Stir in the lemon juice, followed by the lime cream. Fold in the Swiss meringue. Whip the cream until it holds its shape and gently fold it into the mousse. Spoon into 6 cavities of the 1¼-in. (3.2-cm) mold (next to the lime cream) and 8 cavities of the 1½-in. (4-cm) mold. Freeze overnight.

PREPARING THE GENOISE ALMOND SPONGE

Preheat the oven to 340°F (170°C/Gas Mark 3). Beat the almond paste in the stand mixer fitted with the paddle beater until softened. Gradually beat in the eggs. Change to the whisk attachment, add the butter and lemon zest, and whisk on medium speed until pale and thick. Sift in the flour with the baking powder and gently fold in using a flexible spatula. Spread the batter over a lined baking sheet to a thickness of ¾ in. (1.5 cm). Bake for 12 minutes, remove from the oven, and let cool completely. Cut out two 6-in. (16-cm) disks of sponge using the baking rings.

PREPARING THE LEMON SHORTBREAD BASES

Cream together the butter and confectioners' sugar in the stand mixer fitted with the paddle beater. Beat in the egg yolks, add the remaining ingredients, and beat until just combined. Shape the dough into a disk, cover it with plastic wrap, and chill for 30 minutes. Preheat the oven to 340°F (170°C/Gas Mark 3). Roll the dough to a thickness of ⅛ in. (3 mm) and cut

out two 6-in. (16-cm) disks using the baking rings. Place on a lined baking sheet and bake for 10 minutes. Let cool.

PREPARING THE SIPHON SPONGE

Whisk together the egg yolk and sugar in a bowl until pale and thick. Whisk in the lemon juice and water. Add the flour, egg white, and melted butter, and whisk until smooth and pourable. Transfer to the siphon, charge with the cartridges, and shake the siphon to distribute the gas. Using the tip of a knife, pierce five holes in the bottom of the paper cup and lightly grease the cup with neutral oil. Hold the siphon upside down and dispense the mixture to fill the cup halfway. Microwave in three 15-second bursts on medium power.

PREPARING THE YELLOW MARZIPAN COLLAR

Using your hands, work yellow food coloring into the marzipan until evenly distributed. Roll out the marzipan as thinly as possible between the two acetate sheets and cut two strips, 1⅓ in. (3.5 cm) wide and the same length as the circumference of the 6-in. (16-cm) baking rings.

PREPARING THE WHITE CHOCOLATE VELVET SPRAY

Melt the white chocolate and cocoa butter together over a bain-marie until the temperature reaches 122°F (50°C), stirring until smooth. Remove the frozen lemon mousse spheres from the silicone molds. Pour the melted chocolate into the spray gun and spray over the frozen spheres. Clean the spray gun.

PREPARING THE NEUTRAL GLAZE

Heat the neutral glaze, water, and glucose syrup in a saucepan until the temperature reaches 160°F (70°C). Unmold the frozen lime cream from the baking rings and silicone molds. Pour the hot glaze into the spray gun and spray evenly over the lime cream disks and spheres.

ASSEMBLING THE TARTS

For each tart, place a shortbread base on a serving plate and top with a genoise almond sponge disk. Spread a thin layer of lime cream over the sponge and top with a lime cream disk. Arrange the lime cream and lemon mousse spheres randomly over the lime cream disks. Wrap a marzipan collar around each tart and press the ends together to seal. Scatter the Swiss meringue petals and kisses, dried lemon and lime slices, and torn pieces of siphon sponge over the tarts. Decorate with the basil leaves and, if desired, place a spoonful of finger lime "caviar" in the center.

SPICED BABAS WITH ORANGE COMPOTE

Baba, compotée d'oranges, infusion aux épices douces

Serves 6

Active time

2 hours

Chilling time

12 hours

Freezing time

1 hour

Maturing time

12 hours

Cooking time

3¼ hours

Resting time

1 hour

Storage

Up to 3 days before assembling

Equipment

Immersion blender

18-cavity silicone ice ball mold, ¾ in. (2 cm) in dia.

Instant-read thermometer

Ice cream maker

Stand mixer + paddle beater

Pastry bag

2 cylindrical molds, 2 in. (5 cm) in dia., 10 in. (25 cm) long

2 sheets food-safe acetate

3-in. (8-cm) and ¾-in. (2-cm) round cookie cutters

Metal piping tips of different sizes

Kitchen torch

6 serving glasses, 2½ in. (6 cm) in dia. and 4 in. (10 cm) deep

Ingredients

Mascarpone cream marbles

Scant ¼ tsp (0.6 g) gelatin powder

Scant 1 tsp (4.5 ml) water

2 tbsp (30 ml) heavy cream, min. 35% fat

1¼ tsp (6 g) superfine sugar

Seeds of ½ vanilla bean

1¼ tsp (6 ml) orange blossom water

1½ tsp (15 g) mascarpone

2 tbsp (30 ml) heavy cream, min. 35% fat, well chilled

Orange sorbet

1 sheet (2 g) gold strength gelatin, 200 Bloom

Scant 1½ tsp (7 ml) water

Scant ¼ cup (1½ oz./45 g) superfine sugar

⅔ cup (160 ml) orange juice

Babas

2½ tbsp (40 ml) whole milk

¼ oz. (4.5 g) fresh yeast

¾ cup plus 2 tbsp (3½ oz./100 g) all-purpose flour

¼ tsp (1.5 g) fine salt

2½ tsp (10 g) superfine sugar

Scant ¼ cup (2 oz./55 g) lightly beaten egg (about 1 egg)

Seeds of ½ vanilla bean

2 tbsp (1 oz./30 g) butter, melted and cooled

Soaking syrup

1 cup plus 1½ tbsp (275 ml) water

Scant ½ cup (3¼ oz./90 g) superfine sugar

½ vanilla bean

1½ tsp (8 ml) white rum

Zest of ½ orange

Zest of ½ lime

½ stick cinnamon

½ star anise pod

⅔ oz. (20 g) passion fruit puree

2 tbsp (30 ml) orange juice

Caramelized grissini

¹⁄₂₅ oz. (1 g) fresh yeast

⅓ cup (1½ oz./40 g) bread flour

¾ tsp (4 ml) olive oil

1 pinch (0.15 g) fine salt

1 tbsp (15 ml) water

½ tbsp (4 g) vanilla powder

2 tbsp (16 g) confectioners' sugar

Orange compote

4 lb. (1.8 kg) sweet oranges

Scant 1 cup (6 oz./180 g) superfine sugar

Decoration

5¼ oz. (150 g) white couverture chocolate, 35% cacao (preferably Valrhona Ivoire), chopped

18 baby garden cress leaves

PREPARING THE MASCARPONE CREAM MARBLES (1 DAY AHEAD)

Sprinkle the gelatin over the cold water in a bowl and let soak for 10 minutes. Heat 2 tbsp (30 ml) cream in a saucepan with the sugar, vanilla seeds, and orange blossom water until the sugar dissolves. Stir in the gelatin until dissolved. Place the mascarpone in a bowl, pour over the cream mixture, and process with the immersion blender until smooth. Mix in the 2 tbsp (30 ml) well-chilled cream, cover, and chill for 12 hours. The next day, whip to soft peaks and spoon into the ice ball mold. Freeze until solid (about 1 hour), then unmold and store in the freezer.

PREPARING THE ORANGE SORBET (1 DAY AHEAD)

Soak the gelatin in a bowl of cold water until softened. Heat the scant 1½ tsp (7 ml) water, sugar, and one-third of the orange juice in a saucepan until the sugar dissolves. Bring to a simmer, then remove from the heat. Squeeze the gelatin to remove excess water and stir it into the hot syrup until dissolved. Let cool to 86°F (30°C). Add the remaining orange juice, then process with the immersion blender until smooth. Transfer to an airtight container and chill for 12 hours to mature. The next day, churn in the ice cream maker. Store in the freezer.

PREPARING THE BABAS

Heat the milk to lukewarm (95°F/35°C), crumble in the yeast, and stir to dissolve. Place the flour, salt, and sugar in the stand mixer bowl. Add the egg, vanilla seeds, and milk and yeast, then beat until combined. Pour in the melted butter and continue kneading until the dough is smooth and elastic. Transfer the dough to the pastry bag and pipe into the cylindrical molds, filling them two-thirds full. Let rise at room temperature until the dough fills the molds. Preheat the oven to 340°F (170°C/ Gas Mark 3). Bake the babas for about 15 minutes. Remove from the oven and lower the temperature to 325°F (160°C). Turn the babas out of the molds onto a baking sheet and return them to the oven for an additional 15 minutes until dry and golden. Let cool on a wire rack.

PREPARING THE SOAKING SYRUP

Heat all the ingredients together in a saucepan until the sugar dissolves. Bring to a boil, then reduce the heat and let simmer for 30 minutes. Remove from the heat, cover, and let cool to 140°F (60°C). Soak the babas in the syrup. Cover and refrigerate.

PREPARING THE CARAMELIZED GRISSINI

Crumble the yeast into the flour. Add the olive oil, salt, and water, and knead with your hands to make a dough. Shape into a ball, cover with plastic wrap, and let rest for 1 hour at room temperature. Preheat the oven to 325°F (160°C/Gas Mark 3). Pull off pieces of dough about ⅙ oz. (5 g) each and place on the work surface. Using the palm of your hand, roll each piece into a long, very thin stick. Place on a lined baking sheet and dust with the vanilla powder and a little confectioners' sugar.

Bake for 15 minutes, then remove from the oven and increase the temperature to 430°F (220°C/Gas Mark 7). Dust with confectioners' sugar again and return to the oven for 1 minute, or until caramelized. Let cool.

PREPARING THE ORANGE COMPOTE

Peel and segment the oranges (see technique p. 68), working over a bowl to catch the juice. Weigh out about 14 oz. (400 g) of the segments and place in a saucepan with the sugar and juice from the bowl. Stir to combine. Cut out a circle of parchment paper and place it over the orange segments. Cook gently over very low heat for about 2 hours until thick. Remove from the heat and let cool to room temperature.

PREPARING THE WHITE CHOCOLATE DECORATION

Temper the chocolate by melting it in a bowl over a bain-marie until the temperature reaches 113°F (45°C), stirring until smooth. Remove the bowl and stand it in a larger bowl filled with ice water. Stir until the chocolate cools to 79°F–81°F (26°C–27°C). Return the bowl to the bain-marie and raise the temperature of the chocolate to 82°F–84°F (28°C–29°C). Spread the chocolate in a thin layer between the two acetate sheets and let it set slightly without becoming hard (about 5 minutes). Peel off the top acetate sheet and cut out six disks using the 3-in. (8-cm) cutter. Let the disks set until they can be easily removed from the bottom sheet. Gently warm the piping tips using the kitchen torch, then use the base of each tip to cut out holes of different sizes in the disks. Let set completely.

TO SERVE

Drain the babas and cut them into 2-in. (5-cm) slices. Using the ¾-in. (2-cm) cutter, make a hole in the center of each one and place in the serving glasses. Top with the orange compote and a quenelle of orange sorbet. Set a white chocolate disk over each glass and place three mascarpone marbles on each one. Decorate with a few baby cress leaves and add the caramelized grissini. Serve immediately.

MANDARINS, EGG WHITE FOAM, AND OLIVE OIL AND VANILLA ICE CREAM

Mandarine, blancs mousseux et crème glacée à l'huile d'olive et vanille

Serves 6

Active time

2 hours

Cooking time

About 5 hours

Chilling time

1 hour

Storage

Up to 1 day before assembling

Equipment

Food processor (optional)

Instant-read thermometer

Immersion blender

Ice cream maker

Stand mixer + paddle beater and whisk

¾-in. (2-cm), 2-in. (5-cm), and 3-in. (8-cm) round cookie cutters

2 silicone baking mats

Rimmed silicone baking mat

Ingredients

Dried mandarin zest

1 mandarin

Meringues

Scant ¼ cup (1¾ oz./50 g) egg white (about 1⅔ whites)

½ cup (3½ oz./100 g) superfine sugar

⅕ oz. (5 g) dried mandarin zest (see above)

3¾ tsp (15 g) granulated sugar

1 pinch (3 g) ascorbic acid

Vanilla and olive oil ice cream

1⅔ cups (400 ml) whole milk

¼ oz. (8 g) invert sugar

Seeds of 3 vanilla beans

1¼ tsp (6 g) milk powder

⅓ cup (2½ oz./70 g) sugar

5 tsp (1¼ oz./35 g) glucose syrup

1 pinch (2.5 g) stabilizer

Scant ¼ cup (55 ml) olive oil

Mandarin marmalade

8 oz. (220 g) mandarins

½ cup (3½ oz./100 g) sugar, divided

¼ cup (60 ml) lemon juice

¼ tsp (1 g) pectin NH

Mandarin shortbread cookies

1¾ cups (8 oz./225 g) all-purpose flour, divided

1 stick (4 oz./113 g) butter, diced and softened

Scant ½ cup (2oz./55 g) confectioners' sugar

½ cup plus 1 tsp (2 oz./55 g) almond flour

Finely grated mandarin zest, as needed

3½ tbsp (1¾ oz./50 g) lightly beaten egg (1 egg)

Scant ½ tsp (2 g) salt

Madeleine sponge

Scant ½ cup (3½ oz./100 g) lightly beaten egg (2 eggs)

Scant ½ cup (3 oz./85 g) superfine sugar

5 tsp (1¼ oz./35 g) honey

¾ cup plus 2 tbsp (3½ oz./100 g) all-purpose flour

1 tsp (4 g) baking powder

Finely grated mandarin zest, to taste

Generous ⅓ cup (90 ml) olive oil

Lemon and mandarin jelly

2½ tbsp (1 oz./30 g) sugar

2¼ tsp (5 g) agar-agar powder

¾ cup (180 ml) lemon juice

¾ cup (180 ml) water

Finely grated mandarin zest, to taste

Citrus vinaigrette

Scant ½ cup (100 ml) mandarin juice

Scant ½ cup (100 ml) lemon juice

Generous ¾ cup (200 ml) olive oil

3½ oz. (100 g) neutral glaze

Candied mandarins

1 cup (250 ml) water

¼ cup (1¾ oz./50 g) sugar

Juice of 2 mandarins

6 mandarins, peeled and left whole

Egg white foam

2 tsp (10 g) gelatin powder

¼ cup (60 ml) cold water

Scant 2 cups (14 oz./400 g) egg white (about 13 whites)

¾ cup (5 oz./140 g) superfine sugar

¾ tsp (3 g) cream of tartar

1 tsp (3 g) egg white powder (optional)

Cooking spray or 1 tbsp grape-seed oil

To serve

Neutral oil for greasing

1–2 mandarins, peeled and segmented (see technique p. 68)

Red-veined sorrel leaves

Dried mandarin zest

PREPARING THE DRIED MANDARIN ZEST

Preheat the oven to 160°F (70°C/Gas on lowest setting). Wash and remove the zest from the mandarin using a zester. Spread the zest out over a lined baking sheet and place in the oven for 2 hours until completely dry. When cool, chop finely with a knife or in a food processor.

PREPARING THE MERINGUES

Preheat the oven to 175°F (80°C/Gas on lowest setting). Whisk the egg whites and sugar continuously over a bain-marie until the temperature reaches 122°F (50°C). Remove the bowl from the heat and continue to whisk on high speed until the meringue has cooled completely. Spread the meringue over a lined baking sheet in a thin, even layer and sprinkle with the dried mandarin zest, reserving some for decoration. Combine the granulated sugar and ascorbic acid and sprinkle over the meringue. Bake for 2 hours until dry and crisp. When cool, break the meringue into small pieces and store in an airtight container.

PREPARING THE VANILLA AND OLIVE OIL ICE CREAM

Bring the milk and invert sugar to a boil. Stir in the vanilla seeds, milk powder, sugar, glucose syrup, and stabilizer. Add the olive oil and process with the immersion blender until emulsified. Let cool, then churn in the ice cream maker. Freeze in an airtight container until serving.

PREPARING THE MANDARIN MARMALADE

Wash the mandarins and cook them whole in a saucepan of boiling water for about 10 minutes. Drain, cut into pieces, and return to the pan. Add a scant ½ cup (3¼ oz./90 g) of the sugar and the lemon juice and process to a coarse puree using the immersion blender. Cook over low heat, stirring often, until thick. Once the marmalade reaches the desired consistency, combine the remaining sugar with the pectin. Stir into the marmalade and bring to a boil. Let cool.

PREPARING THE MANDARIN SHORTBREAD COOKIES

Place ½ cup (2 oz./55 g) of the flour in the stand mixer bowl. Add the remaining ingredients and beat with the paddle beater until smooth. Add the rest of the flour and mix briefly on low speed. Transfer the dough to the work surface, press down on it, and push with the heel of your hand, smearing it against the work surface until smooth (*fraisage*). Gather the dough into a ball and flatten into a disk ¾ in. (2 cm) thick. Cover with plastic wrap and chill for 1 hour. Preheat the oven to 325°F (160°C/Gas Mark 3). On a lightly floured surface, roll the dough to a thickness of ¹⁄₁₆ in. (2 mm). Cut out six ¾-in. (2-cm) disks and six 2-in. (5-cm) disks using the cookie cutters and place on a silicone mat. Cover with the second mat, top down, and bake for 15 minutes. Remove the top mat and let the cookies cool.

PREPARING THE MADELEINE SPONGE

Preheat the oven to 340°F (170°C/Gas Mark 3). Fit the stand mixer with the whisk and beat the eggs, sugar, and honey together until pale and thick. Whisk in the flour and baking powder until just combined, followed by the mandarin zest and olive oil. Pour the batter into the rimmed silicone baking mat and bake for 12 minutes. Let cool, then cut out six 2-in. (5-cm) disks using the cookie cutter.

PREPARING THE LEMON AND MANDARIN JELLY

Heat all the ingredients together in a saucepan until the sugar and agar-agar dissolve. Briefly bring to a boil, then remove from the heat. Process with the immersion blender. Let set and chill until serving.

PREPARING THE CITRUS VINAIGRETTE

Process all the ingredients together in a bowl using the immersion blender until emulsified. Chill until serving.

PREPARING THE CANDIED MANDARINS

Heat the water, sugar, and mandarin juice in a saucepan until the sugar dissolves, then bring to a boil. Immerse the mandarins in the syrup and cook for 5–10 minutes, depending on their size. Drain the mandarins using a skimmer. Boil the syrup until reduced by half and drizzle over the mandarins. Let cool to room temperature.

PREPARING THE EGG WHITE FOAM

Sprinkle the gelatin over the cold water in a bowl and let soak for 10 minutes. Whisk the egg whites, sugar, cream of tartar, and egg white powder, if using, in the stand mixer until foamy. Heat the gelatin by placing the bowl over a bain-marie until dissolved. With the mixer running, slowly pour the gelatin over the egg whites and whisk continuously until they are almost firm. Cover a large plate with plastic wrap and lightly grease it with cooking spray or oil. Using an offset spatula, spread a layer of egg whites ¾ in. (2 cm) thick over the plate. Cook for a few seconds over a bain-marie until the whites are firm.

TO SERVE

Grease the 3-in. (8-cm) cookie cutter with oil and cut out six disks of egg white foam. Cut out the center of each one to form a ring, using the 2-in. (5-cm) cutter. Set a ring on each serving plate, cut out a segment, and place a candied mandarin in the space. Top with a ¾-in. (2-cm) cookie. Place a 2-in. (5-cm) shortbread disk in the center of each ring. Moisten the sponge disks with the vinaigrette and place on top of the shortbread, then cover with a little marmalade and jelly. Decorate the foam rings with mandarin segments, red-veined sorrel leaves, dried mandarin zest, dots of jelly, and pieces of meringue, leaving space for the ice cream. Using a spoon dipped in hot water, scrape curls of ice cream into rolls and place on the rings. Serve immediately, with the remaining vinaigrette.

KUMQUAT CAKE
Cake au kumquat

Serves 6

Active time
45 minutes

Cooking time
35 minutes

Storage
Up to 3 days

Equipment
Stand mixer + paddle beater

2½ × 8½-in. (6.5 × 22-cm) oblong cake pan, 1¾ in. (4.5 cm) deep

2 × 8¼-in. (5.5 × 21-cm) oblong cake frame, 1 in. (2.5 cm) deep

Ingredients

Candied kumquats
5–6 whole candied kumquats (see technique p. 84)
Flour, for dusting

Syrup
⅔ cup (150 ml) water
½ cup (3½ oz./100 g) sugar
Zest of 3 kumquats

Cake batter
6 tbsp (3 oz./90 g) butter, diced and softened
⅔ cup (3 oz./85 g) confectioners' sugar
⅓ cup (2½ oz./75 g) lightly beaten egg (about 1½ eggs)
¼ cup (1 oz./25 g) almond flour
¾ cup plus 2 tbsp (3¾ oz./105 g) all-purpose flour
1½ tbsp (15 g) cornstarch
1 tsp (3.5 g) baking powder
3½ tsp (17 ml) whole milk
3½ tsp (17 ml) kumquat juice

Calamansi jelly
2½ tsp (3 g) agar-agar powder
2½ tbsp (1 oz./30 g) sugar
1 tbsp (15 ml) orange juice
2 oz. (55 g) calamansi puree

Decoration
Dried candied kumquats (see technique p. 122), thinly sliced

PREPARING THE CANDIED KUMQUATS
Toss the candied kumquats in flour until coated.

PREPARING THE SYRUP
Heat the water, sugar, and kumquat zest in a saucepan until the sugar dissolves. Bring to a boil, remove from the heat, and let cool to room temperature.

PREPARING THE CAKE BATTER
Preheat the oven to 350°F (175°C/Gas Mark 4). Beat the butter and confectioners' sugar together in the stand mixer until light and creamy. Gradually beat in the egg. Add the almond flour, all-purpose flour, cornstarch, and baking powder, and beat until just combined. Beat in the milk and kumquat juice. Transfer the batter to the lined cake pan, filling it three-quarters full. Scatter the candied kumquats randomly over the top. Bake for 35 minutes or until the tip of a knife inserted into the center of the cake comes out clean. Let the cake cool in the pan for 10 minutes, then turn it out onto a wire rack. Spoon the cooled syrup over the cake to soak it, then let it cool completely.

PREPARING THE CALAMANSI JELLY
Combine the agar-agar and sugar in a bowl. Place in a saucepan with the orange juice and calamansi puree, and heat until the agar-agar and sugar dissolve. Bring to a boil, then remove from the heat and let cool.

ASSEMBLING THE CAKE
Place the cake frame on top of the cooled cake and pour in the calamansi jelly. Wait about 10 minutes, or until the jelly has set, then remove the frame. Arrange dried candied kumquat slices over the top of the cake.

SUGAR-GLAZED YUZU MADELEINES

Madeleine au yuzu, glaçage au sucre

Makes 24

Active time
20 minutes

Resting time
2–12 hours

Chilling time
About 25 minutes

Cooking time
11 minutes

Storage
Up to 1 week
in an airtight container

Equipment
Madeleine pan
2 pastry bags + a plain
⅓-in. (8-mm) tip
Immersion blender

Ingredients

Madeleine batter
⅔ cup (5 oz./150 g)
lightly beaten egg
(3 eggs)
⅔ cup (4½ oz./125 g)
superfine sugar
⅛ tsp (0.5 g) fine salt
1¼ tbsp (25 g) acacia
honey
2¾ tsp (12 ml) grape-
seed oil
1 cup plus 1 tbsp
(4½ oz./135 g) all-
purpose flour, plus extra
for dusting
1¾ tsp (7 g) baking
powder
Scant ½ cup (1½ oz./45 g)
almond flour
1½ sticks (6 oz./180 g)
butter, melted and
cooled, plus extra
for greasing
2 tbsp (30 ml) whole milk

Yuzu filling
5 tsp (20 g) superfine
sugar
Scant 1 tsp (3.5 g) pectin
NH
½ tsp (1 g) agar-agar
powder
1½ tbsp (25 ml) yuzu juice
Scant ½ cup (100 ml)
water

Glaze
⅓ cup (1½ oz./45 g)
confectioners' sugar
1 tbsp (15 ml) yuzu juice

PREPARING THE MADELEINE BATTER

Whisk together the eggs, sugar, salt, and honey until combined but not emul-sified. Whisk in the oil. Sift together the all-purpose flour, baking powder, and almond flour, then whisk into the mixture. Finally fold in the melted butter and the milk. Press plastic wrap over the surface of the batter and let it rest in the refrigerator for at least 2 hours, or preferably overnight (12 hours).

PREPARING THE YUZU FILLING

Combine the sugar, pectin, and agar-agar in a bowl. Heat the yuzu juice and water in a saucepan, stir in the agar-agar mixture until dissolved, then bring to a boil. Let boil for 30 seconds, pour into a bowl, and press plastic wrap over the surface. Chill until completely set.

BAKING THE MADELEINES

Grease the madeleine pan with butter and dust lightly with flour. Stir the batter with a spatula to loosen it and spoon into a pastry bag fitted with the plain tip. Pipe the batter into the pan, filling each cavity just over two-thirds full. Before baking, chill for 10 minutes (or until the batter is cold), as this will help the madeleines rise and develop their characteristic "bump." Preheat the oven to 375°F (190°C/Gas Mark 5) and bake for 2 minutes. Reduce the temperature to 340°F (170°C/Gas Mark 3) and bake for an additional 7 minutes. Remove from the oven and immediately turn them out onto a wire rack. Let cool completely.

PREPARING THE GLAZE

Whisk together the confectioners' sugar and yuzu juice in a bowl until the sugar dissolves.

GLAZING AND FILLING THE MADELEINES

Preheat the oven to 340°F (170°C/Gas Mark 3). Place the madeleines, scal-loped side uppermost, on a baking sheet. Brush with the glaze and place in the oven for 1 minute to dry the glaze. Remove the yuzu filling from the refrigerator and process with the immersion blender until fluid. Transfer the filling to a pastry bag without a tip. Make a small hole on the smooth side of each madeleine and fill with the yuzu filling.

KAFFIR LIME PRALINE AND MARSHMALLOW CHOCOLATE BARS

Tablette chocolat combawa, guimauve et praliné

Makes 2

Active time
1 hour

Cooking time
30 minutes

Setting time
2 hours

Storage
Up to 5 days

Equipment
Silicone baking mat

Food processor

Instant-read thermometer

Stand mixer + whisk

Pastry bag + a plain ¼-in. (6-mm) tip

2 citrus slice-shaped chocolate molds, 4 in. (10 cm) in diameter and ¾-in. (1.5 cm) deep, or 2 classic chocolate bar molds (see Chefs' Notes)

Ingredients

Kaffir lime and hazelnut praline

2 tbsp (20 g) whole hazelnuts

1 tbsp (12 g) superfine sugar

¾ tsp (4 ml) water

½ tsp (4 g) glucose syrup

Seeds of 1 vanilla bean

⅛ tsp (0.5 g) fine salt

1/10 oz. (3 g) cocoa butter

½ tsp (1 g) finely grated kaffir lime zest

Kaffir lime marshmallow

Scant ½ tsp (2 g) gelatin powder

Scant 1 tbsp (14 ml) cold water

1 tbsp (15 ml) water

2 tbsp (25 g) superfine sugar

⅔ oz. (18 g) invert sugar, divided

½ tsp (1 g) finely grated kaffir lime zest

Chocolate coating

7 oz. (200 g) dark couverture chocolate, 64% cacao, chopped

PREPARING THE KAFFIR LIME AND HAZELNUT PRALINE

Preheat the oven to 285°F (140°C/Gas Mark 1). Spread the hazelnuts out over a lined baking sheet and roast them in the oven for 20 minutes. Heat the sugar, water, glucose syrup, and vanilla seeds in a saucepan until the sugar dissolves, then boil to a light brown caramel. Stir in the salt and warm nuts, then pour the mixture over the silicone baking mat. Let cool to room temperature. Break the nuts roughly into large chunks and process in the food processor in stages, to avoid overheating the mixture, until a smooth paste is obtained. The temperature should not exceed 95°F (35°C), or the oil in the hazelnuts could separate. Melt the cocoa butter in a bowl over a bain-marie, then mix into the praline paste. Add the kaffir lime zest and let cool to room temperature. Process again to ensure the paste is smooth.

PREPARING THE KAFFIR LIME MARSHMALLOW

Sprinkle the gelatin over the cold water in a bowl and let soak for 10 minutes. Heat the 1 tbsp (15 ml) water, superfine sugar, and ¼ oz. (8 g) of the invert sugar in a saucepan until the sugar dissolves, then continue to cook to 230°F (110°C). Transfer to the stand mixer and add the remaining invert sugar and gelatin. Whisk for 3 minutes on medium speed until the mixture thickens and is light and fluffy. Reduce the speed to low and whisk until cold. Whisk in the kaffir lime zest. Spoon into the pastry bag.

TEMPERING THE COATING CHOCOLATE

Place the chopped chocolate in a bowl over a bain-marie and melt until the temperature reaches 122°F (50°C), stirring until smooth. When the chocolate has melted, stand the bowl in a larger bowl filled with ice water and stir until the chocolate has cooled to 82°F–84°F (28°C–29°C). Return the bowl to the saucepan and raise the temperature of the chocolate to 88°F–90°F (31°C–32°C).

ASSEMBLING THE BARS

Pour a layer of chocolate into the molds and let set for a few minutes. Pipe the marshmallow mixture over the chocolate, filling the molds halfway. Let set for a few minutes until the marshmallow is no longer sticky to the touch. Cover with the praline mixture to within 1/16 in. (2 mm) of the tops of the molds. When the top of the praline has firmed up, cover with the remaining chocolate, removing any excess with a spatula. Let set for 2 hours at room temperature, or until the chocolate pulls away from the sides of the molds. Carefully invert the molds over a flat surface to remove the bars.

CHEFS' NOTES

• This recipe works equally well using classic chocolate bar molds.

• As the marshmallow mixture does not contain egg white, it can be reused. Reheat in the microwave to soften.

LANGOUSTINE WITH FINGER LIME CAVIAR AND CHIA TUILES

Langoustine, citron caviar et tuile de chia

Serves 4

Active time

1½ hours

Soaking time

24 hours

Cooking time

3¾ hours

Infusing time

12 hours

Freezing time

1¼ hours

Storage

Up to 2 days, before assembling

Equipment

Silicone baking mat

Instant-read thermometer

Blender

Food-safe fine-mesh cheesecloth

Disposable pastry bag

Pipette

Mandoline

2 skewers

Ingredients

Chia tuiles

4 tsp (20 ml) water

1 tbsp (10 g) chia seeds

⅔ cup (150 ml) grape-seed oil

Decoction

1 cup (250 ml) cold water

1 bay leaf

½ stick cinnamon

1 star anise pod

1¾ tsp (7.5 g) superfine sugar

2½ tsp (12 g) fine salt

Langoustines

1 cup (250 ml) decoction (see above)

4 extra-large langoustines (Norway lobsters), 5¼–9 oz. (150–250 g) each

Dill oil

Scant ½ cup (115 ml) grape-seed oil

1 oz. (30 g) spinach

2¼ oz. (65 g) fresh dill

Yogurt broth

Scant ½ cup (3½ oz./100 g) Greek yogurt

½ cup (4½ oz./125 g) whole milk plain yogurt

Generous ½ teaspoon (3 g) salt

Fromage frais cream

2 oz. (60 g) curds from the yogurt broth

1 tsp finely chopped shallot

1 tbsp finely chopped chives

½ tsp (4 g) thyme honey

1 tsp (5 ml) white balsamic vinegar

Salt, freshly ground long pepper, and *piment d'Espelette*, to taste

Pickled cucumber

3½ tbsp (50 ml) water

3½ tbsp (50 ml) white vinegar

¼ cup (1¾ oz./50 g) superfine sugar

Scant ½ tsp (2 g) fine salt

2 oz. (60 g) cucumber

Apple *brunoise*

2 oz. (50 g) Granny Smith apple

Juice of 1 lemon

To serve

Drizzle of extra-virgin olive oil

1 finger lime

Baby Kikuna cress, Persinette cress, and borage cress

PREPARING THE CHIA TUILES (1 DAY AHEAD)

Bring the water to a boil, place the chia seeds in a bowl, and pour the boiling water over them. Stir to mix, cover the bowl with plastic wrap, and let soak at room temperature for 24 hours. The next day, preheat the oven to 175°F (80°C/Gas on lowest setting). Spread the chia seeds out over the silicone baking mat in a thin, even layer. Bake for 3 hours or until completely dry. Heat the grape-seed oil in a small, deep skillet to 355°F (180°C). Break the dried chia seeds into even-sized pieces and fry until crisp. Drain on paper towel and store in a dry place until serving.

PREPARING THE DECOCTION (1 DAY AHEAD)

Place ⅔ cup (150 ml) water, the bay leaf, cinnamon stick, and star anise pod in a bowl and place in the freezer until very cold but not frozen. In a saucepan, bring the remaining water, sugar, and salt to a boil. Immediately pour it over the cold water in the bowl to create a thermal shock that helps the salt dissolve. Let infuse for 12 hours in the refrigerator, then strain through a fine-mesh sieve.

PREPARING THE LANGOUSTINES

One hour before preparing the langoustines, measure out 1 cup (250 ml) of the decoction and place in the freezer. Remove the heads from the langoustines and peel them, leaving the last segment of shell and tail end intact (the shells can be reserved for another recipe). Make a small cut down the back of each langoustine and pull out the dark thread (intestinal tract). Gently immerse the langoustines in the decoction and let marinate for 4 minutes. Remove, pat dry, cover with plastic wrap, and keep chilled.

PREPARING THE DILL OIL

Heat the oil to 185°F (85°C). Pour it into the blender, add the spinach and dill, and process to a fine puree. Strain through the cheesecloth into a bowl. Transfer to the pastry bag and suspend the bag, tip pointing downward, for 2 hours to allow any solids to settle at the bottom. Snip off the tip of the bag to make a small hole and let the solids drain out. Fill the pipette with the remaining oil. (Store any leftover oil in a cool place, away from light, for use in another recipe.)

PREPARING THE YOGURT BROTH AND FROMAGE FRAIS CREAM

Heat the yogurts and salt in a saucepan until the yogurt curdles. Strain through the cheesecloth into a bowl to separate the curds from the whey (the yogurt broth). Chill the yogurt broth and the curds in separate bowls. Weigh out 2 oz. (60 g) of the curds, stir with a spoon to loosen them, and stir in the shallot, chives, honey, and vinegar. Season to taste with salt, long pepper, and *piment d'Espelette*. Chill until serving.

PREPARING THE PICKLED CUCUMBER

Prepare a brine by heating the water, vinegar, sugar, and salt in a saucepan until the sugar and salt dissolve. Bring to a boil, remove from the heat, cover, and let cool. Chill until using. Wash the cucumber. Using the mandoline, shave it lengthwise into very thin slices (1/16 in./1.5 mm thick). Cut out the centers to remove the seeds, immerse the slices in the brine, and let marinate for 5 minutes. Wrap the slices around the skewers to make mini rolls (see photograph).

PREPARING THE APPLE BRUNOISE

Peel the apple and cut it into 1/16-in. (2-mm) dice. Coat with the lemon juice to prevent browning.

TO FINISH

Gently warm the yogurt broth, add a few drops of the dill oil, and stir without emulsifying. To cook the langoustines, coat a skillet with a drizzle of olive oil and set over high heat. When hot, add the langoustines, bellies uppermost, and sear without turning for 2–3 minutes until the bellies are just opaque. Remove from the skillet and season with salt and pepper. Cut the finger lime in half and scoop out the caviar-like pulp. Drain the apple *brunoise*.

TO SERVE

Place a spoonful of the fromage frais cream in each serving dish and top with a langoustine, back uppermost. Spoon over a little apple *brunoise*, followed by a little finger lime caviar. Arrange the pickled cucumber rolls and chia tuiles attractively around the langoustines. Divide the yogurt broth between the dishes, sprinkle with a few cress leaves or microgreens, and serve.

GRAPEFRUIT YULE LOG

Bûche au pamplemousse

Serves 6

Active time

1½ hours

Freezing time

3 hours

Chilling time

1 hour

Cooking time

10 minutes

Storage

Up to 24 hours in the refrigerator

Equipment

Instant-read thermometer

Immersion blender

Rigid food-safe acetate sheet rolled into a ¾-in. (2-cm) dia. tube, 10 in. (25 cm) long, held in place with adhesive tape

Channel (canelle) knife

Ingredients

Grapefruit crémeux

3½ sheets (7 g) gold-strength gelatin, 200 Bloom

5½ oz. (155 g) white chocolate, chopped

1 cup (250 ml) whole milk

1¾ oz. (50 g) superfine sugar, divided

3 tbsp (1¾ oz./50 g) egg yolk (about 2½ yolks)

Scant ⅔ cup (140 ml) grapefruit juice

Pear mousse

2 sheets (4 g) gold-strength gelatin, 200 Bloom

⅔ cup (5 oz./150 g) lightly beaten egg (3 eggs)

Scant ½ cup (4¼ oz./120 g) egg yolk (6 yolks)

½ cup (3½ oz./100 g) superfine sugar

14 oz. (400 g) pear puree

1 stick plus 3 tbsp (5½ oz./160 g) butter

Joconde sponge

1 cup (4¾ oz./135 g) confectioners' sugar

Scant 1½ cups (4¾ oz./135 g) almond flour

¾ cup (6¼ oz./180 g) lightly beaten egg (about 3½ eggs)

½ cup (4 oz./120 g) egg white (4 whites)

1½ tbsp (18 g) superfine sugar

¼ cup (1¼ oz./35 g) all-purpose flour, sifted

2 tbsp (28 g) butter, melted and cooled

Grapefruit syrup

3½ tbsp (50 ml) water

¼ cup (1¾ oz./50 g) sugar

3½ tbsp (50 ml) grapefruit juice

Decoration

1 white grapefruit

1 pink grapefruit

1 pear in syrup (canned)

Affilla cress leaves

PREPARING THE GRAPEFRUIT CRÉMEUX

Soak the gelatin in a bowl of cold water until softened. Place the white chocolate in a separate bowl. Heat the milk in a saucepan with half the sugar until the sugar dissolves, then bring to a boil. Meanwhile, whisk together the egg yolks and remaining sugar until pale and thick. When the milk comes to a boil, whisk a little into the egg yolk mixture. Pour the egg yolk mixture into the saucepan and cook, stirring continuously with a spatula, until the custard coats the spatula and the temperature reaches 180°F (82°C). Remove from the heat. Weigh out 5 oz. (140 g) and place in a bowl. Squeeze the gelatin to remove excess water and stir it into the custard in the bowl, then pour the mixture over the white chocolate. Process with the immersion blender until smooth, then mix in the grapefruit juice. Weigh out 14 oz. (400 g) and use to fill the acetate tube. Freeze for 3 hours.

PREPARING THE PEAR MOUSSE

Soak the gelatin in a bowl of cold water until softened. Whisk together the eggs, egg yolks, and sugar in a bowl until pale and thick. Place the egg mixture in a saucepan with the pear puree and bring to a simmer, whisking continuously. As soon as the mixture begins to bubble, remove it from the heat. Squeeze the gelatin to remove excess water and whisk it in until dissolved. Immerse the base of the saucepan in a bowl filled with ice water and cool the mixture until the temperature reaches 113°F (45°C), stirring regularly. Stir in the melted butter. Chill for 1 hour before assembling.

PREPARING THE JOCONDE SPONGE

Preheat the oven to 350°F (180°C/Gas Mark 4). Whisk together the confectioners' sugar, almond flour, and lightly beaten eggs in a mixing bowl until creamy and thick. Wash and dry the whisk. Whisk together the egg whites and superfine sugar until they hold firm peaks. Using a flexible spatula, gently fold the whites into the almond flour mixture. Sift in the all-purpose flour and fold in. Finally, fold in the melted butter. Spread the batter across a lined baking sheet to a thickness of ½ in. (1 cm) and bake for 9 minutes. Let cool.

PREPARING THE GRAPEFRUIT SYRUP

Heat the water and sugar in a saucepan until the sugar dissolves. Bring to a boil, then stir in the grapefruit juice. Let cool completely in the refrigerator.

PREPARING THE DECORATIONS

To make the candied grapefruit zest, remove the zest from the grapefruits using the channel knife (see technique p. 64). To remove bitterness from the zest, blanch it three times in boiling water: drain, immerse in ice water, and blanch in fresh water each time. Drain the pear from its syrup and heat the syrup in a separate saucepan. Bring to a boil, add the zest, and cook for 1 minute. Remove the zest from the syrup and let drain on a plate lined with paper towel. Peel and segment both grapefruits (see technique p. 68) and set the segments aside. Cut the pear into ¼-in. (5-mm) dice.

ASSEMBLING THE YULE LOG

Cut the Joconde sponge into a 10 × 16-in. (25 × 40-cm) rectangle. Brush the grapefruit syrup over the sponge, then spread it with a ¼-in. (5-mm) layer of pear mousse, leaving a 2-in. (5-cm) border at one short side to make it easier to seal the log when rolled. Scatter the diced pear over the mousse. Take the crémeux from the freezer and remove from the acetate tube. Place at the short side of the sponge where the mousse has been spread to the edge and roll the sponge up around it. Arrange the grapefruit segments attractively over the top and scatter with the candied grapefruit zest and a few affilla cress leaves.

CHEFS' NOTES

To roll the log up more easily,
place the sponge on a sheet of parchment
paper before spreading with the pear mousse
and use the parchment to help you roll.
This will prevent the sponge from breaking.

KING CRAB WITH POMELOS, AVOCADO, AND GRAPEFRUIT CLOUDS

Crabe royal et pomélos, purée d'avocat et nuage de pamplemousse

Serves 4

Active time
1 hour

Cooking time
1 hour

Storage
Up to 2 days
in the refrigerator, before
assembling

Equipment
Food processor

Food-safe acetate sheet

2-in. (5-cm) round cookie
cutter

Immersion blender

2-cup (500-ml) whipping
siphon + 1 N$_2$O gas
cartridge

Blender

Pipette or pastry
bag + a small plain tip

Kitchen torch

Ingredients
Spicy mayonnaise
1¾ tsp (10 g) egg yolk
(about ½ yolk)

½ tsp (2.5 g) Dijon
mustard

½ tsp (2.5 g) very finely
grated horseradish

Scant ½ cup (100 ml)
grape-seed oil

1 tsp (5 ml) lime juice

2 tbsp (1½ oz./40 g) Thai
chili paste (nam prik pao)

Salt and freshly ground
pepper

**Cucumber powder
(optional)**
7 oz. (200 g) cucumber

Grapefruit veils
1 sheet (2 g) gold-
strength gelatin,
200 Bloom

Scant ½ cup (100 ml)
grapefruit juice

2½ tsp (10 g) superfine
sugar

½ tsp (1 g) agar-agar
powder

Grapefruit clouds
1 sheet (2 g) gold-
strength gelatin,
200 Bloom

1½ tbsp (25 ml) whole
milk

Seeds of ½ vanilla bean

2½ tsp (10 g) superfine
sugar

Scant ½ cup (100 ml)
pink grapefruit juice

Avocado puree
4½ oz. (125 g) Hass
avocado flesh

1 tsp (5 ml) grape-seed oil

½ tsp (3 ml) lime juice

½ tsp (1.5 g) *piment
d'Espelette* (or to taste)

Salt and freshly ground
pepper

To serve
11 oz. (320 g) cooked king
crab merus

1½ oz. (40 g) honey
pomelo

Kikuna cress, Persinette
cress, and borage cress

Angel hair (Chinese long
chilies, dried and finely
shredded), to taste

PREPARING THE SPICY MAYONNAISE

Whisk together the egg yolk, mustard, and horseradish in a mixing bowl. Season with salt and pepper. Whisking continuously, add the oil drop by drop until the mixture begins to thicken. Once the egg yolk and oil have emulsified, drizzle in the remaining oil in a thin stream, whisking continuously, until the mayonnaise is thick, creamy, and smooth. Whisk in the lime juice to stabilize it. In a separate bowl, beat the chili paste to loosen it, then gradually stir in the mayonnaise until combined. Cover and chill until serving.

PREPARING THE CUCUMBER POWDER (OPTIONAL)

Preheat the oven to 425°F (220°C/Gas Mark 7). Wash the cucumber and cut it into quarters lengthwise, without peeling. Place on a lined baking sheet and roast for about 1 hour until blackened. Let cool completely. Pulse to a powder in the food processor and store in an airtight container.

PREPARING THE GRAPEFRUIT VEILS

Soak the gelatin in a bowl of cold water until softened. Heat the grapefruit juice in a saucepan and stir in the sugar and agar-agar powder until dissolved. Bring to a boil for 1 minute, then remove from the heat. Squeeze the gelatin to remove excess water and stir into the hot liquid until dissolved. Pour the mixture over the acetate sheet placed on a rimmed baking sheet, in a layer 1/16 in. (2 mm) thick, and chill until set. Cut out four disks using the cookie cutter and chill until serving.

PREPARING THE GRAPEFRUIT CLOUDS

Soak the gelatin in a bowl of cold water until softened. Warm the milk, vanilla seeds, and sugar in a saucepan until the sugar dissolves, then remove from the heat. Squeeze the gelatin to remove excess water and stir into the hot liquid. When the gelatin has dissolved, stir in the grapefruit juice. Process with the immersion blender until smooth, then strain through a fine-mesh sieve into a bowl. Transfer to the siphon and charge it with the cartridge. Shake the siphon to distribute the gas, then chill until serving.

PREPARING THE AVOCADO PUREE

Place all the ingredients in the blender and puree. Taste and adjust the seasonings, then press through a fine-mesh sieve so the mixture is perfectly smooth. Transfer to the pipette or pastry bag and chill until serving.

TO SERVE

Shell the king crab merus and cut each one into three pieces. Cover two out of the three pieces with spicy mayonnaise and brown using the kitchen torch. If you do not have a kitchen torch, place under a broiler preheated to 375°F (190°C) for 2 minutes. Peel and segment the pomelo (see technique p. 68) and cut the segments into pieces. Sear the top edges with the kitchen torch. If using cucumber powder, dust each serving plate with a little powder using a fine-mesh sieve. If desired, place a circle of parchment paper in the center of each plate before dusting to leave it clear. Arrange the crab pieces and pomelo segments attractively on each plate, place a grapefruit veil on top of the crab, and pipe small mounds of avocado puree around. Finally, hold the siphon upside down and dispense some of the mixture onto each plate to form a "cloud." Garnish with the assorted cress leaves and a tangle of angel hair shreds.

BUDDHA'S-HAND MILLE-FEUILLE

Millefeuille à la main de bouddha

Serves 6

Active time
4½ hours

Chilling time
8 hours

Freezing time
20 minutes

Cooking time
1 hour 10 minutes

Storage
Up to 2 days in the refrigerator

Equipment
4-in. (10-cm) square baking dish

Mandoline

Instant-read thermometer

Immersion blender

Silicone baking mat or lined baking sheet

Food processor

Stand mixer + dough hook

2 pastry bags

Ingredients

Gianduja cubes

1¾ oz. (50 g) gianduja paste (see technique p. 114)

Candied Buddha's-hand

1 Buddha's-hand

Scant ½ cup (100 ml) water

½ cup (3½ oz./100 g) superfine sugar

Seeds of 1 vanilla bean

Gianduja crémeux

Scant ¼ tsp (1 g) gelatin powder

1¼ tsp (6 ml) cold water

2 tbsp (30 ml) whole milk

Scant ¼ cup (55 ml) heavy cream, min. 35% fat

2 tsp (8 g) superfine sugar

1 tbsp (20 g) egg yolk (1 yolk)

1½ oz. (45 g) gianduja paste (see technique p. 114)

1 tbsp (14 g) butter

Caramel powder

½ cup (3½ oz./100 g) superfine sugar

Puff pastry layers

For the *détrempe* (water dough)

3¼ cups (14 oz./400 g) all-purpose flour, sifted

Generous ¾ cup (200 ml) water

2½ tsp (12 g) fine salt

4 tbsp (2 oz./60 g) butter, softened

Generous ½ tsp (3 ml) white vinegar

For laminating

3 sticks (12½ oz./350 g) butter, preferably 84% fat

Lemon diplomat cream

½ tsp (2.5 g) gelatin powder

1 tbsp (15 ml) cold water

Scant ⅔ cup (140 ml) whole milk

1 tbsp plus 2 tsp (1 oz./30 g) egg yolk (about 1½ yolks)

Scant ¼ cup (1½ oz./45 g) superfine sugar

5 tsp (15 g) custard powder

3 tbsp (45 ml) lemon juice

Scant ½ cup (112 ml) heavy cream, min. 35% fat

PREPARING THE GIANDUJA CUBES

Line the baking dish with plastic wrap. Spread the gianduja paste over the plastic wrap in an even layer about ¼ in. (5 mm) thick. Press plastic wrap over the surface and chill for at least 4 hours. Remove the gianduja from the dish and peel away the plastic wrap. Using a chef's knife, cut the gianduja into ¼-in. (5-mm) cubes.

PREPARING THE CANDIED BUDDHA'S-HAND

Preheat the oven to 140°F (60°C/Gas on lowest setting). Using the mandoline, cut the Buddha's-hand into wafer-thin slices (approximately 1 mm thick). Heat the water, sugar, and vanilla seeds in a saucepan until the sugar dissolves. Bring to a boil, immerse the slices in the hot syrup, and leave until translucent. Drain and set half the slices aside. Place the other half on a lined baking sheet. Dry in the oven for about 40 minutes. Let cool, then store in an airtight container until assembling.

PREPARING THE GIANDUJA CRÉMEUX

Sprinkle the gelatin over the cold water in a bowl and let soak for 10 minutes. Heat the milk, cream, and sugar in a saucepan until the sugar dissolves, then bring to a boil. Whisk in the egg yolk and cook until the temperature reaches 185°F (85°C), whisking continuously. Remove from the heat and whisk in the gelatin until dissolved. Pour over the gianduja paste in a bowl and process with the immersion blender until smooth. Let the mixture cool to 95°F (35°C), then add the butter and process until smooth. Press plastic wrap over the surface and chill until assembling.

PREPARING THE CARAMEL POWDER

Heat the sugar in a heavy saucepan, without adding any water, until it dissolves and forms a golden caramel. Immediately pour over the silicone mat or baking sheet and let cool completely. Break the caramel into pieces and grind to a fine powder in the food processor.

PREPARING THE PUFF PASTRY LAYERS

To make the *détrempe*, place the flour, water, salt, softened butter, and vinegar in the stand mixer and mix until smooth. Place between two sheets of parchment paper and roll into an 8 × 12-in. (20 × 30-cm) rectangle. Chill for 1 hour. Roll the laminating butter between two sheets of parchment paper into an 8 × 10-in. (20 × 25-cm) rectangle and chill for 1 hour.
Roll the *détrempe* into a rectangle twice as long as the butter. Place the butter on one side of the dough and fold the other side over to enclose the butter completely. Press down on the edges to seal them. With one short side facing you, roll the dough into a 10 × 24-in. (25 × 60-cm) rectangle. Make a double turn by folding the shorter sides of the dough toward the center, one-third down from the top and two-thirds up from the bottom, then fold the dough in half. Rotate it 90° clockwise and roll into a rectangle twice as long as it is wide. Give it a

single turn by folding it into three, then rotate it 90° clockwise. The dough has now had two and a half turns. Cover with plastic wrap and chill for 1 hour. Give the dough two more single turns, cover with plastic wrap and chill for an additional 2 hours. Divide the dough into three equal pieces and roll each one into a 6 × 10-in. (15 × 25-cm) rectangle, ½ in. (1 cm) thick. Place on a lined baking sheet and roll a dough docker over it, or prick with a fork. Place in the freezer for 20 minutes. Preheat the oven to 340°F (170°C/Gas Mark 3). Cover the three rectangles with a sheet of parchment paper and place another baking sheet on top to prevent the pastry from rising unevenly in the oven. Bake for 30 minutes until the pastry is golden; uncover the rectangles and return them to the oven to brown a bit more, if necessary. Transfer one of the rectangles to a wire rack to cool. Sprinkle the remaining two with the caramel powder and bake uncovered for an additional 2 minutes until caramelized. Transfer to the rack and let cool before assembling.

PREPARING THE LEMON DIPLOMAT CREAM

Sprinkle the gelatin over the cold water in a bowl and let soak for 10 minutes. Bring the milk to a boil. Whisk together the egg yolks and sugar in a bowl until pale and thick, then whisk in the custard powder and lemon juice. Slowly whisk one-third of the boiling milk into the egg yolk mixture, pour it back into the saucepan, and bring to a boil, whisking vigorously. Continue to boil, still whisking, for 2–3 minutes. Remove from the heat and whisk in the gelatin until dissolved. Transfer to a bowl, press plastic wrap over the surface, cool, and chill. Before assembling the mille-feuille, whip the cream until it holds its shape. Whisk the chilled custard to loosen it, then gently fold in the cream using a flexible spatula.

ASSEMBLING THE MILLE-FEUILLE

Using a serrated knife, trim the cooled puff pastry layers to form rectangles measuring 4 × 8 in. (10 × 20 cm). Place a caramelized rectangle on a board, caramelized side down. Spoon the diplomat cream and gianduja crémeux into the pastry bags and pipe them out lengthwise over the pastry in alternate lines, to cover it completely. Place the non-caramelized pastry rectangle on top and cover with alternate lines of the two creams. Finish with the remaining puff pastry rectangle, placing it caramelized side up. Carefully transfer the mille-feuille to a serving plate and place it on its side. Pipe a few mounds of the remaining diplomat cream on top and decorate with the candied Buddha's-hand, arranging the slices like flowers and alternating the dried and non-dried slices. Garnish with a few gianduja cubes.

BERGAMOT PUFF PASTRY BRIOCHE KNOTS

Chignons feuilletés à la bergamote

Makes 10

Active time
2½ hours

Chilling time
Overnight + 4 hours

Freezing time
10 minutes

Cooking time
20 minutes + making
the marmalade

Rising time
2½ hours

Storage
Up to 24 hours

Equipment
Stand mixer + dough hook
10 individual Parisian
brioche molds
Pastry bag

Ingredients

Bergamot marmalade
4½ oz. (125 g) bergamots
1⅓ cups (9 oz./255 g)
sugar, divided
¼ cup (60 ml) water
½ cup (125 ml) apple juice
Scant ½ cup (100 ml)
lemon juice
⅜ tsp (1.5 g) pectin NH

**Puff pastry brioche
dough**
⅓ cup (2½ oz./75 g)
lightly beaten egg (about
1½ eggs)
⅓ cup (75 ml) whole milk
⅓ oz. (10 g) fresh yeast,
crumbled
1 cup plus 3 tbsp
(5¼ oz./150 g) all-
purpose flour
Generous ½ teaspoon
(3 g) salt
5 tsp (20 g) superfine
sugar
2 tbsp (25 g) butter,
melted and cooled, plus
extra for the molds
1 stick plus 2 tbsp
(5¼ oz./150 g) butter,
preferably 84% fat

Syrup
3½ tbsp (50 ml) water
¼ cup (2 oz./50 g)
superfine sugar

Decoration
Candied bergamot, diced

PREPARING THE BERGAMOT MARMALADE (1 DAY AHEAD)

Make the bergamot marmalade (see technique p. 101), using the ingredients
listed.

PREPARING THE PUFF PASTRY BRIOCHE DOUGH (1 DAY AHEAD)

Place the eggs, milk, and yeast in the bowl of the stand mixer. Add the flour,
followed by the salt, sugar, and melted butter, then knead for 2 minutes on
low speed. Increase the speed to medium and knead for 5 minutes. Shape
the dough into a ball, cover with plastic wrap, and refrigerate overnight.
The next day, roll the dough into an 8 × 16-in. (20 × 40-cm) rectangle and
place in the freezer for 10 minutes. Place the 84% fat butter between two
sheets of parchment paper and roll it into an 8-in. (20-cm) square. Place
the butter in the center of the dough and fold the two short ends over it
to meet in the center, enclosing the butter completely. Roll the dough into
an 8 × 24-in. (20 × 60-cm) rectangle with one short side facing you. Give
the dough a single turn by folding it in three, then rotate it 90° clockwise.
Cover the dough with plastic wrap and chill for 2 hours. Roll the dough
and give it another single turn, cover with plastic wrap, and chill for an
additional 2 hours.

SHAPING AND BAKING THE KNOTS

Grease the brioche molds with butter. Roll the dough to a thickness of ¼ in.
(5 mm) and cut into ten 2¼ × 6-in. (6 × 15-cm) rectangles. Cut each rectangle
lengthwise into three strips ¾ in. (2 cm) wide, leaving the tops of the strips
attached. Braid the strips. Spoon the marmalade into the pastry bag and
pipe out a little marmalade over the loose ends of the braids. Roll the braids
up toward the attached ends so the marmalade is enclosed in the center.
Pinch the bases to seal the knots and place them in the molds. Let rise for
2½ hours in a warm place (82°F/28°C). Toward the end of the rising time,
preheat the oven to 340°F (170°C/Gas Mark 3). Bake the brioche knots for
15–20 minutes until golden.

PREPARING THE SYRUP

While the brioche knots bake, heat the water and sugar in a saucepan until
the sugar dissolves. Bring to a boil, then remove from the heat.

ASSEMBLING THE BRIOCHE KNOTS

Remove the brioche knots from the oven and immediately brush them with
the syrup. Sprinkle over the diced candied bergamot. Let cool for a few minutes before unmolding onto a wire rack. Serve warm or cold.

PORTO-VECCHIO ICE CREAM CONES

Face u caldu, cornet de Porto-Vecchio

Serves 6

Active time

45 minutes

Maturing time

12 hours + 4 hours

Cooking time

3 hours

Storage

Up to 3 days
in an airtight container
(cones), or in the freezer
(ice cream and sorbet)

Equipment

Instant-read thermometer

Immersion blender

Ice cream maker

Silicone half-sphere mold,
1¼ in. (3 cm) in dia. and
¾ in. (1.5 cm) deep

Waffle cone maker and
cone roller

3 pastry bags + a fluted
¾-in. (18-mm) tip

Ingredients

**Corsican hazelnut
praline ice cream**

Generous 1 cup (255 ml)
whole milk

2 tbsp (15 g) skim milk
powder

1 oz. (30 g) glucose
powder, divided

2½ tbsp (1 oz./30 g)
superfine sugar, divided

1 pinch (1.5 g) stabilizer
(super neutrose or
stab2000)

2 tbsp (30 ml) heavy
cream, min. 35% fat

1½ oz. (40 g) hazelnut
praline paste

Citron sorbet

⅓ cup (2¾ oz./75 g)
superfine sugar

½ oz. (15 g) invert sugar

1 oz. (25 g) glucose
powder

1 pinch (1.5 g) stabilizer
(super neutrose or
stab2000)

Scant ⅔ cup (145 ml)
water

Scant ⅔ cup (140 ml)
citron juice

Candied citron zest

Scant ½ cup (100 ml)
water

½ cup (3½ oz./100 g)
superfine sugar

1 oz. (30 g) citron zest, cut
into 18 very thin strips (see
technique p. 66)

Waffle cones

¾ cup plus 3 tbsp
(3½ oz./110 g) all-purpose
flour

¼ cup (2 oz./55 g)
superfine sugar

⅛ tsp (0.5 g) salt

Scant ½ cup (110 ml) hot
water

2 tbsp (1 oz./30 g) butter,
softened

1⁄10 oz. (3 g) liquid soy
lecithin

To serve

Hazelnuts, preferably
Corsican, halved

Skin from the hazelnuts

PREPARING THE HAZELNUT ICE CREAM (1 DAY AHEAD)

Heat the milk in a saucepan until the temperature reaches 77°F (25°C). Stir in the milk powder. When the temperature reaches 86°F (30°C), stir in half the glucose powder and half the sugar until dissolved. Combine the remaining sugar and glucose powder in a bowl. Keep heating and when the temperature reaches 95°F (35°C), add the cream and praline paste. At 113°F (45°C), stir in the remaining sugar and glucose powder until dissolved. Continue to cook until the temperature reaches 185°F (85°C). Remove from the heat and process with the immersion blender until smooth. Transfer to an airtight container and let mature for 12 hours in the refrigerator. The next day, churn in the ice cream maker. Freeze in an airtight container.

PREPARING THE CITRON SORBET

Combine the superfine sugar, invert sugar, glucose powder, and stabilizer in a bowl. Heat the water in a saucepan until the temperature reaches 104°F (40°C), then add the sugar mixture and stir until dissolved. Continue to cook until the temperature reaches 185°F (85°C), then cool quickly in the refrigerator. Let mature for at least 4 hours. Add the citron juice and process with the immersion blender until smooth, then churn in the ice cream maker. Freeze in an airtight container.

PREPARING THE CANDIED CITRON ZEST

Preheat the oven to 105°F (40°C/Gas on lowest setting). Heat the water and sugar in a saucepan until the sugar dissolves, then bring to a boil. Immerse the citron zest strips in the hot syrup for 2 minutes, then drain. Place them in the cavities of the half-sphere mold in a curved shape. Place in the oven for 2 hours, or until completely dry. Let cool completely, then store in a dry place until serving.

PREPARING THE WAFFLE CONES

Combine the flour, sugar, and salt in a bowl and mix in the hot water until smooth. Stir in the butter and soy lecithin until well blended. Let rest for 10 minutes at room temperature. Cook 6 cones in the waffle cone maker until uniformly golden, shaping each one around the cone roller as soon as it is cooked. Let the cones cool completely, then store them in an airtight container.

TO SERVE

Place the ice cream and citron sorbet in two separate pastry bags and snip off the tips to make relatively large holes. Place these two bags side by side inside the third pastry bag fitted with the fluted tip. Working in a circular motion, pipe out about 4¼ oz. (120 g) of ice cream and sorbet into each cone. Decorate with hazelnut halves, a little hazelnut skin, and three pieces of candied citron zest.

CHEFS' NOTES

For an even more decadent treat and the full Corsican experience, top the cones with crushed canistrelli cookies.

YOGURT AND GRANOLA PARFAITS WITH CALAMANSI PEARLS

Yogourt, perles de kalamansi et granola

Serves 4

Active time
30 minutes

Fermentation time
8–10 hours (or 2 hours in the oven)

Cooking time
20–25 minutes

Freezing time
1 hour

Storage
Up to 2 days in the refrigerator

Equipment
Instant-read thermometer

8 glass yogurt jars
(or 4 yogurt jars and 4 serving glasses)

Yogurt maker (optional)

Pipette

Ingredients

Homemade yogurt
2 cups (500 ml) whole milk

¼ cup (2 oz./60 g) skim milk powder

Seeds of 1 vanilla bean

¼ cup (2 oz./60 g) plain yogurt

Granola
Generous 1 tsp (8 g) acacia honey

1½ tsp (7.5 ml) coconut oil

⅓ cup (25 g) rolled oats

1 cup (15 g) puffed brown rice

2 tbsp (15 g) peeled pistachios

1 tbsp (10 g) whole hazelnuts, preferably from Piedmont

Scant 2½ tsp (8 g) golden sesame seeds

Scant 1 tbsp (8 g) sunflower seeds

1 tbsp (10 g) Zante currants

1 tbsp (10 g) dried cranberries

Calamansi pearls
Grape-seed oil

Scant 1 tbsp (2 g) gelatin powder

1 tbsp (15 ml) cold water

Scant ½ cup (100 ml) calamansi juice

3¾ tsp (15 g) superfine sugar

¾ tsp (1.5 g) agar-agar powder

Scant ¼ tsp (0.5 g) turmeric

Calamansi reduction
1¼ cups (300 ml) calamansi juice

Sugar, if needed

PREPARING THE HOMEMADE YOGURT (1 DAY AHEAD)

Heat the milk, milk powder, and vanilla seeds in a saucepan until the temperature reaches 180°F (82°C). Remove from the heat and let cool to 113°F (45°C). Place the yogurt in a bowl and whisk in one-quarter of the vanilla milk. Pour back into the saucepan and stir until smooth. Pour into 4 yogurt jars, place in the yogurt maker (without lids), and let ferment for 8–10 hours (the longer the fermentation, the tangier the flavor of the yogurt). If you do not have a yogurt maker, preheat the oven to 105°F (40°C) and place the uncovered jars inside. Let ferment for 2 hours, then turn the oven off and leave the jars inside for an additional 6 hours without opening the oven door. Cover the jars with lids and chill until serving.

PREPARING THE GRANOLA

Preheat the oven to 300°F (150°C/Gas Mark 2). Warm the honey until fluid and combine with the coconut oil in a small bowl. Place the remaining ingredients, except for the currants and cranberries, in a mixing bowl, add the honey and coconut oil, and stir until combined. Spread the granola out over a lined baking sheet and bake for 25–30 minutes until golden brown, stirring every 10 minutes. Let the granola cool slightly on the baking sheet, mix in the currants and cranberries, and let cool completely. Store in an airtight container in a cool, dry place.

PREPARING THE CALAMANSI PEARLS

Fill a tall, narrow container with grape-seed oil and place in the freezer for 1 hour. Sprinkle the gelatin over the water in a bowl and let soak for 10 minutes. When the oil is well chilled, heat the remaining ingredients, including the soaked gelatin, in a saucepan until the sugar, agar-agar, and gelatin dissolve. Bring to a boil, remove from the heat, and let cool to lukewarm. Transfer to the pipette and release drop by drop into the cold oil—as the warm calamansi mixture hits the cold oil, it will form pearls, due to the thermal shock. Strain through a fine-mesh sieve and rinse well under cold water to remove the oil (the pearls will not burst). Chill until serving.

PREPARING THE CALAMANSI REDUCTION

Bring the calamansi juice to a simmer in a saucepan and cook until it has reduced to one-fifth of its original volume. Taste and add sugar, if necessary. Chill until serving.

ASSEMBLING THE PARFAITS

Holding each empty yogurt jar or serving glass at an angle, add a layer of yogurt, followed by a layer of granola and a layer of calamansi pearls. Repeat the layers, finishing with a layer of yogurt. Top with a spoonful of calamansi reduction, a few calamansi pearls, and a little granola.

STONE FRUITS

APRICOT, PISTACHIO, AND GREEN ALMOND TART

Tarte abricot, pistaches et amandes fraîches

Serves 6

Active time
30 minutes

Cooking time
13 hours

Chilling time
3 hours

Storage
Up to 2 days
in the refrigerator

Equipment
8-in. (20-cm) tart ring,
¾ in. (2 cm) deep

Mandoline

7-in. (18-cm) cardboard
plate

Ingredients

Candied rosemary

10 sprigs (10 g) fresh
rosemary

1 egg white, lightly beaten

Superfine sugar as
needed

Egg wash

1 tbsp (20 g) egg yolk
(1 yolk)

1 tsp (5 ml) heavy cream,
min. 35% fat

¼ tsp (1 g) fine salt

**Almond shortcrust
pastry**

4 tbsp (2 oz./60 g) butter,
diced

1 cup (4 oz./120 g)
all-purpose flour

2½ tbsp (1 oz./30 g)
superfine sugar

Scant ⅓ cup (1 oz./30 g)
almond flour

Seeds of 1 vanilla bean

¼ tsp (1.5 g) *fleur de sel*

1 tbsp plus 2 tsp (25 g)
lightly beaten egg
(½ egg)

**Almond and pistachio
cream**

¼ cup (1¾ oz./50 g)
superfine sugar

4 tbsp (2 oz./60 g) butter,
softened

Scant ⅓ cup (1 oz./30 g)
almond flour

Scant ¼ cup (20 g)
pistachio flour

1½ tsp (5 g) cornstarch

Scant 1 tsp (4 g) pistachio
butter

3½ tbsp (1¾ oz./50 g)
lightly beaten egg (1 egg)

To assemble

1¼ lb. (600 g) fresh
apricots

⅔ oz. (20 g) neutral
glaze

1 tsp (5 ml) water

⅓ oz. (10 g) fresh
almonds

5 tsp (10 g) pistachio flour

1¼ tbsp (10 g)
confectioners' sugar

Sechuan Cress

PREPARING THE CANDIED ROSEMARY (1 DAY AHEAD)

Preheat the oven to 120°F (50°C/Gas on lowest setting with the door propped open). Wash the rosemary and remove the leaves. Brush the leaves with a thin layer of egg white and coat in the sugar, shaking off any excess. Spread them across a lined baking sheet, well separated, and dry in the oven for 12 hours.

PREPARING THE EGG WASH

Whisk the ingredients together in a bowl and chill until using.

PREPARING THE ALMOND SHORTCRUST PASTRY

Rub the butter into the flour with your fingertips until the mixture has the texture of coarse crumbs. Add the sugar, almond flour, vanilla seeds, and *fleur de sel*. Mix in the egg, gather the dough together and lightly push down on it with the heel of your hand, smearing it against the work surface until smooth (*fraisage*). Shape it into a ball, flatten slightly, cover with plastic wrap, and chill for 1 hour. Place the tart ring on a lined baking sheet and press the dough across the base and up the sides of the ring in an even layer. Chill for 2 hours. Preheat the oven to 300°F (150°C/Gas Mark 2) and blind-bake the tart shell for 20 minutes. Remove it from the oven and increase the temperature to 340°F (170°C/Gas Mark 3). Remove the ring and neaten any irregular pastry edges using a fine grater. Brush the pastry all over with the egg wash and return to the oven for 10 minutes, until just golden.

PREPARING THE ALMOND AND PISTACHIO CREAM

Mix the sugar and butter together using a flexible spatula. Stir in the almond flour, pistachio flour, cornstarch, and pistachio butter. Gradually stir in the egg and spoon into the tart shell, spreading it in an even layer.

ASSEMBLING THE TART

Preheat the oven to 325°F (160°C/Gas Mark 3). Wash and halve the apricots and remove the pits. Cut each half in two and arrange the quarters over the cream in concentric circles, rounded sides down. Bake for 25 minutes, remove from the oven, and let cool to room temperature. Whisk together the neutral glaze and water and brush a thin layer over the tart. Tap the almond shells firmly with the back of the blade of a chef's knife. Remove the almonds and peel off the thin outer skin using a paring knife. Slice the almonds thinly using the mandoline. Sprinkle the tart with the pistachio flour, place the 7-in. (18-cm) cardboard plate in the center and dust the pastry edges with the confectioners' sugar. Remove the plate and scatter over the candied rosemary, sliced almonds, and cress.

PEACH FLOWER TART

Fleur de pêche

Serves 8

Active time
1½ hours

Chilling time
2 hours 20 minutes

Cooking time
35–40 minutes

Infusing time
10 minutes

Storage
Up to 24 hours in the refrigerator

Equipment
7-in. (18-cm) tart ring, ¾ in. (2 cm) deep

Instant-read thermometer

Mandoline

Ingredients

Sweet shortcrust pastry

5 tbsp (2½ oz./75 g) butter, diced, plus more for the ring

1 cup (4½ oz./125 g) all-purpose flour

⅓ cup (1½ oz./45 g) confectioners' sugar

2½ tbsp (15 g) almond flour

Seeds of ½ vanilla bean

¼ tsp (1 g) salt

2 tbsp (1 oz./30 g) lightly beaten egg (about ⅔ egg)

1¾ oz. (50 g) white chocolate, chopped

Syrup

⅓ cup (80 ml) water

Scant ½ cup (3 oz./80 g) sugar

2 tsp (10 ml) lemon juice

Peaches in red wine

3 white peaches

3 yellow peaches

1½ tbsp (25 ml) red wine, preferably Syrah

3 tbsp (1¼ oz./35 g) sugar

Seeds of ½ vanilla bean

Lemon verbena cream

1 sheet (2 g) gold-strength gelatin, 200 Bloom

3 tbsp (45 ml) heavy cream, min. 35% fat

1 tsp (3 g) loose lemon verbena tea

⅓ cup (75 ml) heavy cream, min. 35% fat, well chilled

2 tsp (5 g) confectioners' sugar

Decoration

Fresh lemon verbena leaves

PREPARING THE SHORTCRUST PASTRY

Rub the butter into the all-purpose flour with your fingertips until the mixture resembles coarse crumbs. Add the sugar, almond flour, vanilla seeds, and salt and mix in the egg to make a smooth dough. Cover with plastic wrap and chill for 2 hours. Preheat the oven to 340°F (170°C/Gas Mark 3). Grease the tart ring with butter and place on a lined baking sheet. Roll the dough to a thickness of ⅛ in. (3 mm) and line the tart ring with it. Blind-bake for 15–20 minutes. Melt the chocolate in a bowl over a bain-marie and as soon as you remove the tart shell from the oven, brush it with a thin layer of the chocolate.

PREPARING THE SYRUP

Heat the water, sugar, and lemon juice in a saucepan until the sugar dissolves, then bring to a boil. Remove from the heat and let cool.

PREPARING THE PEACHES IN RED WINE

Wash the peaches, stand them upright and cut off a ¾-in. (2-cm) slice on either side of the pit. Set the slices aside in the syrup for decoration. Weigh out 4½ oz. (130 g) of the remaining peach flesh and cut it into ½-in. (1-cm) dice. Warm the wine, sugar, and vanilla seeds in a saucepan over low heat until the sugar dissolves, add the diced peach, cover, and cook for about 20 minutes until tender. Let cool.

PREPARING THE LEMON VERBENA CREAM

Soak the gelatin in a bowl of cold water until softened. Heat the 3 tbsp (45 ml) cream in a saucepan, remove from the heat, add the tea, and let infuse for 10 minutes. Strain through a fine-mesh sieve, return to the saucepan, and reheat. Squeeze the gelatin to remove excess water and stir it into the verbena cream until dissolved. Let cool to 68°F (20°C). Just before serving, whip the well-chilled cream with the sugar until it holds its shape, then fold into the verbena cream. If you do this too far in advance, the cream will become too firm to pour.

ASSEMBLING THE TART

Drain the diced peaches from the wine and spoon them into the tart shell. Pour over the verbena cream and chill for 20 minutes until set. Remove the reserved peach slices from the syrup, drain, and slice them with a mandoline very thinly lengthwise. Dip them in the syrup to prevent browning. Roll them up tightly into "roses" and arrange attractively over the tart. Decorate with lemon verbena leaves.

NECTARINE AND LEMON VERBENA RELIGIEUSES

Religieuse nectarine, verveine

Serves 6

Active time

1½ hours

Chilling time

13½ hours

Infusing time

20 minutes

Cooking time

45 minutes

Storage

12 hours

Equipment

Immersion blender

Instant-read thermometer

Small food processor (optional)

6-cavity silicone ice ball mold, 1¼ in. (3.2 cm) in dia., 1 in. (2.8 cm) deep

2 pastry bags + ½-in. (10-mm) and ⅓-in. (8-mm) plain tips

2-in. (5-cm) round cookie cutter

2 food-safe acetate sheets

Stand mixer + whisk

Ingredients

Vanilla ganache

2¾ oz. (80 g) white chocolate, chopped

Scant ¼ cup (55 ml) heavy cream, min. 35% fat

Seeds of 1 vanilla bean

¾ tsp (6 g) glucose syrup

¼ oz. (7 g) invert sugar

Scant ½ cup (112 ml) heavy cream, min. 35% fat, well chilled

Lemon verbena pastry cream

Generous ⅔ cup (165 ml) whole milk

1 oz. (30 g) fresh lemon verbena leaves

2 tbsp (1¼ oz./35 g) egg yolk (about 2 yolks)

2½ tbsp (1 oz./30 g) superfine sugar

4 tsp (13 g) cornstarch

2 tsp (10 g) butter, diced

Nectarine balls

½ ripe yellow nectarine

½ ripe white nectarine

Nectarine compote

½ ripe yellow nectarine

½ ripe white nectarine

1 oz. (30 g) nectarine puree

Seeds of ½ vanilla bean

2½ tsp (10 g) superfine sugar

⅛ tsp (0.5 g) agar-agar powder

Craquelin

2 tbsp (25 g) butter, softened

2½ tbsp (1 oz./30 g) light brown sugar

3 tbsp (1 oz./30 g) all-purpose flour

Choux pastry

¼ cup (60 ml) whole milk

3 tbsp (1¾ oz./50 g) butter, diced

¼ tsp (1 g) salt

½ tsp (2 g) superfine sugar

⅓ cup (1½ oz./40 g) all-purpose flour

¼ cup plus 1 tsp (2 oz./65 g) lightly beaten egg (about 1⅓ eggs)

1¼ tsp (6 ml) whole milk, hot

White chocolate disks

10½ oz. (300 g) white couverture chocolate

Vegan jelly coating

2 tbsp (25 g) superfine sugar

1 tbsp (13 g) vegan gelatin, or 2 tbsp (13 g) agar-agar

1 cup (250 ml) water

Chocolate ganache flowers

Vanilla ganache (see left)

6 white chocolate disks (see left)

1 yellow nectarine

1 white nectarine

Decoration

Vanilla powder, for dusting

PREPARING THE VANILLA GANACHE (1 DAY AHEAD)

Place the white chocolate in a bowl. In a saucepan, heat the scant ¼ cup (55 ml) cream with the vanilla seeds, glucose syrup, and invert sugar and bring to a boil. Pour the hot cream over the white chocolate, one third at a time, and process with the immersion blender until smooth. Mix in the well-chilled cream, cover, and chill for 12 hours.

PREPARING THE LEMON VERBENA PASTRY CREAM

In a saucepan, heat the milk until the temperature reaches 176°F (80°C). Remove from the heat, add the lemon verbena leaves, cover, and let infuse for 20 minutes. Remove the leaves and bring the milk to a boil. Whisk together the egg yolks, sugar, and cornstarch in a bowl until pale and thick. Slowly pour one-third of the boiling milk into the egg yolk mixture, whisking continuously. Return to the saucepan and whisk to a boil. Let boil for about 2 minutes, still whisking. Transfer to a bowl, press plastic wrap over the surface, and let cool in the refrigerator. When cooled to 95°F (35°C), stir in the butter until smooth. Press plastic wrap over the surface and chill until assembling.

PREPARING THE NECTARINE BALLS

Wash and peel the nectarines (see technique p. 34), remove the pits, and cut into pieces. Using the immersion blender or a small food processor, process the fruit to a smooth puree. Weigh out 1 oz. (30 g) of the puree for the compote and set aside. Pour the remaining puree into the ice ball mold (you need six balls) and freeze until coating.

PREPARING THE NECTARINE COMPOTE

Wash and peel the nectarines (see technique p. 34) and remove the pits. Weigh out 4½ oz. (125 g) of the fruit and cut it into 1/16-in. (2-mm) dice (brunoise). Place the dice in a saucepan with the nectarine puree, vanilla seeds, and half the sugar and cook gently until the fruit is very tender but not quite reduced to a puree. Combine the remaining sugar with the agar-agar in a bowl, stir into the compote until dissolved, and bring to a boil. Transfer to a bowl and chill until assembling.

PREPARING THE CRAQUELIN

Place the butter and brown sugar in a bowl and mix together with your hands. Add the flour and lightly mix it in. Roll the paste out between two sheets of parchment paper until 1/20-in. (1.5 mm) thick. Freeze flat, still between the sheets, while you prepare the choux pastry.

PREPARING THE CHOUX PASTRY

Preheat the oven to 340°F (170°C/Gas Mark 3). Heat the ¼ cup (60 ml) milk, butter, salt, and sugar in a saucepan until the butter melts. Bring to a fast boil, remove from the heat, and add all the flour at once. Beat with a spatula until smooth. Return to a low heat to dry the mixture, stirring with a spatula until it leaves the sides of the pan and no longer sticks to the spatula. Remove from the heat, wait 1 minute, then mix in the egg a little at a time, incorporating each addition before you add the next, and stirring until the pastry is smooth, shiny, and drops off the spatula in thick ribbons. Add the hot milk and stir in. Transfer to the pastry bag with the ½-in. (10-mm) tip and pipe out six choux puffs, about 2 in. (5 cm) in diameter, onto a greased baking sheet. Using the cookie cutter, cut out six 2-in. (5-cm) disks of craquelin and lay one on top of each choux puff. Bake for about 30 minutes until golden brown. Transfer to a wire rack and let cool.

PREPARING THE WHITE CHOCOLATE DISKS

Temper the chocolate (see p. 131). Spread the chocolate into a very thin layer between the two acetate sheets. Let set for a few minutes until firm but not hard, then carefully peel off the top sheet and cut out six 2-in. (5-cm) disks using the cookie cutter. Let set completely at room temperature.

PREPARING THE JELLY COATING

Unmold the frozen nectarine balls and spear each with a toothpick. Return to the freezer while you prepare the coating. Combine the sugar and gelatin in a bowl and place in a saucepan with the water. Heat until the sugar and gelatin dissolve and the temperature reaches 195°F (90°C). Dip each ball twice into the coating, place on a plate, and remove the toothpicks. Chill for 30 minutes before assembling to allow the balls to thaw and the jelly to set.

PREPARING THE CHOCOLATE GANACHE FLOWERS

Whip the ganache in the stand mixer to soften it. Spoon it into the pastry bag with the 1/3-in. (8-mm) tip, place the white chocolate disks on a baking sheet, and pipe the ganache over them to resemble flower petals. Wash and halve the nectarines and remove the pits. Leaving the peel on, cut the fruit into small, very thin slices and carefully place the slices, peel down and alternating the colors, between the ganache petals. Chill for at least 30–35 minutes before assembling.

ASSEMBLING THE RELIGIEUSES

Using a serrated knife, neatly cut the tops off the choux buns. Fill the bases with 1½ oz. (40 g) of pastry cream and ⅔ oz. (20 g) of compote and replace the tops. Carefully place a chocolate ganache flower on each and a nectarine ball in the center. Decorate by dusting lightly with vanilla powder.

NECTARINE MELBA

Brugnon Melba

Serves 10

Active time
2 hours

Maturing time
36 hours

Drying time
24–36 hours

Cooking time
20 minutes

Soaking time
10 minutes

Chilling time
12 hours

Equipment
Food processor
Instant-read thermometer
Ice cream maker
Food dehydrator (optional)
Immersion blender
Pastry bag + flat or Saint-Honoré tip

Ingredients

Fresh almond jelly
⅔ cup (3½ oz./100 g) shelled fresh almonds
½ cup (125 ml) whole milk, lukewarm, plus more as needed
1 tbsp (12 g) superfine sugar
¼ tsp (1 g) pectin NH
Generous ¼ tsp (1 g) cornstarch

Nectarine ice cream
½ sheet (1 g) gold-strength gelatin, 200 Bloom
4 tsp (20 ml) water
2½ tbsp (1 oz./30 g) superfine sugar
Seeds of 1 vanilla bean
3½ oz. (100 g) pitted nectarine, diced

Dried raspberries
⅓ oz. (10 g) fresh raspberries

Poached nectarines
4 nectarines
2 cups (500 ml) water
¾ cup (5 oz./150 g) superfine sugar

Mascarpone cream
¼ cup (60 ml) heavy cream, min. 35% fat
1 tbsp (12 g) superfine sugar
Seeds of ¼ vanilla bean
2½ tsp (12 ml) orange blossom water
2 tbsp (1 oz./30 g) mascarpone
Generous ¼ tsp (1.25 g) gelatin powder
Scant 2 tsp (9 ml) water
¼ cup (60 ml) heavy cream, min. 35% fat, well chilled

Decoration
Olive oil
Green oxalis (shamrock leaves)
Whole almonds

PREPARING THE ALMOND JELLY (1 DAY AHEAD)

Finely grind the almonds with the milk in the food processor. Let mature for 24 hours in the refrigerator. The next day, strain through a fine-mesh sieve, measure the almond milk, and add more milk to make a scant ⅔ cup (145 ml) if needed. Pour into a saucepan. Mix together the sugar, pectin, and cornstarch, add to the milk and bring to a simmer, stirring continuously until the pectin mixture dissolves. Pour into a bowl, press plastic wrap over the surface, and chill until serving.

PREPARING THE ICE CREAM (1 DAY AHEAD)

Soak the gelatin in a bowl of cold water until softened. Heat the water, sugar, and vanilla seeds in a saucepan until the sugar dissolves. Bring to a boil and remove from the heat. Squeeze the gelatin to remove excess water and stir it into the hot syrup until dissolved. Let cool at room temperature for 20 minutes, or until the temperature of the syrup reaches 104°F (40°C). Blend with the diced nectarine in the food processor until smooth. Let mature for 12 hours in the refrigerator in a covered container. The next day, churn in the ice cream maker and freeze in an airtight container until serving.

PREPARING THE DRIED RASPBERRIES (1 DAY AHEAD)

Preheat the oven to 120°F (50°C/Gas on lowest setting with the door propped open). Wash the raspberries, cut them in half, and spread them over a lined baking sheet. Place in the oven for 12–24 hours or until they are dry and crisp—the time will depend on your oven and the size of the raspberries. Alternatively, use a food dehydrator. Let the raspberries cool. Crumble and store in an airtight container until serving.

PREPARING THE POACHED NECTARINES (1 DAY AHEAD)

Wash the nectarines, cut them in half, and remove the pits. Heat the water and sugar in a saucepan until the sugar dissolves and the temperature reaches 176°F (80°C). Add the nectarines and gently poach them for 20 minutes. Remove from the heat and let the nectarines cool to room temperature in the syrup. Preheat the oven to 120°F (50°C/Gas on lowest setting with the door propped open). Carefully remove the peel. Chill the nectarines and syrup in a covered container. Spread the peel across a lined baking sheet and place in the oven for 12 hours or until completely dry. Chill in a covered container until serving.

PREPARING THE MASCARPONE CREAM (1 DAY AHEAD)

Sprinkle the gelatin over the cold water in a bowl and let soak for 10 minutes. Heat the first ¼ cup (60 ml) cream with the sugar, vanilla seeds, and orange blossom water in a saucepan until the sugar dissolves. Stir in the gelatin until dissolved. Pour over the mascarpone in a bowl and process with the immersion blender until smooth. Mix in the well-chilled cream, cover, and chill for 12 hours.

ASSEMBLING THE MELBA

Whip the mascarpone cream until it holds its shape and spoon it into the pastry bag. Place a spoonful of almond jelly in the center of each serving dish and top with a poached nectarine half, rounded side down. Add a scoop of nectarine ice cream in the center and cover with a nectarine half, rounded side up. Cover the ice cream with a piped ring of mascarpone cream. Pour a little poaching syrup around each nectarine and sprinkle with a few drops of olive oil. Decorate with dried raspberry pieces and green oxalis leaves. Grate almonds over the melba and gently push two pieces of dried peel upright into the whipped cream. Serve immediately.

CHEFS' NOTES

• This dried raspberry recipe makes the amount you will need for the melba, but the dried raspberries keep well in an airtight container, so you can multiply the quantities to have extra on hand. Alternatively, you can purchase store-bought dried raspberries. Raspberries and nectarine peel (from the poached nectarines) can be dried at the same time in the oven.

• To pipe the mascarpone cream into a perfect ring, place the plates on a rotating cake turner and pipe as the plate turns.

MIRABELLE PLUM PANNA COTTA

Pannacotta à la mirabelle

Serves 8

Active time
1 hour

Cooking time
40 minutes

Freezing time
35 minutes

Storage
Up to 24 hours
in the refrigerator

Equipment
Fabric tea bag

Silicone baking mat with a
leaf impression

Instant-read thermometer

8 serving glasses

Ingredients

Mirabelle jam

14 oz. (400 g) mirabelle
plums

3 tbsp (2 oz./60 g) honey

1 oz. (30 g) rosemary

Crumb topping

¼ cup (1¼ oz./35 g)
confectioners' sugar

Generous ¼ cup
(1½ oz./45 g) cornstarch

Scant ¼ cup (20 g)
almond flour

¼ tsp (1 g) *fleur de sel*

2 tbsp (1¼ oz./35 g)
butter, diced

1¼ oz. (35 g) white
chocolate, chopped

⅕ oz. (5 g) almond
praline paste

1¼ cups (1¼ oz./35 g)
puffed rice

Leaf tuiles

2 tbsp (25 g) butter,
softened

3 tbsp (25 g)
confectioners' sugar

5½ tsp (25 g) egg white
(scant 1 white)

2½ tbsp (25 g) all-
purpose flour

Panna cotta

5 sheets (10 g) gold-
strength gelatin,
200 Bloom

3 cups plus 4 tsp
(770 ml) heavy cream,
min. 35% fat

⅓ cup (2½ oz./75 g)
superfine sugar

Seeds of 2 vanilla beans

Decoration

A few fresh mirabelle
plums

Small rosemary sprigs

CHEFS' NOTES

• Chilling only half of the panna cotta
to 50°F (10°C) at a time prevents
it from setting too much before
assembling the glasses.

• If mirabelle plums are not available,
use another sweet, small variety like
Sugar-Baby or cherry plums.

PREPARING THE MIRABELLE JAM
Wash the mirabelles, cut them in half, and remove the pits. Place in a sauce-pan with the honey. Place the rosemary in the fabric tea bag and add. Cook until the mirabelles are soft and have a thick, jam-like consistency. Remove the rosemary and let cool.

PREPARING THE CRUMB TOPPING
Preheat the oven to 325°F (160°C/Gas Mark 3). Combine the sugar, corn-starch, almond flour, and *fleur de sel* in a bowl. Work in the butter with your fingertips until the mixture resembles coarse crumbs. Spread across a lined baking sheet and bake for 15 minutes. Let cool. Melt the chocolate and almond praline paste together in a saucepan and stir in the puffed rice and crumbs. Transfer to a plate and let cool.

PREPARING THE TUILES
Preheat the oven to 340°F (170°C/Gas Mark 3). Stir all the ingredients together in a bowl until smooth. Spread the mixture across the leaf impres-sions in the silicone mat using an offset spatula and bake for 10–12 minutes. Immediately turn the leaves out and, if desired, drape over a rolling pin so they cool in a curved shape.

PREPARING THE PANNA COTTA
Prepare the panna cotta when you are ready to assemble the desserts. Soak the gelatin in a bowl of cold water until softened. In a saucepan over low heat, infuse the cream, sugar, and vanilla seeds for 15 minutes. When the temperature of the cream cools to 140°F (60°C), squeeze the gelatin to remove excess water and stir it in until dissolved.

ASSEMBLING THE PANNA COTTA
Spoon 1¾ oz. (50 g) of jam into each serving glass and freeze for 10 minutes. Chill half the panna cotta by transferring it to a bowl and setting it over a larger bowl filled with ice water. Cool the panna cotta to around 50°F (10°C) to help prevent the vanilla seeds from sinking to the bottom. Remove the glasses from the freezer and tilt them at an angle by propping them up in "nests" of crumpled paper towel or use egg cartons. Pour 1¾ oz. (50 g) of the chilled panna cotta into each glass and freeze for 15–20 minutes, keeping the glasses at an angle. Cool the remaining panna cotta to around 50°F (10°C) over a bowl of ice water as before. Remove the glasses from the freezer and tilt them the opposite way still in their "nests." Pour 1¾ oz. (50 g) panna cotta into each glass to make a V-shape and freeze for an additional 15 minutes. Break the crumb topping into small pieces and place in the V. Wash the mirabelles, cut them in half, and remove the pits. Set a few over the crumbs in each glass and decorate with a small rosemary sprig and the leaf tuiles.

GREENGAGE PLUM TURNOVERS

Chausson aux prunes Reine-Claude

Serves 6

Active time
7½ hours

Chilling time
7½ hours

Resting time
1 hour

Cooking time
50 minutes

Storage
Up to 24 hours

Equipment
Stand mixer + dough hook
Silicone baking mat (optional)
Food processor
5-in. (13-cm) round fluted pastry cutter

Ingredients

Puff pastry

For the *détrempe* (water dough)
3¼ cups (14 oz./400 g) all-purpose flour, sifted
Generous ¾ cup (200 ml) water
2½ tsp (12 g) fine salt
4 tbsp (2 oz./60 g) butter, softened
Generous ½ tsp (3 ml) white vinegar

For laminating
3 sticks (12½ oz./350 g) butter, preferably 84% fat

Greengage plum compote
¾ lb. (350 g) greengage plums
3½ tbsp (1½ oz./40 g) superfine sugar
1 tbsp (20 g) butter
Seeds of 1 vanilla bean

Caramel powder
½ cup (3½ oz./100 g) superfine sugar

Egg wash
3½ tbsp (1¾ oz./50 g) lightly beaten egg (1 egg)
2½ tbsp (1½ oz./40 g) egg yolk (2 yolks)
3½ tbsp (50 ml) milk

CHEFS' NOTES

If greengages are unavailable, use another variety of sweet, juicy plum.

PREPARING THE PUFF PASTRY

To make the *détrempe*, beat the flour, water, salt, butter, and vinegar together in the stand mixer until you have a smooth dough. Place the dough between two sheets of parchment paper and roll it into an 8 × 16-in. (20 × 40-cm) rectangle. Chill for at least 30 minutes. Place the laminating butter between two sheets of parchment paper and roll or flatten it into an 8-in. (20-cm) square. Let rest at room temperature for 1 hour. Roll the dough into a rectangle twice as long as the butter. Place the butter on one side of the dough and fold the other side over, enclosing the butter completely. Press down on the edges to seal them well. Roll the dough into a rectangle three times as long as it is wide and, with one short side facing you, fold into three. Rotate it 90° clockwise to give it a single turn. Cover with plastic wrap and chill for 2 hours. Give the dough two more single turns as above, for a total of three, chilling it for 2 hours after each turn.

PREPARING THE GREENGAGE COMPOTE

Wash and halve the greengages and remove the pits. Heat the sugar in a saucepan, without adding any water, until it dissolves and cooks to a golden caramel. Stir in the butter until melted, then add the greengages and vanilla seeds. Cook over low heat for about 15 minutes until the greengages have softened. Remove from the heat.

PREPARING THE CARAMEL POWDER

Heat the sugar in a saucepan, without adding any water, until it dissolves and cooks to a golden caramel. Pour over the silicone baking mat or a lined baking sheet and let cool. Break up into small pieces and pulse to a powder in the food processor.

ASSEMBLING THE TURNOVERS

Roll the dough to a thickness of about ⅛ in. (4 mm) and cut out six disks using the pastry cutter. Roll the centers of the disks a little with a rolling pin to make them oval. Whisk the egg wash ingredients together and brush the pastry edges with it so they can be sealed when the filling has been added. Spoon 1¾ oz. (50 g) of the compote into the center of each oval, fold the pastry over the filling, and press the edges together to seal. Turn the parcels over, place on a lined baking sheet, and brush with the egg wash. Chill for 1 hour. Preheat the oven to 350°F (175°C/Gas Mark 4). Brush the turnovers again with egg wash and with the tip of a knife, score a sunray pattern on top of each. Bake for about 30 minutes until golden. As soon as the turnovers come out of the oven, dust them with the caramel powder, and return them to the oven for 3 minutes to melt the caramel.

YELLOW PLUM CLAFOUTIS

Clafoutis aux prunes jaunes

Serves 5

Active time

15 minutes

Cooking time

30 minutes

Storage

Up to 2 days
in the refrigerator

Equipment

7-in. (18-cm) round baking
dish, 2 in. (5 cm) deep

Ingredients

1 tbsp (20 g) lightly salted
butter, softened

¼ cup (1¾ oz./50 g)
superfine sugar

Fruit and clafoutis batter

1¼ lb. (540 g) yellow
plums

1½ eggs

¼ cup (1¾ oz./50 g)
superfine sugar

Seeds of 1 vanilla bean

½ cup (1¾ oz./50 g)
almond flour

½ cup (2¼ oz./65 g)
all-purpose flour

⅔ cup (160 ml) whole
milk

Scant 3 tbsp
(1½ oz./40 g) crème
fraîche

3 tbsp (1½ oz./40 g)
lightly salted butter,
melted and cooled

Confectioners' sugar
for dusting

PREPARING THE BAKING DISH

Grease the inside of the baking dish with the softened butter and dust with
the sugar until coated.

PREPARING THE FRUIT AND CLAFOUTIS BATTER

Wash and halve the plums, removing the pits. Whisk together the eggs,
sugar, vanilla seeds, and almond flour until just combined. Whisk in the
all-purpose flour, followed by the milk and crème fraîche. Finally whisk in
the melted butter.

BAKING THE CLAFOUTIS

Preheat the oven to 400°F (210°C/Gas Mark 6). Arrange the plum halves in
a single layer over the base of the baking dish, rounded sides up. Carefully
pour the batter over the plums and bake for 10 minutes. Reduce the oven
temperature to 350°F (180°C/Gas Mark 4) and continue to bake for an
additional 20 minutes. Serve at room temperature lightly dusted with confectioners' sugar.

CHEFS' NOTES

The clafoutis can be accompanied with vanilla whipped
cream. Whip ⅔ cup (150 ml) heavy cream (min. 35% fat) with
4 tsp (10 g) confectioners' sugar and the seeds of 1 vanilla
bean until the cream holds its shape. Spoon into a serving
dish and serve with the clafoutis.

BASQUE CAKE WITH DAMSON PLUM CREAM

Gâteau basque aux quetsches

Serves 6

Active time
1 hour

Chilling time
15 minutes

Freezing time
30 minutes

Cooking time
30-40 minutes

Storage
Up to 2 days
in the refrigerator

Equipment
Stand mixer + paddle
beater

Food processor

Inexpensive silicone
baking mat to make the
stencil

6-in. (16-cm) cake ring

Ingredients

Sweet shortcrust pastry

1²/3 cups (7 oz./200 g)
flour

2 tsp (8 g) baking powder

½ tsp (2 g) *fleur de sel*

Generous ²/3 cup
(4½ oz./130 g) superfine
sugar

1 stick plus 2 tbsp
(5 oz./140 g) butter,
diced

¼ cup (2½ oz./70 g) egg
yolk (about 4 yolks)

Finely grated zest of
½ lemon

Damson plum cream

7 oz. (200 g) damson
plums

2 tbsp (1 oz./30 g) lightly
beaten egg (about
²/3 egg)

3¾ tsp (15 g) sugar

1½ tbsp (15 g) cornstarch

½ tbsp (6 g) butter, diced

Egg wash

1 egg, lightly beaten

Decoration

Damson plum jam,
as needed

CHEFS' NOTES

• To emboss the top of the cake
with a checkered pattern as in the
photograph, place a textured silicone
baking mat on the baking sheet
before setting the cake ring on it.

• The Basque cross stencil needs
to be cut from a silicone baking mat,
so buy an inexpensive mat and
cut other stencils in different shapes
from it to use for other cakes.

PREPARING THE PASTRY

Beat the flour, baking powder, *fleur de sel*, sugar, and butter in the stand mixer until the mixture is crumbly. Beat in the egg yolks and lemon zest until combined. Gather the dough into a ball with your hands and knead it lightly until smooth. Cover with plastic wrap and chill for 15 minutes. Roll out enough of the dough on a lightly floured surface to cut into a 6-in. (16-cm) circle, 1/16 in. (2 mm) thick. Place flat in the freezer. Roll the remaining pastry to make three more circles: two 6 in. (16 cm) in diameter, ⅛ in. (3 mm) thick, and one 6 in. (16 cm) in diameter, ¼ in. (5 mm) thick. Cut a 5-in. (12-cm) hole in the center of the ¼-in. (5-mm)-thick circle. Place these flat in the freezer as well.

PREPARING THE DAMSON PLUM CREAM

Wash and halve the damson plums and remove the pits. Pulse to a puree in the food processor. Weigh out 5¼ oz. (150 g) of the puree and heat in a saucepan. Meanwhile, whisk together the egg, sugar, and cornstarch until pale and thick. Whisk a little of the hot puree into the whisked mixture, return it to the saucepan, and bring to a boil, whisking continuously. Let boil for 1 minute, then remove from the heat and stir in the butter. Transfer to a bowl and cool quickly in the refrigerator.

PREPARING THE BASQUE CROSS STENCIL

Cut a stencil of a Basque cross about 5½ in. (14 cm) in diameter from the silicone mat. Place the stencil in the center of the thinnest (1/16 in./2 mm) circle of pastry and trace around the outline of the cross with the tip of a knife, cutting all the way through the pastry. Remove the cut-out cross and fit the stencil in its place.

ASSEMBLING AND BAKING THE CAKE

Preheat the oven to 340°F (170°C/Gas Mark 3). Place the cake ring on a lined baking sheet and the pastry circle with the stencil in the ring. Brush the pastry with a thin layer of egg wash and place one of the ⅛-in. (3-mm)-thick pastry circles over it. Brush with egg wash and place the ¼-in. (5-mm)-thick pastry circle with the 5-in. (12-cm) hole on top. Fill the hole with 5¼ oz. (150 g) of the damson plum cream, smoothing it in an even layer using an offset spatula. Brush the pastry around the cream with egg wash. Top with the second ⅛-in. (3-mm)-thick pastry circle to seal the cream inside the cake. Bake for 30–40 minutes until golden. Let the cake cool in the ring for 10 minutes. Invert it onto a serving plate so the stencil is now on top and lift off the ring. Carefully remove the stencil and fill the space with damson plum jam.

CHERRIES JUBILEE

Jubilé de cerises

Serves 6

Active time
1 hour

Maturing time
12 hours

Cooking time
10 minutes

Equipment
Instant-read thermometer
Immersion blender
Ice cream maker
Silicone baking mat

Ingredients

Vanilla ice cream
¹⁄₁₀ oz. (3 g) stabilizer
1¾ oz. (50 g) glucose powder
Scant 1½ cups (370 ml) whole milk
2 vanilla beans, split lengthwise and seeds scraped
Scant 3½ tbsp (25 g) milk powder
⅓ cup (2¾ oz./75 g) superfine sugar
1 tbsp plus 1 tsp (14 g) dextrose powder
Generous ¼ cup (65 ml) heavy cream, min. 35% fat
¼ cup (2¼ oz./65 g) egg yolk (about 3 yolks)

Crisp tuiles
¼ cup (2 oz./55 g) egg white (about 2 whites)
⅓ cup (1½ oz./45 g) confectioners' sugar
2½ tbsp (25 g) all-purpose flour
Scant 1 cup (240 ml) water
1½ tbsp (22 g) butter
Scant ½ tsp (2 g) salt

Flambéed cherries
1¼ lb. (600 g) cherries
3 tbsp (2 oz./60 g) honey
½ cup (2½ oz./70 g) turbinado sugar
7 oz. (200 g) cherry puree
4¼ tbsp (2 oz./60 g) butter
2 tbsp plus 2 tsp (50 ml) kirsch

PREPARING THE VANILLA ICE CREAM (1 DAY AHEAD)

Combine the stabilizer and glucose powder in a bowl. Heat the milk with the vanilla beans and seeds in a saucepan until the temperature reaches 77°F (25°C). Stir in the milk powder until smooth, then heat until the temperature reaches 86°F (30°C). Stir in the sugar and dextrose powder until dissolved. Continue heating to 95°F (35°C), whisk in the cream and egg yolks, and stir over the heat until the temperature reaches 113°F (45°C). Stir in the stabilizer and glucose powder. When the temperature reaches 185°F (85°C), take the saucepan off the heat and remove the vanilla beans. Process with the immersion blender until smooth. Cool, transfer to a covered bowl or other container, and let mature in the refrigerator for 12 hours. The next day, process once more with the immersion blender, then churn in the ice cream maker. Transfer to an airtight container and freeze until serving.

PREPARING THE CRISP TUILES

Preheat the oven to 340°F (170°C/Gas Mark 3). Whisk together the egg whites, confectioners' sugar, and flour in a mixing bowl. Bring the water, butter, and salt to a boil in a saucepan. Whisking continuously, add the whisked egg whites, and return to a boil. Immediately pour over the silicone mat and spread into a thin, even layer using an offset spatula. Bake for about 10 minutes or until golden and crisp. Let cool completely before breaking into pieces.

PREPARING THE FLAMBÉED CHERRIES

Wash and dry the cherries and remove the stems. Halve and remove the pits. Heat the honey and turbinado sugar in a deep skillet until dissolved. Add the cherries and cook briefly until the cherries release their juices. Add the cherry puree and cook until the juices have reduced to a thick syrup. Stir in the butter and, when melted, add the kirsch. Flambé carefully with a long-reach lighter.

TO SERVE

Serve the cherries warm with the vanilla ice cream and a piece of crisp tuile on the side.

BLACK FOREST GÂTEAU

Forêt-noire

Serves 8

Active time
2 hours

Cooking time
10 minutes

Freezing time
Overnight

Thawing time
3 hours

Storage
Up to 2 days
in the refrigerator

Equipment
Instant-read thermometer

Stand mixer + paddle
beater

Pastry bag

2 food-safe acetate
sheets

4 × 9½-in. (10 × 24-cm)
silicone Yule log (bûche)
mold, 3¼ in. (8.3 cm)
deep (preferably a
Silikomart "Fôret" mold)

Velvet spray gun

Ingredients
Chocolate sponge

⅔ oz. (18 g) dark
chocolate, 64% cacao
(preferably Valrhona
Manjari), chopped

2 tbsp (1¼ oz./35 g)
butter, softened

2½ tbsp (20 g)
confectioners' sugar

¼ cup (2¼ oz./65 g) egg
yolk (about 3 yolks)

1 tbsp (10 g) all-purpose
flour

1¼ tsp (3 g) unsweetened
cocoa powder

¼ cup (2 oz./55 g) egg
white (about 2 whites)

5 tsp (20 g) superfine
sugar

Cherry jelly

10½ oz. (300 g) fresh
cherries, pitted and
quartered

3½ oz. (100 g) cherry
puree

1½ tsp (6 g) pectin NH

5 tsp (20 g) superfine
sugar

1 tbsp (15 ml) kirsch

Mascarpone cream

1 tbsp (16 g) mascarpone

Scant ½ cup (100 ml)
heavy cream, min. 35%
fat, well chilled

Seeds of ⅓ vanilla bean

1¼ tbsp (10 g)
confectioners' sugar

Chocolate mousse

5 oz. (140 g) dark
chocolate, 64% cacao
(preferably Valrhona
Manjari), chopped

Generous ½ cup (130 ml)
heavy cream, min. 35%
fat

2 tbsp (30 ml) whole milk

2½ tbsp (1 oz./30 g)
sugar

⅓ cup (3 oz./90 g) egg
yolk (about 4½ yolks)

Scant 1 cup (230 ml)
heavy cream, min. 35%
fat, well chilled

Chocolate sheets

1 lb. 2 oz. (500 g) dark
chocolate, 64% cacao
(preferably Valrhona
Manjari), chopped

Chocolate spray

2½ oz. (70 g) dark
chocolate, 64% cacao
(preferably Valrhona
Manjari), chopped

1 oz. (30 g) cocoa butter,
chopped

Decoration

A few cherries (fresh or
in syrup)

PREPARING THE CHOCOLATE SPONGE

Preheat the oven to 350°F (180°C/Gas Mark 4). Melt the chocolate until the temperature reaches 95°F (35°C) in a bowl over a bain-marie. Cream the butter and confectioners' sugar together in the stand mixer. Add the egg yolks and beat until the mixture is creamy and thick. Beat in the melted chocolate, followed by the flour and cocoa powder. Whisk the egg whites and superfine sugar together until they hold firm peaks and gently fold them into the batter. Spread the batter over a lined baking sheet and bake for 10 minutes.

PREPARING THE CHERRY JELLY

Wash the cherries, quarter them, and remove the pits. Warm the cherry puree in a saucepan. Combine the pectin and sugar in a bowl and stir into the puree until dissolved. Let boil for 30 seconds, remove from the heat, and stir in the cherries and kirsch. Let cool slightly, then transfer to the pastry bag and chill in the refrigerator until assembling.

PREPARING THE MASCARPONE CREAM

Place the mascarpone in a bowl and whisk in a little of the cream to loosen it. Whisk in the vanilla seeds, followed by the remaining cream and confectioners' sugar. Whisk until the cream holds its shape and chill until assembling.

PREPARING THE CHOCOLATE MOUSSE

Place the chocolate in a bowl. Heat the generous ½ cup (130 ml) cream with the milk and half the sugar in a saucepan until the sugar dissolves, then bring to a boil. Whisk the egg yolks and remaining sugar in a bowl until pale and thick. When the cream comes to a boil, pour a little into the egg yolk mixture, whisking continuously. Return to the saucepan and whisk continuously over the heat, until the temperature of the custard reaches 181°F–185°F (83°C–85°C). Pour over the chocolate and whisk until melted. Set the bowl over a larger bowl filled with ice water and let cool, stirring often, to 95°F (35°C). Whisk the well-chilled cream until it holds its shape and fold it into the mousse. Chill until assembling.

PREPARING THE CHOCOLATE SHEETS

Temper the chocolate (see p. 140). Using a rolling pin, roll the chocolate into a thin layer between the two acetate sheets. Let set for a few minutes until firm but not hard, then carefully peel off the top sheet. Cut the chocolate into five 3½ × 9-in. (9 × 23-cm) rectangles (½ in./1 cm shorter in width and length than your Yule log mold).

ASSEMBLING THE GÂTEAU

Line your mold with a first layer of chocolate mousse about ¼ in. (5 mm) thick. Place two chocolate sheets over the mousse, followed by a layer of mascarpone cream and another chocolate sheet. Pipe the cherry jelly over the chocolate sheet. Cover the jelly with another chocolate sheet, add another layer of mascarpone cream, followed by the final chocolate sheet. Finish with the chocolate sponge, trimmed so it fits just inside the mold. Freeze overnight.

PREPARING THE VELVET FINISH

Unmold the gâteau. Melt the chocolate and cocoa butter together in a bowl over a bain-marie until the temperature reaches 113°F (45°C). Transfer it to the spray gun and spray over the gâteau for a velvet-like finish. Let the gâteau thaw for at least 3 hours before serving.

DECORATING THE GÂTEAU

Decorate with fresh cherries or well-drained cherries in syrup and serve immediately.

TAGGIASCA OLIVE TAPENADE SWIRLS

Pain feuilleté aux olives Taggiasche

**Makes 12,
to serve 6**

Active time
7½ hours

Resting time
1½ hours

Chilling time
6 hours

Rising time
2 hours

Cooking time
20 minutes

Storage
3 days in an airtight container

Equipment
Stand mixer + dough hook
Instant-read thermometer
Food processor
Muffin pan with 2½-in. (6.5-cm) cups

Ingredients

Dough
For the *détrempe* (water dough)
3¼ cups (14 oz./400 g) bread flour
¾ cup plus 2½ tbsp (215 ml) water
1½ tsp (7 g) salt
⅙ oz. (4 g) fresh yeast

For laminating
1 stick plus 2 tbsp (5 oz./145 g) butter, preferably 84% fat

Taggiasca tapenade
4½ oz. (125 g) Taggiasca olives
1 tbsp (8 g) capers
1 oz. (30 g) anchovy fillets
½ clove garlic, peeled
3 tbsp (40 ml) olive oil

Beurre noisette
3 tbsp (1¾ oz./50 g) butter
1 tsp (4 g) *fleur de sel*

CHEFS' NOTES

• Toasted ground almonds can be added to the tapenade to prevent it from separating and boost its flavor. Toast ½ cup (1¾ oz./50 g) ground almonds for 10 minutes in a preheated 325°F (160°C/Gas Mark 3) oven. Let cool before stirring into the tapenade.

• In summer, you can also add a few fresh basil leaves to the tapenade.

PREPARING THE DOUGH
To make the *détrempe*, knead the flour, water, salt, and yeast in the stand mixer on low speed for about 6 minutes until the temperature of the dough reaches 81°F (27°C). Cover the bowl and let the dough rest for 1 hour at room temperature. Transfer it to a work surface and flatten the dough with your hand to burst any air bubbles trapped inside. Roll into an 8 × 12-in. (20 × 30-cm) rectangle, place on a lined baking sheet, cover, and chill for 2 hours. Toward the end of the chilling time, flatten the 84% fat butter for laminating into a 6-in. (15-cm) square using a rolling pin. Cover with plastic wrap and let rest at room temperature for 30 minutes. Place the *détrempe* on the work surface with one short side facing you. Place the butter on one half of the dough and fold the other half over the butter to enclose it completely. Press the edges together to seal and then give the dough a quarter turn so the seal is perpendicular to you. Roll the dough on a lightly floured surface into a rectangle 16–17½ in. (40–45 cm) long. Fold up the bottom third from one short side, fold the top third down over it, and rotate the folded dough 90° to the right (a single turn). Cover with plastic wrap and chill for 2 hours. Repeat the rolling and folding to give the dough another single turn. Cover it with plastic wrap and chill for an additional 2 hours.

PREPARING THE TAGGIASCA TAPENADE
Pit the olives and process them with the other ingredients to make a paste.

PREPARING THE BEURRE NOISETTE
Heat the butter in a saucepan until it melts. When it begins to turn golden, stop the cooking by immersing the base of the pan in cold water. Stir in the salt and strain the butter through a fine-mesh sieve.

ASSEMBLING AND BAKING THE SWIRLS
On a lightly floured surface, roll the dough into a 10 × 16½-in. (26 × 42-cm) rectangle, ⅛ in. (3.5 mm) thick. Spread the tapenade over it in a thin layer using an offset spatula. Cut the dough into twelve 1⅓ × 10-in. (3.5 × 26-cm) strips, roll up the strips from one short side, and place flat in the muffin pan cavities. Let rise for 2 hours at warm room temperature (about 79°F/26°C) until doubled in size. Preheat the oven (without steam) to 450°F (230°C/Gas Mark 8). Warm the *beurre noisette*, brush it onto the swirls, and bake for 20 minutes until golden brown. Turn out and let cool on a wire rack.

FRUITS WITH SEEDS

TARTE TATIN

Serves 4

Active time

40 minutes

Cooking time

55 minutes

Chilling time

About 1 hour

Freezing time

10 minutes

Storage

Up to 2 days in the refrigerator

Equipment

Instant-read thermometer

6-in. (16-cm) round cake pan, 2 in. (5 cm) deep

Food processor

6-in. (16-cm) tart ring

Pastry bag + a plain ⅔-in. (16-mm) tip

2 food-safe acetate sheets

3 in. (8-cm) round cookie cutter

Mandoline

6-in. (16-cm) round cake board or serving plate

Velvet spray gun (optional)

Ingredients

Syrup-poached apples

Juice of ¼ lemon

1¼ lb. (600 g) King of the Pippins apples

Scant 1 cup (220 ml) water

⅔ cup (4½ oz./125 g) superfine sugar

1 stick plus 2 tsp (4½ oz./125 g) butter

Seeds of 1½ vanilla beans

Tatin apple topping

¼ cup (2 oz./55 g) superfine sugar

1 tbsp (15 g) butter

¾ tsp (4 ml) olive oil

Seeds of 1½ vanilla beans

Scant ⅛ tsp (0.5 g) ground cinnamon

Speculaas shortbread

1 tbsp (15 g) butter

5 tsp (20 g) superfine sugar

2 tbsp (20 g) muscovado or rapadura sugar

4 eggs

½ cup plus 1 tbsp (2½ oz./70 g) all-purpose flour

¼ tsp (1 g) baking powder

Scant 2 tsp (3.5 g) finely grated orange zest

⅛ tsp (0.5 g) salt

Generous ½ tsp (1.5 g) ground cinnamon

⅛ tsp (0.5 g) ground nutmeg

Scant ⅛ tsp (0.5 g) ground cloves

¼ tsp (0.5 g) green anise seeds

⅛ tsp (0.5 g) *quatre-épîces* spice mix (or allspice, ground mixed spice, or pumpkin pie spice)

¾ tsp (4 ml) whole milk

Speculaas shortbread crust

3 tbsp (2½ oz./45 g) butter

5¾ oz. (160 g) roughly ground speculaas shortbread (see left)

Vanilla cream

1 tbsp (15 ml) heavy cream, min. 35% fat, well chilled

1¾ tsp (8 g) crème fraîche

1¼ tbsp (10 g) confectioners' sugar

Seeds of 1 vanilla bean

Decoration

⅓ oz. (10 g) white couverture chocolate, 35% cacao (preferably Valrhona Ivoire), chopped

⅓ oz. (10 g) Granny Smith apple

3½ oz. (100 g) neutral glaze

1½ tbsp (25 ml) water

Small piece of edible gold leaf

PREPARING THE POACHED APPLES

Add the lemon juice to a bowl of cold water. Wash and peel the apples. Quarter them and remove the cores. Immerse the apples in the acidulated water to prevent them from browning. Heat the scant 1 cup (220 ml) water, sugar, butter, and vanilla seeds in a saucepan until the sugar dissolves and the butter melts. Working in batches, cook the apple quarters in the butter and syrup until they are almost tender when pierced with the tip of a knife. Transfer to a wire rack to drain, cover with plastic wrap, and set aside at room temperature.

PREPARING THE TATIN TOPPING

Preheat the oven to 325°F (160°C/Gas Mark 3). Make a dry caramel by heating the sugar in a heavy-bottomed saucepan over low heat, without adding water, until it dissolves to form a syrup. Boil until the syrup becomes a golden-brown caramel and the temperature reaches a maximum of 340°F (170°C). Stir in the butter and oil, followed by the vanilla seeds and cinnamon. Immediately pour the caramel into the cake pan, tilting the pan so it coats the base evenly. Arrange the apple quarters over the caramel in concentric circles, packing them tightly together. Bake for 20 minutes. Let cool, then carefully pour out any excess juice. Chill until assembling.

PREPARING THE SHORTBREAD AND MAKING THE CRUST

To make the shortbread, cream the butter, superfine sugar, and muscovado sugar together. Mix in the eggs one at a time, then add the flour, baking powder, orange zest, salt, and spices. Finally, stir in the milk. Transfer the dough to the work surface, press down on it and push with the heel of your hand, smearing it against the work surface until smooth (*fraisage*). Roll between two sheets of parchment paper to a thickness of approximately ⅛ in. (3–4 mm). Chill for about 25 minutes. Preheat the oven to 300°F (155°C/Gas Mark 2), remove the top sheet of parchment, place on a baking sheet, and bake for 25 minutes. Let cool completely. Grind coarsely in the food processor into roughly ⅟₁₆-in. (2-mm) pieces. To make the crust, melt the butter in a saucepan and gradually stir in the shortbread pieces using a flexible spatula. Place the tart ring on a lined baking sheet, transfer the shortbread to the ring, and press it down using the back of a spoon into a flat, even layer. Chill to firm up the butter.

PREPARING THE VANILLA CREAM

Whip the heavy cream with the crème fraîche, confectioners' sugar, and vanilla seeds until the cream holds its shape. Spoon into the pastry bag and keep chilled.

PREPARING THE DECORATIONS

Melt the chocolate in a bain-marie until the temperature reaches 113°F (45°C). Spread it into a thin layer between the two acetate sheets and let set for a few minutes in the freezer. When the chocolate is hard, remove the top sheet. Warm the base of the cookie cutter slightly and cut out a chocolate disk. Return the disk to the freezer while you prepare the apple. Wash the apple and slice it very thinly using the mandoline. Keep the slices immersed in a bowl of cold water with a little lemon juice added to prevent browning. Drain and pat the slices dry, then arrange them in an overlapping circle over the chocolate disk. Trim off any apple extending beyond the chocolate to make a neat edge.

ASSEMBLING THE TART

Place the shortbread crust on the cake board or serving plate and remove the tart ring. Remove the apple topping from the refrigerator and, to ensure it will release easily, gently heat the bottom of the pan by immersing it briefly in hot water or setting it over a low heat. Carefully invert the apple topping over the crust and remove the pan. Combine the neutral glaze and water in a saucepan and heat until the temperature reaches 140°F (60°C). Brush a thin layer of glaze over the apples or use a spray gun. Place the apple-covered chocolate disk in the center of the tart and pipe a mound of vanilla cream in the center of the disk. Top the cream with a small piece of gold leaf. Pipe the remaining cream into small bowls to serve alongside the tart.

TONKA-FLAVORED APPLE CRUMBLE

Crumble fleur de pomme tonka

Serves 6

Active time

2 hours

Chilling time

30 minutes + chilling the oil for the apple caviar

Cooking time

15 minutes

Storage

Up to 24 hours in the refrigerator before assembling

Equipment

Instant-read thermometer

Syringe or pipette

Mandoline

Ingredients

Apple compote

1 lb. 2 oz. (500 g) apples

½ tbsp (8 g) butter

¼ cup (1¾ oz./50 g) sugar

Seeds of 1 vanilla bean

1 tonka bean, finely grated

Water, as needed

Almond and tonka bean crumble

⅓ cup (1¼ oz./35 g) almond flour

⅓ cup (2½ oz./45 g) all-purpose flour

2½ tbsp (1 oz./30 g) turbinado sugar

½ tonka bean, finely grated

4 tbsp (2 oz./60 g) butter, diced

Apple caviar

2 cups (500 ml) grape-seed oil

1½ tbsp (25 ml) water

2 tbsp (25 g) sugar

Scant ½ cup (115 ml) apple juice

2 tsp (4 g) agar-agar powder

Apple flower petals

Scant ½ cup (100 ml) Granny Smith or another apple juice

2 tsp (10 ml) lemon juice

4 apples

PREPARING THE APPLE COMPOTE

Peel and core the apples, and cut them into ½-in. (1-cm) dice. Melt the butter in a saucepan, add the rest of the ingredients, and cook to make a compote (see technique p. 94).

PREPARING THE CRUMBLE

Combine the flours, sugar, and tonka bean in a bowl. Add the butter and rub it in using your fingertips until the mixture has the texture of coarse crumbs. Cover with plastic wrap and chill for about 30 minutes. Preheat the oven to 340°F (170°C/Gas Mark 3). Spread the crumble mixture across a lined baking sheet and bake for 15 minutes.

PREPARING THE APPLE CAVIAR

Fill a tall, narrow container with grape-seed oil and chill until the temperature reaches 39.2°F (4°C). When the oil is well chilled, heat the water and sugar in a saucepan until the sugar dissolves. Bring to a boil, stir in the apple juice and agar-agar, then bring back to a boil for 30 seconds. Cool to lukewarm. Transfer to the syringe or pipette and release drop by drop into the cold oil—as the warm mixture hits the cold oil, it will form caviar-like pearls, due to the thermal shock. Strain through a fine-mesh sieve and rinse well under cold water to remove the oil (the pearls will not burst). Chill until serving.

PREPARING THE APPLE FLOWER PETALS

Combine the apple juice and lemon juice in a bowl. Wash and quarter the apples and remove the cores. Using the mandoline, cut the apple quarters into wafer-thin slices (approximately 1 mm thick) ¾ in. (2 cm) long. Immerse in the apple and lemon juice to prevent the slices from browning.

TO SERVE

Reheat the apple compote over low heat. Place about ⅔ oz. (20 g) of the crumble in the base of each serving dish and spoon the compote on top, spreading it into an even layer. Drain the apple slices and arrange them over the compote overlapping in concentric circles to form flower shapes. Place the apple caviar in the center of each flower and over the petals and compote.

CHEFS' NOTES

For an impeccably neat presentation, place a cookie cutter in the center of each serving dish. Spread a layer of crumble into it and top with an even layer of apple compote before carefully lifting off the cutter.

PEAR TIRAMISU

Tiramisu aux poires

Serves 6

Active time

3–3½ hours

Chilling time

12 hours

Maturing time

12 hours

Cooking time

20 minutes

Infusing time

20 minutes

Storage

Up to 24 hours in the refrigerator before assembling

Equipment

Instant-read thermometer

Immersion blender

Ice cream maker

Silicone baking mat

4-cup (1-L) whipping siphon + 2 N₂O gas cartridges and a plain nozzle

2 food-safe acetate sheets

2-in. (5-cm) round cookie cutter

Pastry bag + a plain ⅓-in. (8-mm) tip

Ingredients

Chocolate crémeux

¼ cup (60 ml) whole milk

¼ cup (65 ml) heavy cream, min. 35% fat

1 tbsp (20 g) egg yolk (1 yolk)

5 tsp (20 g) superfine sugar

2 oz. (55 g) dark chocolate, 70% cacao, chopped

Pear sorbet

3½ tbsp (50 ml) water

2½ tsp (7 ml) lemon juice

3½ tbsp (1½ oz./40 g) superfine sugar, divided

⅔ oz. (20 g) glucose powder

1 pinch (1.5 g) sorbet stabilizer

9 oz. (250 g) pear puree

Flourless chocolate and almond sponge

1¾ oz. (50 g) dark couverture chocolate, 50% cacao, chopped

1 tbsp (15 g) butter

1 oz. (25 g) raw almond paste, 50% almonds

Scant 2¾ tsp (15 g) egg yolk (about ¾ yolk)

Scant ⅓ cup (2¼ oz./65 g) egg white (about 2 whites)

2 tbsp (25 g) superfine sugar

Vanilla mascarpone cream

⅔ cup (5 oz./150 g) lightly beaten egg (3 eggs)

¼ cup (1¾ oz./50 g) turbinado sugar

1 cup (9 oz./250 g) mascarpone

Seeds of 1 vanilla bean

Chocolate decoration

10½ oz. (300 g) dark couverture chocolate, 66% cacao

Chocolate syrup

3½ tbsp (50 ml) water

¼ cup (1¾ oz./50 g) superfine sugar

1½ tbsp (10 g) cacao nibs

1½ tbsp (10 g) unsweetened cocoa powder

Vanilla pear *brunoise*

1 pear

4 tsp (20 ml) lemon juice

Seeds of 1 vanilla bean

Decoration

2 Bartlett (Williams) pears

3 tbsp (40 ml) lemon juice

To serve

Unsweetened cocoa powder, for dusting

PREPARING THE CHOCOLATE CRÉMEUX (1 DAY AHEAD)

In a saucepan, bring the milk and cream to a boil. Meanwhile, whisk the egg yolk and sugar together until pale and thick. Whisk in a little of the hot milk and cream, pour the mixture into the saucepan, and stir continuously over medium heat until the temperature reaches 181°F (83°C). Place the chocolate in a bowl, pour the custard over it, and process with the immersion blender until smooth. Transfer to a covered container, cool, and chill for at least 12 hours (ideally overnight).

PREPARING THE PEAR SORBET (1 DAY AHEAD)

Heat the water, lemon juice, and 2½ tbsp (1 oz./30 g) of the sugar in a saucepan until the sugar dissolves. Stir the glucose powder, stabilizer, and remaining sugar together in a bowl. Add to the saucepan, stir to dissolve, then remove from the heat and let cool completely. Stir in the pear puree, transfer to a covered container, and let mature in the refrigerator for 12 hours. The next day, churn in the ice cream maker. Store in the freezer.

PREPARING THE SPONGE

Preheat the oven to 350°F (180°C/Gas Mark 4). Melt the chocolate and butter together over a bain-marie until the temperature reaches 122°F–131°F (50°C –55°C). Microwave the almond paste in a mixing bowl on high for 20 seconds to soften it. Mix in the egg yolk until smooth, then stir in the melted chocolate and butter. In a separate bowl, whisk the egg whites until they hold soft peaks. Whisk in the sugar until the peaks are firm. Using a flexible spatula, gently fold the whites into the chocolate and almond mixture. Spread the batter into an even layer over the silicone baking mat and bake for 7–8 minutes. Carefully invert the sponge onto a wire rack and remove the silicone mat. Let cool completely.

PREPARING THE VANILLA MASCARPONE CREAM

Whisk the eggs and sugar together over a bain-marie until pale and thick. Remove the bowl from the bain-marie and place on the work surface. In a separate bowl, whisk the mascarpone to loosen it, then whisk in the vanilla seeds. Using a flexible spatula, gently fold the mascarpone into the eggs and sugar. Transfer to the siphon, seal, and refrigerate until serving.

PREPARING THE CHOCOLATE DECORATION

Temper the chocolate (see p. 140). Spread it in a thin layer over one acetate sheet and place the other sheet on top. When the chocolate is just set but not hard, peel off the top sheet and cut the chocolate into tall, thin triangles with approximately ¾-in. (2-cm) bases and 3½-in. (9-cm) sides. Let set completely.

PREPARING THE CHOCOLATE SYRUP

Heat the water, sugar, and cacao nibs in a saucepan until the sugar dissolves. Bring to a boil. Remove from the heat, cover with plastic wrap, and let infuse for 20 minutes. Strain through a fine-mesh sieve, then stir in the cocoa powder until dissolved.

PREPARING THE VANILLA-SCENTED PEAR BRUNOISE

Peel and core the pear. Cut the flesh into 1/16-in. (2-mm) dice (*brunoise*). Place the lemon juice and vanilla seeds in a bowl, add the diced pear, and stir gently until coated.

PREPARING THE PEAR DECORATION

Wash, dry, quarter, and core the pear without peeling it. Using a sharp knife, cut the quarters lengthwise into thin slices about ½ in. (1 cm) wide and 2–2½ in. (5–6 cm) long. Coat the slices in lemon juice to prevent browning.

ASSEMBLING THE TIRAMISU

Cut the sponge into rounds using the cookie cutter. Brush them with the chocolate syrup until soaked and place slightly off-center on serving plates. Pipe spirals of crémeux over the sponge, cover with the pear *brunoise*, and top with a half-scoop of sorbet. Charge the siphon with the gas cartridges and fit with the plain nozzle. Shake to distribute the gas and cover each serving completely with a spiral of mascarpone cream. Dust the plates and mascarpone cream with sifted cocoa powder, then arrange the chocolate triangles and pear strips attractively around, pushing them gently into the cream to fix them in place. Serve immediately.

PEARS BELLE HÉLÈNE

Poire façon Belle Hélène

Serves 8

Active time
45 minutes

Maturing time
12 hours

Cooking time
45 minutes

Chilling time
30 minutes

Storage
Up to 3 days before assembling

Equipment
Instant-read thermometer

8 × 12-in. (20 × 30-cm) rimmed baking sheet

Ice cream maker

2 × silicone molds with ring-shaped cavities, 3 in. (7.5 cm) external dia. and 2 in. (6 cm) internal dia.

2-in. (5-cm) and 1¼-in. (3-cm) round cookie cutters

2 silicone baking mats

Immersion blender

Cutting tube ¾ in. (2 cm) in dia. and 4 in. (10 cm) long (or apple corer)

Ingredients

Vanilla ice cream

½ cup plus 2 tsp (135 ml) whole milk

2 tbsp plus 1 tsp (35 ml) heavy cream, min. 35% fat

2 tbsp (1¼ oz./35 g) egg yolk (about 2 yolks)

3 tbsp (1¼ oz./35 g) superfine sugar

2 tsp (10 g) milk powder

Seeds of ½ vanilla bean

Almond tuiles

Scant ¼ cup (20 g) sliced almonds

3¾ tsp (15 g) superfine sugar

2½ tsp (5 g) all-purpose flour

1 ¼ tsp (6 g) egg white (about ⅕ white)

Seeds of ½ vanilla bean

1 tsp (5 g) butter, melted and cooled

Poached pears

6¾ cups (1.6 L) water

2⅔ cups (1 lb. 2 oz./500 g) superfine sugar

Seeds of 2 vanilla beans

Scant ½ tsp (2 ml) lemon juice

⅒ oz. (2 g) lemon zest

1 cinnamon stick

8 pears, preferably Conference

Belle Hélène sauce

6 oz. (170 g) dark chocolate, 70% cacao (preferably Valrhona Guanaja), chopped

Scant ⅔ cup (140 ml) whole milk

½ cup (125 ml) heavy cream, min. 35% fat

2½ tbsp (1 oz./30 g) superfine sugar

Generous 1 tbsp (20 g) butter

⅟₂₀ oz. (1.5 g) tonka bean

Apple filling

3½ oz. (100 g) Granny Smith apples

Seeds of ½ vanilla bean

2 tsp (10 ml) lime juice

⅒ oz. (3 g) finely grated lime zest

PREPARING THE VANILLA ICE CREAM (1 DAY AHEAD)

Bring the milk and cream to a boil in a saucepan. Meanwhile, whisk together the egg yolks and sugar in a bowl until pale and thick. Whisk in the milk powder and vanilla seeds. When the milk mixture comes to a boil, pour a little into the egg yolk mixture, whisking continuously. Pour the mixture into the saucepan and cook, stirring constantly with a spatula, until the custard coats the spatula and the temperature reaches 181°F (83°C). Strain through a fine-mesh sieve into a bowl, press plastic wrap over the surface, and cool quickly in the refrigerator. Let mature for 12 hours in the refrigerator. The next day, place the rimmed baking sheet in the freezer until well chilled. Remove the ice cream from the refrigerator and churn it in the ice cream maker. Fill 8 cavities of the ring molds with ice cream and freeze until serving. Spread the remaining ice cream across the chilled baking sheet to a thickness of ¼ in. (5 mm) and freeze until quite firm. Cut out eight 2-in. (5-cm) disks using the larger cookie cutter, then cut out the centers using the smaller one to make rings. Freeze until serving.

PREPARING THE ALMOND TUILES

Preheat the oven to 300°F (150°C/Gas Mark 2). Combine the almonds, sugar, and flour in a bowl. Using a spatula, stir in the egg white, vanilla seeds, and butter. Spoon eight ⅓-oz. (10-g) mounds of batter onto a silicone baking mat, leaving plenty of space between them. Place the second silicone mat on top to flatten them into thin, irregular shapes. Bake for 10 minutes, then lift off the top mat and, using the 2-in. (5-cm) cutter, cut a hole from the center of each tuile. Return to the oven for 5 minutes until lightly golden. Let cool.

POACHING THE PEARS

Place the water, sugar, vanilla seeds, lemon juice, lemon zest, and cinnamon stick in a large saucepan. Heat until the sugar dissolves, then bring to a boil. Meanwhile, wash and peel the pears, leaving the stems attached. When the syrup comes to a boil, reduce the heat and add the pears. Cut a circle of parchment paper slightly larger than the diameter of the saucepan, place it over the pears, and let poach for about 15 minutes or until almost tender. Remove from the heat and let the pears cool to room temperature in the syrup.

PREPARING THE BELLE HÉLÈNE SAUCE

Place the chocolate in a bowl. In a saucepan, heat the milk, cream, and sugar until the sugar dissolves, then bring to a boil. Pour over the chocolate, stirring until melted. Stir in the butter, finely grate in the tonka bean, and process with the immersion blender until smooth. Set aside.

PREPARING THE APPLE FILLING

Wash and core the apples. Cut them into very small dice (*brunoise*), without peeling them. Place in a bowl and stir in the vanilla seeds, lime juice, and lime zest until combined. Push the cutting tube (or corer) into the base of each poached pear until it reaches the center, to remove the core and hollow out the pear. Fill the centers of the pears with the apple *brunoise*.

ASSEMBLING THE PEARS

Warm the Belle Hélène sauce in a saucepan. Place a large ice cream ring in each serving bowl and set a poached pear inside it. Slip a tuile over the top of each pear, tilting it slightly, then do the same with the smaller ice cream ring. Pour a little sauce into each bowl alongside the pear and serve immediately.

QUINCE ÉCLAIRS

Éclairs aux coings

Makes 6

Active time
2 hours

Setting time
At least 1 hour

Cooking time
1 hour 10 minutes

Freezing time
2 hours

Storage
Up to 24 hours
in the refrigerator

Equipment
Silicone éclair mold with
six 1 × 5-in. (2.5 × 13-cm)
cavities, 1 in. (2.5 cm)
deep

2 pastry bags + a plain
½-in. (15-mm) tip

Ingredients

Quince jelly

2¼ lb. (1 kg) quinces

Sugar, as needed

Scant ½ tsp (2 g) tartaric
acid dissolved in ½ tsp
(2 ml) water, or a scant
½ tsp (2 ml) lemon juice

Quince tatin topping

1 cup (7 oz./200 g) sugar

5 tbsp (3 oz./80 g) butter,
diced

1¼ lb. (600 g) diced
cooked quince from the
jelly (see above)

Choux pastry

¼ cup (60 ml) water

Generous ¼ cup (65 ml)
whole milk

Generous ½ tsp (3 g) salt

3 tbsp (1¾ oz./50 g)
butter, diced

⅔ cup (2½ oz./75 g) all-
purpose flour, sifted

½ cup (4½ oz./125 g)
lightly beaten egg (about
2½ eggs)

Decoration

1 cup (9 oz./250 g) crème
fraîche, preferably from
Isigny

Baby watercress leaves

PREPARING THE QUINCE JELLY

Prepare the jelly (see technique p. 104) using the ingredients listed and cutting the quinces into ½-in. (1-cm) cubes. Reserve 1¼ lb. (600 g) of the cooked cubes for the topping and make the jelly with the remainder. Let set for at least 1 hour before using.

PREPARING THE QUINCE TATIN TOPPING

Preheat the oven to 325°F (160°C/Gas Mark 3). Make a dry caramel by heating the sugar in a heavy-bottomed saucepan over low heat, without adding water, until it dissolves to form a syrup. Boil until the syrup becomes a pale gold caramel. Remove from the heat and gradually whisk in the butter to prevent further cooking. Divide the caramel between the cavities in the éclair mold, pouring about 1¼ oz. (35 g) into each one. Add the reserved quince cubes, filling the cavities to the top. Bake for 30 minutes, then let cool to room temperature. Freeze for 2 hours to make unmolding easier.

PREPARING THE CHOUX PASTRY

Preheat the oven to 350°F (180°C/Gas Mark 4). Heat the water, milk, salt, and butter in a saucepan until the butter melts. Bring to a full boil, remove from the heat, and add all the flour, beating vigorously with a spatula until smooth. Return the saucepan to low heat and stir continuously to dry out the mixture. Beat for 10 seconds, or until the mixture is no longer sticking to the sides of the pan. Transfer to a mixing bowl to prevent further cooking. Using the spatula, gradually mix in the beaten eggs, incorporating each addition before you add the next and beating until smooth and glossy. To check the consistency, draw a line through the batter with the spatula—it should close up slowly. If too stiff, beat in a little extra egg. Transfer the choux pastry to the pastry bag and pipe 5-in. (12-cm) lengths onto a lightly greased baking sheet. Bake for 30–40 minutes, without opening the oven door during the first 20 minutes, until the éclairs are risen, dry to the touch, and golden brown. Cool on a wire rack.

ASSEMBLING AND DECORATING THE ÉCLAIRS

Split the éclairs in half lengthwise. Fill with a thin layer of crème fraîche, followed by a thin layer of quince jelly. Carefully turn the quince tatin toppings out of the mold and set one on top of each éclair. Pipe small dots of crème fraîche over the topping and decorate with baby watercress leaves. Place the other half of each éclair on top, if desired.

FIGS IN RED WINE JELLY WITH STILTON ICE CREAM

Figues sur gelée de vin rouge et crème glacée au Stilton

Serves 6

Active time
1 hour

Maturing time
12 hours

Chilling time
1 hour

Equipment
Instant-read thermometer

Ice cream maker

Autumn leaf motif punch, about 2 in. (5 cm) tall and wide

Velvet spray gun

Ingredients

Stilton ice cream
7 oz. (200 g) Stilton cheese

Scant 1 cup (240 ml) whole milk

Generous ¾ cup (190 ml) heavy cream, min. 35% fat

¼ cup (2½ oz./75 g) egg yolk (about 4 yolks)

2½ tbsp (1 oz./30 g) superfine sugar

1 tbsp (20 g) flower honey

Red wine jelly
7 sheets (14 g) gelatin

1¼ cups (300 ml) red wine (preferably Maury AOC) or tawny port

Autumn leaves
1 sheet rice paper

3½ oz. (100 g) cocoa butter

2 tsp (8 g) natural powdered red food coloring

2 tsp (8 g) natural powdered yellow food coloring

To serve
6 fresh figs

⅓ cup (2 oz./60 g) raisins

Scant 1 cup (3½ oz./100 g) walnut halves

Red-veined sorrel leaves

PREPARING THE STILTON ICE CREAM (1 DAY AHEAD)

Crumble the Stilton into small pieces. Combine the milk and cream in a saucepan and bring to a boil. Meanwhile, whisk together the egg yolks and sugar in a bowl until pale and thick. Slowly pour one-third of the hot milk and cream into the yolk mixture, whisking continuously. Pour the mixture into the saucepan and cook until the temperature reaches 181°F (83°C), stirring constantly. Stir in the honey and Stilton, transfer to a covered container, and let mature in the refrigerator for 12 hours. The next day, churn in the ice cream maker. Freeze in an airtight container until serving.

PREPARING THE RED WINE JELLY

Soak the gelatin in a bowl of cold water until softened. Bring the wine to a boil in a saucepan, then remove from the heat. Squeeze the gelatin to remove excess water and stir it into the hot wine until dissolved. Immediately divide between six serving bowls. Cool, then chill for at least 1 hour until set.

PREPARING THE AUTUMN LEAVES

Using the leaf paper punch, cut six leaves out of the rice paper. Melt the cocoa butter in a bowl over a bain-marie. Divide between two bowls and stir the red food coloring into one bowl and the yellow food coloring into the other. Let cool to 86°F (30°C). Using the velvet spray gun, spray one color at a time over the rice paper leaves, allowing one color to shade into the other.

TO SERVE

Just before serving, quarter the figs and arrange them over the set jelly. Add a quenelle of Stilton ice cream and top with a rice paper autumn leaf. Sprinkle with raisins, walnut halves, and a few red-veined sorrel leaves. Serve immediately.

MELON GAZPACHO

Gaspacho de melon

Serves 6

Active time
30 minutes

Chilling time
2 hours

Cooking time
10 minutes

Storage
Up to 2 days

Equipment
Blender

Silicone mold imprinted with a leaf design

Ingredients

Melon gazpacho

2¼ lb. (1 kg) orange-fleshed melon

15 basil leaves

2½ tbsp (40 ml) olive oil

Cayenne pepper, to taste

1 tbsp (15 ml) raspberry vinegar

Salt and freshly ground pepper

Parmesan tuiles

1½ tbsp (20 g) egg white (about ⅔ white)

1 tbsp (20 g) butter, melted and cooled

2 tbsp (20 g) all-purpose flour

¼ cup (25 g) grated Parmesan

Pata negra chips

4 slices "pata negra" cured Ibérico ham to serve

18 basil leaves

PREPARING THE MELON GAZPACHO

Halve the melon, remove the seeds (see technique p. 37), and cut off the rind. Cut the flesh into pieces and blend with the remaining ingredients until smooth. Refrigerate for at least 2 hours or until serving.

PREPARING THE PARMESAN TUILES

Preheat the oven to 350°F (180°C/Gas Mark 4). Whisk together the egg white, butter, and flour in a bowl. Add the grated Parmesan and stir to combine. Spread the batter over the leaf imprints in the silicone mold and bake for 10 minutes until golden. Immediately unmold onto a wire rack.

PREPARING THE PATA NEGRA CHIPS

Sear the slices of pata negra ham in a dry skillet until crisp. Remove from the pan and let cool.

TO SERVE

Pour about 7 oz. (200 g) of gazpacho into each soup plate. Break the pata negra chips into pieces and scatter over the gazpacho. Add 3 basil leaves and a Parmesan leaf tuile. Serve immediately.

WATERMELON GRANITA

Granité de pastèque

Serves 6

Active time

10 minutes

Cooking time

5 minutes

Freezing time

About 2 hours

Storage time

Up to 2 weeks
in the freezer

Equipment

Refractometer
(optional, see Chefs' Notes)

Ingredients

²/₃ cup (160 ml) water

Scant ½ cup
(2¾ oz./80 g) superfine
sugar

Generous 3 cups (760 ml)
watermelon juice, or
1½ lb. (760 g) fresh
watermelon flesh blended
to a puree

Heat the water and sugar in a saucepan until the sugar dissolves. Bring to a boil, remove from the heat, and let cool completely.

Stir in the watermelon juice or pureed flesh. Transfer to a shallow container and place in the freezer.

When ice crystals begin to form around the edges (after about 1 hour), remove the granita from the freezer and scrape the ice crystals away from the edges to break them up, using a fork.

Return to the freezer and repeat the freezing and scraping process every 30 minutes or so, doing this as many times as necessary to obtain the slushy texture of a granita.

CHEFS' NOTES

The advantage of using a refractometer is that you can adjust the amount of sugar to give a reading of 17° Brix. This means the granita will be more stable and, as a result, will melt less quickly.

FOIE GRAS WITH GRAPE SAUCE VIERGE AND CARDAMOM BROTH

Foie gras sauté, vierge de raisin et bouillon cardamome noire

Serves 4

Active time
30 minutes

Chilling time
At least 2 hours

Cooking time
10 minutes

Infusing time
30 minutes

Ingredients

Grape sauce vierge

4¼ oz. (120 g) Muscat grapes

1¼ oz. (35 g) golden raisins

2½ tsp (12 ml) olive oil

1 kaffir lime leaf

Juice of ¼ lime

Freshly ground white pepper

Cardamom broth

1 cup (250 ml) water

1 tbsp (15 ml) rice vinegar

3½ tbsp (50 ml) mirin

Scant ⅓ cup (70 ml) sake

4 tsp (20 ml) fish sauce

2 tsp (10 ml) yuzu juice

⅓ oz. (10 g) fresh ginger, preferably organic

½ pod black cardamom

¼ oz. (7 g) fresh basil

3 kaffir lime leaves

1½ tbsp (25 ml) soy sauce

Scant ¼ tsp (0.5 g) Sichuan peppercorns

To assemble

⅔ oz. (20 g) snow peas

1¾ oz. (50 g) shiitake mushrooms

3½ oz. (100 g) enoki mushrooms

4 scallions

8½ oz. (240 g) foie gras escalope

Grape-seed oil

Salt and freshly ground pepper

Basil cress

PREPARING THE GRAPE SAUCE VIERGE

Peel and halve the Muscat grapes and remove the seeds. Cut the golden raisins in two. Combine the grapes and raisins in a bowl with the remaining ingredients. Press plastic wrap over the surface and chill for at least 2 hours.

PREPARING THE CARDAMOM BROTH

Combine all the broth ingredients in a saucepan and bring to a boil. Remove from the heat, cover with plastic wrap, and let infuse for 30 minutes. Strain through a fine-mesh sieve and reserve at room temperature until using.

ASSEMBLING THE DISH

Fill a bowl with ice water. Wash the snow peas and cook them in a saucepan of boiling salted water for 2–3 minutes. Remove with a skimmer and plunge immediately into the ice water to stop the cooking. Using the skimmer, transfer the peas to paper towel to drain. Drain, slice them thinly, and set aside. Clean the mushrooms, slice the shiitakes thinly, and cut off the bases of the enokis. Wash the scallions and cut them into pieces. Warm the cardamom broth over low heat and add the scallions. Using a sharp knife, cut the foie gras into squares. Add a splash of grape-seed oil to a skillet, place over low heat, and brown the foie gras on both sides. Season with salt and pepper, drain, and set aside on paper towel. Sauté the shiitakes in a little grape-seed oil. Add the sliced snow peas and lightly season with salt and pepper. Drain the scallions from the cardamom broth, add the enoki mushrooms to the broth, and poach for a few seconds. Divide the mushrooms and scallions between four serving bowls, top with the foie gras and a spoonful of grape sauce vierge. Pour broth around the foie gras and sprinkle with basil cress. Serve immediately.

KIWIFRUIT VACHERIN

Vacherin kiwi

Serves 6

Active time

45 minutes

Maturing time

12 hours

Chilling time

12 hours

Cooking time

16 hours

Freezing time

1 hour

Storage

Up to 2 days before
assembling

Equipment

Instant-read thermometer

Immersion blender

Ice cream maker

4 pastry bags + a plain
¼-in. (6-mm) tip

3½-in. (9-cm) silicone
cube mold

Ingredients

Kiwifruit sorbet

½ sheet (1 g) gold-
strength gelatin,
200 Bloom

4½ oz. (130 g) kiwifruits

¼ oz. (8 g) fresh lemon
verbena leaves

3½ tbsp (1½ oz./40 g)
superfine sugar

1½ tbsp (25 ml) water

¾ tsp (4 ml) lemon juice

Mascarpone ice cream

3½ tbsp (1½ oz./40 g)
superfine sugar

1 pinch (1 g) super
neutrose stabilizer

Scant ½ cup (100 ml)
water

2 tsp (10 ml) lemon juice

¼ cup (2 oz./60 g)
mascarpone

**Vanilla mascarpone
whipped cream**

1⅛ sheets (2.25 g)
gold-strength gelatin,
200 Bloom

1½ tbsp (25 ml) whole
milk

2 tbsp (25 g) superfine
sugar

Seeds of ½ vanilla bean

3½ tbsp (1¾ oz./50 g)
mascarpone

Scant 1 cup (220 ml)
heavy cream, min. 35%
fat, well chilled

Dried kiwifruit

2 kiwifruits

**Reduced-sugar
meringue**

¼ cup (1¾ oz./50 g)
superfine sugar

Scant ¼ tsp (0.5 g)
xanthan gum

Scant ¼ cup
(1¾ oz./50 g) egg white
(about 1⅔ whites)

Decoration

2 kiwifruits (1 green,
1 gold), peeled and
quartered lengthwise

PREPARING THE KIWIFRUIT SORBET (1 DAY AHEAD)

Soak the gelatin in a bowl of cold water until softened. Peel the kiwifruits and wash the lemon verbena. Cut the kiwifruits into approximately ¾-in. (2-cm) pieces. Heat the sugar, water, and lemon juice in a saucepan until the sugar dissolves, then bring to a simmer. Remove from the heat and add the lemon verbena. Squeeze the gelatin to remove excess water and stir it into the hot syrup until dissolved. Cover with plastic wrap and let cool to 104°F (40°C). Pour over the kiwifruits in a bowl and reduce to a puree using the immersion blender. Press plastic wrap over the surface and let mature in the refrigerator for 12 hours. The next day, churn in the ice cream maker and freeze until serving.

PREPARING THE MASCARPONE ICE CREAM (1 DAY AHEAD)

Mix the sugar and stabilizer together and place in a saucepan with the water and lemon juice. Heat until the sugar and stabilizer dissolve, then bring to a boil. Remove from the heat and let the mixture cool to 104°F (40°C). Pour it over the mascarpone in a bowl and process with the immersion blender until smooth. Press plastic wrap over the surface and let mature in the refrigerator for 12 hours. The next day, churn in the ice cream maker and freeze until serving.

PREPARING THE MASCARPONE CREAM (1 DAY AHEAD)

Soak the gelatin in a bowl of cold water until softened. Heat the milk, sugar, and vanilla seeds in a saucepan until the sugar dissolves, then bring to a boil. Remove from the heat, squeeze the gelatin to remove excess water, and stir it in until dissolved. Pour over the mascarpone in a bowl and process with the immersion blender until smooth. Add the well-chilled cream and process again with the immersion blender until smooth. Chill for 12 hours.

PREPARING THE DRIED KIWIFRUIT (1 DAY AHEAD)

Preheat the oven to 140°F (60°C/Gas on lowest setting). Peel the kiwifruits and cut them crosswise into ¼-in. (5-mm) slices. Spread the slices out over a lined baking sheet and place in the oven for 12 hours or until completely dry, turning the slices over occasionally. If using a gas oven, prop the door open so the slices do not dry out too quickly.

PREPARING THE MERINGUE

Preheat the oven to 175°F (80°C/Gas on lowest setting). Combine the sugar and xanthan gum in a bowl. In a separate bowl, whisk the egg whites until frothy, then whisk in the sugar and xanthan gum a third at a time. Continue whisking until a stiff, shiny meringue is obtained. Spoon the meringue into a pastry bag with a ¼-in. (6-mm) tip. Pipe out three 3½-in. (9-cm) squares with a thickness of about ⅓ in. (8 mm), and four thin 12-in. (30-cm) long cylinders onto a lined baking sheet. Bake for 4 hours until dry and crisp but not colored.

ASSEMBLING THE VACHERIN

Place a meringue square in the base of the cube mold. Transfer the kiwifruit sorbet to one of the pastry bags and pipe the sorbet over the meringue. Smooth into an even layer using an offset spatula and place a second meringue square on top. Transfer the mascarpone ice cream to a pastry bag and pipe over the second meringue square. Smooth into an even layer with the offset spatula. Top with the third meringue square, then freeze for 1 hour. Remove the mascarpone cream from the refrigerator and whip until it just holds its shape. Spoon it into another pastry bag. Remove the vacherin from the freezer and unmold it onto a serving plate. Cover one side with the whipped cream, smoothing it over with a spatula. Break the meringue cylinders into different lengths and place them vertically side by side over the cream, lightly pressing them to fix them in place. Repeat on the other three sides. Finally, cover the top of the vacherin with a layer of whipped cream and decorate with fresh and dried kiwifruit slices.

BERRIES
AND RHUBARB

STRAWBERRIES WITH STRAWBERRY AND BASIL SORBET

Fraises fraîches, jus glacé et sorbet fraise basilic

Serves 6

Active time
40 minutes

Drying time
12 hours

Maturing time
12 hours

Cooking time
5½ hours

Chilling time
2 hours

Freezing time
1½ hours

Storage
Up to 2 days before assembling

Equipment
Food processor
Instant-read thermometer
Immersion blender
Ice cream maker
Pastry bag

Ingredients

Basil powder
1 oz. (25 g) basil leaves

Strawberry and basil sorbet
½ sheet (1 g) gold-strength gelatin, 200 Bloom

3½ oz. (100 g) Fraises des Bois

1¾ oz. (50 g) strawberries, preferably Gariguette

¹⁄₁₀ oz. (3.5 g) basil leaves

2 tbsp (30 ml) water

1¾ tsp (8 ml) lemon juice

¼ cup (1¾ oz./50 g) superfine sugar

Strawberry paper
Scant ¼ tsp (0.6 g) gelatin powder

¾ tsp (4 ml) cold water

¾ tsp (3 g) superfine sugar

¼ tsp (1 g) pectin NH

1¾ oz. (50 g) strawberries, preferably Gariguette

1½ tbsp (25 ml) water

Reduced-sugar meringue petals (optional)
2 tbsp (1 oz./30 g) egg white (1 white)

3¾ tsp (15 g) superfine sugar

5½ tsp (15 g) confectioners' sugar, sifted

Basil powder, for dusting

Chilled strawberry juice
1½ lb. (750 g) sweet strawberries, preferably Gariguette

1 cup (7 oz./200 g) superfine sugar

To assemble
1¾ oz. (50 g) Fraises des Bois

6¼ oz. (180 g) Mara des Bois strawberries

8½ oz. (240 g) strawberries, preferably Gariguette

8½ oz. (240 g) pineberries (pineapple-flavored white strawberries)

Basil cress and red-veined sorrel leaves

PREPARING THE BASIL POWDER (1 DAY AHEAD)

Preheat the oven to 115°F (45°C/Gas on lowest setting with the door propped open). Wash the basil and remove the leaves from the stems. Fill a bowl with ice-cold water. Bring a saucepan of water to a boil, add the basil leaves, and let boil for a few seconds. Drain with a skimmer and plunge the leaves into the ice-cold water. Gently pat them dry with paper towel and spread them across a lined baking sheet. Place in the oven for about 12 hours or until dry. Blend to a fine powder in the food processor and store in an airtight container.

PREPARING THE SORBET (1 DAY AHEAD)

Soak the gelatin in a bowl of cold water until softened. Wash and hull all the strawberries and halve or quarter them depending on their size. Wash the basil and place it in a bowl with the strawberries. Heat the water, lemon juice, and sugar in a saucepan until the sugar dissolves, then bring to a simmer. Remove from the heat, squeeze the gelatin to remove excess water and stir it into the hot syrup until dissolved. Cover the saucepan with plastic wrap and let the syrup cool until the temperature reaches 104°F (40°C). Pour it over the strawberries and basil and process with the immersion blender until smooth. Press plastic wrap over the surface and let mature in the refrigerator for 12 hours. The next day, churn in the ice cream maker, then freeze in an airtight container.

PREPARING THE STRAWBERRY PAPER

Preheat the oven to 175°F (80°C/Gas on lowest setting). Sprinkle the gelatin over the ¾ tsp (4 ml) cold water and let soak for 10 minutes. Combine the sugar and pectin in a bowl. Wash and hull the strawberries and puree them in the food processor with the 1½ tbsp (25 ml) water. Heat the puree until the temperature reaches about 113°F (45°C), stir in the sugar and pectin until dissolved, and bring to a boil. Let boil for a few seconds, then remove from the heat, and stir in the gelatin until dissolved. Pour over a nonstick baking sheet and cook in the oven for 2 hours. Cut into even-sized pieces while still warm, fold into pleats, and drape over shapes of your choice. Let dry until serving.

PREPARING THE MERINGUE PETALS (OPTIONAL)

Preheat the oven to 175°F (80°C/Gas on lowest setting). Place the egg white and superfine sugar in a bowl over a bain-marie and heat until the temperature reaches 131°F (55°C), whisking continuously. Remove from the heat and whisk until the egg white holds its shape. Add the confectioners' sugar and fold it in using a flexible spatula until the meringue is firm and glossy. Spoon the meringue into the pastry bag and pipe out small mounds, about ½ in. (1 cm) in diameter, on a lined baking sheet. Using a spatula, flatten the mounds to make small petals. Dust with a little basil powder and bake for 1½ hours until dry. Store in a dry place until serving.

PREPARING THE STRAWBERRY JUICE

Wash and hull the strawberries and place in a heatproof bowl with the sugar, stirring to combine. Cover the bowl with plastic wrap and cook gently over a bain-marie for 2 hours to allow the strawberries to break down. Strain through a fine-mesh sieve without pressing down on the berries. When well-drained, cool in the refrigerator, then freeze for about 1½ hours, until well chilled but not frozen.

ASSEMBLING THE DESSERT

Wash and hull the strawberries and halve all of them except for the tiny Fraises des Bois. Arrange the strawberries attractively in serving dishes and pour the chilled strawberry juice over them. Top each one with a quenelle of sorbet and scatter over the meringue petals, if using. Decorate with the strawberry paper and basil cress or red-veined sorrel leaves. Finally, dust lightly with basil powder and serve immediately.

STRAWBERRY LAYER CAKE

Fraisier

Serves 6

Active time

2½ hours

Cooking time

3 hours 10 minutes

Chilling time

1 hour 20 minutes

Freezing time

30 minutes

Storage

Up to 24 hours in the refrigerator

Equipment

Food processor

2 sheets food-safe acetate

6-in. (16-cm) cake ring, 1¾ in. (4.5 cm) deep

Stand mixer + paddle beater and whisk

2 pastry bags

Ingredients

Strawberry juice

1 lb. 2 oz. (500 g) strawberries

Soaking syrup

⅔ cup (150 ml) strawberry juice

4 tsp (20 ml) simple syrup

Pistachio praline paste

½ cup (2 oz./60 g) shelled pistachios

¼ cup (1½ oz./40 g) whole almonds

½ cup (3½ oz./100 g) sugar

Strawberry marzipan collar

Scant ½ cup (100 ml) strawberry juice

3½ oz. (100 g) marzipan, chopped

Pastry cream

Generous ¾ cup (200 ml) whole milk

3 tbsp (2 oz./50 g) egg yolk (about 2½ yolks)

3½ tbsp (1½ oz./40 g) superfine sugar

2½ tbsp (25 g) cornstarch

Genoise sponge

5¾ oz. (165 g) almond paste, 50% almonds, chopped

Scant ½ cup (3½ oz./100 g) lightly beaten egg (2 eggs)

3 tbsp (1½ oz./40 g) butter, diced and softened

Finely grated zest of ½ lemon

2½ tbsp (25 g) all-purpose flour

¾ teaspoon (3 g) baking powder

Mousseline cream

¾ lb. (350 g) pastry cream (see above)

1 stick plus 2 tbsp (5¼ oz./150 g) butter, diced and softened

Decoration

1 lb. 2 oz. (500 g) strawberries

1 cup (3½ oz./100 g) pistachio powder

PREPARING THE STRAWBERRY JUICE

Wash and hull the strawberries. Place them in a fine-mesh sieve over a heat-resistant bowl and cover airtight with plastic wrap. Cook over a bain-marie for 3 hours so all the juice from the strawberries runs into the bowl.

PREPARING THE SOAKING SYRUP

Mix the strawberry juice and simple syrup together.

PREPARING THE PISTACHIO PRALINE PASTE

Preheat the oven to 325°C (160°C/Gas Mark 3). Spread the pistachios and almonds over a lined baking sheet and roast them in the oven for 10 minutes. Heat the sugar in a heavy saucepan over low heat without adding any water. Once the sugar dissolves to a syrup, boil it until it becomes a golden caramel. Stir in the pistachios and almonds, pour over a sheet of parchment paper, and let cool. Break the caramelized nuts roughly into large chunks and process to a smooth paste in the food processor.

PREPARING THE MARZIPAN COLLAR

Reduce the strawberry juice in a saucepan until it is thick and sticky. Let cool for about 20 minutes before working it into the marzipan until tinted a natural pink. Roll between the two acetate sheets to a thickness of about 1/16 in. (2 mm). Cut into a 2½-in. (6-cm)-wide strip the same length as the circumference of the cake ring.

PREPARING THE PASTRY CREAM

In a saucepan, heat the milk over medium heat. Meanwhile, whisk together the egg yolks, sugar, and cornstarch in a bowl until pale and thick. When the milk comes to a boil, slowly pour one-third into the egg yolk mixture, whisking continuously. Pour the mixture into the saucepan, bring to a boil, whisking vigorously, and let boil for 2–3 minutes, still whisking. Transfer to a bowl, press plastic wrap over the surface, and let cool for 20 minutes in the refrigerator.

PREPARING THE GENOISE SPONGE

Preheat the oven to 340°F (170°C/Gas Mark 3). Beat the almond paste in the stand mixer with the paddle beater until softened, then gradually beat in the eggs. Change to the whisk, add the butter and lemon zest, and whisk on medium speed until pale and thick. Sift in the flour with the baking powder and fold in until just combined. Spread the batter across a lined baking sheet to a thickness of ¾ in. (1.5 cm). Bake for 12 minutes, remove from the oven, and let cool completely.

PREPARING THE MOUSSELINE CREAM

Whisk the pastry cream until smooth. Add the softened butter and beat until light and creamy.

ASSEMBLING THE CAKE

Wash and hull the strawberries, leaving them whole. Cut out two 6-in. (16-cm) disks from the sponge and place one in the cake ring. Brush the sponge with soaking syrup and cover with a layer of mousseline cream. Arrange 9 oz. (250 g) of the strawberries over the cream, trimming the ends if they are too tall, and using the trimmings to fill any spaces around the sides. Spoon some of the pistachio praline paste into one of the pastry bags and pipe it out randomly between the strawberries. Cover the berries with another layer of mousseline cream and add the second sponge disk, which should reach the top of the ring. Brush syrup over the sponge and cover with a very fine layer of mousseline cream. Chill for 1 hour. Weigh the remaining mousseline cream and mix with 10% of its weight in praline paste. Transfer to the second pastry bag and pipe out small balls touching each other onto a lined baking sheet. Freeze for 30 minutes. Dust the balls with pistachio powder. Remove the cake ring. Cut the strawberries into different size pieces and arrange over the top with the mousseline cream balls. Wrap the marzipan collar around the cake fluting the top edge attractively.

CHEFS' NOTES

When making the mousseline cream, the pastry cream and butter should be the same temperature (around 64°F–68°F/18°C–20°C) for best results.

RASPBERRY OPÉRA CAKES

Opéra framboise

Serves 6

Active time

2 hours

Cooking time

5–8 minutes

Chilling time

2 hours 20 minutes

Storage

Up to 3 days in the refrigerator

Equipment

14½ × 4½-in. (37 × 11-cm) rectangular cake frame, 1 in. (2.5 cm) deep

Immersion blender

Instant-read thermometer

2 food-safe acetate sheets

Ingredients

Raspberry confit with seeds

7 oz. (200 g) fresh raspberries

5 tsp (20 g) superfine sugar, divided

½ tsp (2 g) pectin NH

2 tsp (10 ml) lemon juice

Joconde sponge

1⅓ cups (4½ oz./125 g) almond flour

Scant 1 cup (4½ oz./125 g) confectioners' sugar

¼ cup (1¼ oz./35 g) all-purpose flour

⅓ oz. (10 g) invert sugar

¾ cup (6 oz./170 g) lightly beaten egg (about 3½ eggs), divided

2 tbsp (25 g) butter, melted and cooled, plus extra for the frame

½ cup (4 oz./110 g) egg white (about 3⅔ whites)

2 tbsp (25 g) superfine sugar

Whipped vanilla ganache

2¾ oz. (80 g) white chocolate, chopped

Scant ¼ cup (55 ml) heavy cream, min. 35% fat

¾ tsp (6 g) glucose syrup

¼ oz. (7 g) invert sugar

Seeds of 1 vanilla bean

Scant ½ cup (110 ml) heavy cream, min. 35% fat, well chilled

Chocolate and raspberry ganache

3 oz. (85 g) milk chocolate, 39% cacao, chopped

3½ oz. (100 g) raspberry puree

1 tsp (8 g) glucose syrup

2½ tbsp (1 oz./30 g) superfine sugar

2 tbsp (1 oz./30 g) butter, preferably 84% butterfat

Raspberry crémeux

1¼ sheets (2.5 g) gold-strength gelatin, 200 Bloom

4 oz. (110 g) raspberry puree, divided

2 tbsp (1¼ oz./35 g) egg yolk (scant 2 yolks)

3½ tbsp (1½ oz./40 g) superfine sugar

3½ tbsp (1¾ oz./50 g) lightly beaten egg (1 egg)

3 tbsp plus 2 tsp (2 oz./55 g) butter, diced

Raspberry soaking syrup

Generous ¾ cup (200 ml) water

1 cup (7 oz./200 g) superfine sugar

3½ oz. (100 g) raspberry puree

Glaze

3½ oz. (100 g) neutral glaze

4 tsp (20 ml) water

Decorations

3½ oz. (100 g) dark chocolate, 70% cacao

Edible gold luster dust

PREPARING THE RASPBERRY CONFIT

Heat the raspberries with three-quarters of the sugar in a saucepan until the sugar dissolves. Combine the remaining sugar and pectin in a bowl, add to the saucepan, and bring to a boil. Remove from the heat and stir in the lemon juice. Transfer to a bowl and chill for 2 hours.

PREPARING THE JOCONDE SPONGE

Preheat the oven to 450°F (230°C/Gas Mark 8). Grease the cake frame with butter and place it on a lined baking sheet. Sift the almond flour, confectioners' sugar, and all-purpose flour together into a mixing bowl, add the invert sugar, and half the eggs. Whisk with an electric hand beater for 15 minutes until the mixture is creamy and light. Whisk in the remaining eggs and melted butter. Clean the beaters and whisk the egg whites in a separate bowl, gradually adding the sugar, until holding firm peaks. Using a flexible spatula, gently fold the whites into the batter. Fill your frame with batter, spreading it into an even layer. Bake for 5–8 minutes, until lightly golden. Let cool slightly, remove the frame, and cut the sponge crosswise into three equal-sized layers.

PREPARING THE WHIPPED VANILLA GANACHE

Place the white chocolate in a heat-resistant bowl. Combine the scant ¼ cup (55 ml) cream, glucose syrup, invert sugar, and vanilla seeds in a saucepan and bring to a boil. Pour the hot cream over the white chocolate one-third at a time and process with the immersion blender until smooth. Mix in the cold cream and chill until assembling.

PREPARING THE CHOCOLATE AND RASPBERRY GANACHE

Melt the chocolate until the temperature reaches 95°F (35°C) in a bowl over a bain-marie. Heat the raspberry puree, glucose syrup, and sugar until the sugar dissolves, then continue to cook to 95°F (35°C). Pour the melted chocolate into the raspberry puree and stir with a flexible spatula until the mixture is glossy and smooth. Add the butter and process with the immersion blender until smooth.

PREPARING THE RASPBERRY CRÉMEUX

Soak the gelatin in a bowl of cold water until softened. In a saucepan, bring 3¼ oz. (90 g) of the raspberry puree to a boil. Meanwhile, whisk the egg yolks, sugar, and egg together until pale and thick. Slowly add the hot puree, whisking continuously. Return to the saucepan and cook, stirring continuously, until the temperature reaches 180°F (82°C). Remove from the heat, squeeze the gelatin to remove excess water, and stir it into the hot mixture until dissolved. Stir in the remaining raspberry puree. Let the mixture cool to 95°F (35°C), then add the butter and process with the immersion blender until smooth.

PREPARING THE RASPBERRY SOAKING SYRUP

Heat the water and sugar in a saucepan until the sugar dissolves, then bring to a boil. Remove from the heat and stir in the raspberry puree. Let cool completely.

PREPARING THE GLAZE

Whisk together the neutral glaze and water.

PREPARING THE CHOCOLATE DECORATION

Temper the chocolate (see p. 130). Brush some over one piece of sponge in a thin layer and spread the remaining chocolate into a thin layer between the acetate sheets. Let set for a few minutes, peel off the top sheet, and cut the chocolate into six 1¼ × 4½-in. (3 × 11-cm) rectangles.

ASSEMBLING THE OPÉRA CAKES

Place the chocolate-coated sponge in the cake frame, chocolate-side down. Moisten the sponge with the soaking syrup, then spread with the chocolate and raspberry ganache. Top with a second sponge layer and moisten with syrup. Spread the crémeux over and top with the third sponge layer. Moisten with syrup, cover with the vanilla ganache, then chill for at least 20 minutes or until the ganache is firm. Spread the raspberry confit evenly over the vanilla ganache and coat with a layer of the glaze. Using a sharp knife, cut the assembled cake into six 2½ × 4½-in. (6 × 11-cm) rectangles. Top each with a chocolate rectangle and decorate with a dot of gold dust in the center.

BLACKBERRY CHARLOTTE

Charlotte aux mûres et biscuits de Reims

Serves 6

Active time
40 minutes

Cooking time
8–10 minutes

Chilling time
3 hours

Storage
Up to 2 days
in the refrigerator

Equipment
2 pastry bags + plain
⅔-in. (16-mm) tip

Food processor

6-in (16-cm) round
silicone mold

Instant-read thermometer

Silicone ice ball mold with
at least 5 cavities, 1 in.
(2.5 cm) in dia.

7-in (18-cm) cake ring,
2½ in. (6 cm) deep

Round cake board slightly
larger than the cake ring

Ingredients
Ladyfinger sponge

1 tbsp plus 2 tsp
(1 oz./30 g) egg yolk
(about 1½ yolks)

3 tbsp (1¼ oz./35 g)
superfine sugar, divided

Seeds of ½ vanilla bean

2 tbsp (20 g) all-purpose
flour, sifted

3 tbsp plus 1 tsp
(1½ oz./45 g) egg white
(about 1½ whites)

2 tbsp (20 g) potato
starch, sifted

Confectioners' sugar, for
dusting

Blackberry insert

1 sheet (2 g) gold-
strength gelatin,
200 Bloom

5¾ oz. (160 g) fresh
blackberries

Juice of ¼ lime

Generous 1 tbsp (15 g)
superfine sugar

½ tsp (2 g) pectin
325 NH 95

Blackberry mousse

1½ sheets (3 g)
gold-strength gelatin,
200 Bloom

2 oz. (60 g) strained fresh
blackberry puree

2½ tsp (12 ml) lemon
juice

3½ tbsp (1½ oz./40 g)
superfine sugar

Generous ⅔ cup
(5¾ oz./165 g) fromage
blanc (if unavailable,
substitute Greek yogurt
or quark)

Generous ⅔ cup (165 ml)
heavy cream, min. 35%
fat

Blackberry soaking syrup

¼ cup (60 ml) water

1¼ tsp (5 g) sugar

½ oz. (15 g) fresh
blackberries

Finely grated zest of
¼ lime

To assemble

1 package *biscuits
roses de Reims* (pink
champagne biscuits)

13 oz. (375 g) fresh
blackberries

Confectioners' sugar, for
dusting

Edible red oxalis (wood
sorrel) leaves

Red-veined sorrel leaves

Dried rose bud petals

PREPARING THE LADYFINGER SPONGE

Preheat the oven to 350°F (180°C/Gas Mark 4). Whisk together the egg yolks, 2 tbsp (1 oz./25 g) of the superfine sugar, and vanilla seeds until pale and thick. Gently fold in the flour. Whisk the egg whites until holding soft peaks, add the remaining superfine sugar, and whisk until the peaks are firm. Fold in the potato starch. Using a flexible spatula, fold the two mixtures together and spoon into the pastry bag with the ⅔-in. (16-mm) tip. Pipe out in a spiral onto a lined baking sheet into two 6-in (16-cm) disks, ¾ in. (1.5 cm) thick. Dust with confectioners' sugar and let sit briefly until the sugar dissolves. Repeat this twice more, then bake for 8–10 minutes until pale golden. Let cool completely.

PREPARING THE BLACKBERRY INSERT

Soak the gelatin in a bowl of cold water until softened. Wash the blackberries, then crush them with the lime juice using a fork or in the food processor. Mix the sugar and pectin in a bowl and place in a saucepan with the crushed blackberries. Heat until the sugar dissolves, bring to a simmer, and remove from the heat. Squeeze the gelatin to remove excess water and stir it in until dissolved. Pour into the round silicone mold and freeze until assembling.

PREPARING THE BLACKBERRY MOUSSE

Soak the gelatin in a bowl of cold water until softened. Meanwhile, heat the blackberry puree, lemon juice, and sugar in a saucepan until the sugar dissolves, then cook until the temperature reaches 176°F (80°C). Remove from the heat, squeeze the gelatin to remove excess water, and stir it in until dissolved. Let the mixture cool to 113°F (45°C). Meanwhile, place the fromage blanc in a bowl. In a separate bowl, whip the cream until it holds its shape. Pour the blackberry mixture over the fromage blanc and stir with a flexible spatula until combined. Fold in the whipped cream. Transfer the mousse to the pastry bag without a tip and pipe it into 5 of the cavities of the ice ball mold, filling them completely. Freeze until the balls are solid. Keep the pastry bag with the remaining mousse chilled until assembling.

PREPARING THE BLACKBERRY SOAKING SYRUP

Heat the water and sugar in a saucepan until the sugar dissolves, then bring to a boil. Let cool to room temperature. Wash the blackberries and crush them in a bowl using a fork, pour the syrup over them, and add the lime zest. Blend in the food processor, then chill until assembling.

ASSEMBLING THE CHARLOTTE

Place the cake ring on the cake board and line the ring with the *biscuits rose de Reims*, placing them tightly together. Lightly brush the sponge disks with the soaking syrup and place one in the base of the ring. Cover with a ¾-in. (2-cm) layer of mousse and top with the second sponge disk. Place the blackberry insert over the sponge and finish with another ¾-in. (2-cm) layer of mousse, smoothing it in an even layer with an offset spatula. Chill for about 3 hours, or until the mousse has set completely. Wash and dry the blackberries. Unmold the frozen balls of mousse and arrange them over the charlotte with the blackberries. Dust with confectioners' sugar and decorate with red oxalis leaves, red-veined sorrel leaves, and dried rose bud petals.

BLACK CURRANT PAVLOVAS

Pavlova yaourt cassis

Makes 6

Active time
2 hours

Maturing time
6 hours

Cooking time
3–4 hours

Freezing time
6 hours

Equipment
Instant-read thermometer

Ice cream maker

6 silicone half-sphere
molds, 2¾ in. (7 cm)
in dia.

3 pastry bags + plain
⅓-in. (8-mm) and ½-in.
(12-mm) tips

Food processor

Ingredients

**Black currant frozen
yogurt**
¾ cup (5 oz./140 g)
sugar

⅔ oz. (20 g) stabilizer

1 cup (245 ml) whole milk

2 tbsp (1 oz./30 g) skim
milk powder, 0% fat

2 tbsp (20 g) dextrose
powder

2½ tbsp (40 ml) heavy
cream, min. 35% fat

⅔ oz. (20 g) invert sugar

2 cups (1 lb. 2 oz./500 g)
plain yogurt

7 oz. (200 g) black
currant puree

Swiss meringue
Neutral oil for greasing

Scant ½ cup
(3½ oz./100 g) egg white
(about 3 whites)

1 cup (7 oz./200 g)
superfine sugar

Black currant compote
½ tsp (2 g) pectin NH

2 tbsp (25 g) sugar

7 oz. (200 g) black
currants

Fromage blanc cream
Generous ¾ cup
(200 ml) heavy cream,
min. 35% fat

2 tbsp (25 g) sugar

7 oz. (200 g) fromage
blanc (if unavailable,
substitute Greek yogurt
or quark)

Finely grated zest of
½ lemon

Seeds of ½ vanilla bean

Decoration
Black currants

Red-veined sorrel leaves

PREPARING THE BLACK CURRANT FROZEN YOGURT

Mix the sugar and stabilizer together. In a saucepan, heat the milk, milk powder, dextrose powder, and cream until the temperature reaches 104°F (40°C). Stir in the sugar and stabilizer, followed by the invert sugar, and cook to 185°F (85°C). Remove from the heat, transfer to a covered container, and, when cool, let mature for 6 hours in the refrigerator. When the mixture is well chilled, stir in the yogurt, then churn in the ice cream maker. Using a flexible spatula, stir in the black currant puree to create a marbled effect. Store in the freezer until serving.

PREPARING THE SWISS MERINGUE

Preheat the oven to 175°F (80°C/Gas on lowest setting). Grease the mold with oil. Place the egg whites in a heatproof bowl over a bain-marie, add the sugar, and immediately begin whisking on high speed to prevent the whites cooking. Continue whisking until the temperature reaches 122°F (50°C), then transfer the bowl to the work surface and whisk on high speed until you have a firm meringue. Spoon it into a pastry bag fitted with the ⅓-in. (8-mm) tip and beginning at the bottom of each cavity in the mold and working your way up and around the sides in a spiral, pipe the meringue into "nests." Bake for 3–4 hours until crisp and dry.

PREPARING THE BLACK CURRANT COMPOTE

Combine the pectin and sugar in a bowl. Puree the black currants in the food processor, pour into a saucepan, and heat until the temperature reaches 104°F (40°C). Stir in the pectin and sugar until dissolved, then boil for 1 minute. Let cool.

PREPARING THE FROMAGE BLANC CREAM

Whip the cream with the sugar until holding its shape. Fold in the fromage blanc, followed by the lemon zest and vanilla seeds. Chill until serving.

ASSEMBLING THE PAVLOVAS

Carefully remove the meringue nests from the molds and scrape the bottom of each on a fine grater to make a flat base. Place on serving plates and fill with frozen yogurt and a little black currant compote. Using a pastry bag fitted with the ½-in. (12-mm) tip, pipe mounds of cream over the compote. Spoon the remaining compote into the third pastry bag without a tip and pipe a ring of compote over the meringue shell rims. Decorate with a few black currants and red-veined sorrel leaves. Serve immediately.

BLUEBERRY CHEESECAKE

Cheesecake aux myrtilles

Serves 8

Active time
1 hour

Chilling time
1 hour (and ideally overnight)

Cooking time
2 hours

Resting time
1 hour

Storage
Up to 2 days
in the refrigerator

Equipment
Stand mixer + paddle beater

Food processor

6-in. (16-cm) baking ring, 3 in. (8 cm) deep

Instant-read thermometer

Ingredients

Sweet shortcrust pastry

6 tbsp (3 oz./90 g) butter, diced

3½ tbsp (1½ oz./45 g) brown sugar

2 tbsp (1 oz./30 g) lightly beaten egg (about 1 medium egg)

1 cup plus 2 tbsp (5¼ oz./150 g) all-purpose flour

Scant ¼ cup (20 g) almond flour

Scant ½ tsp (1 g) ground cinnamon

1 pinch *fleur de sel*

3 tbsp (1¾ oz./50 g) clarified butter, melted

Cream cheese filling

Scant 3 cups (1½ lb./665 g) cream cheese

¼ cup plus 1 tsp (2¼ oz./65 g) lightly beaten egg (about 1½ medium eggs)

¾ cup (4¾ oz./135 g) superfine sugar

3 tbsp (45 ml) heavy cream, min. 35% fat

Blueberry puree

3 tbsp (1¼ oz./35 g) superfine sugar

½ tsp (2 g) pectin

5¾ oz. (165 g) blueberry puree

Decoration

Confectioners' sugar, for dusting

Blueberries

Small pieces of edible gold leaf

PREPARING THE SWEET SHORTCRUST PASTRY

Beat the butter, brown sugar, and egg in the stand mixer until smooth. Add the all-purpose flour, almond flour, cinnamon, and *fleur de sel* and beat until just combined. Bring the dough together with your hands, shape it into a disk, cover with plastic wrap, and chill for 1 hour. Preheat the oven to 350°F (180°C/Gas Mark 4). Roll the pastry on a lightly floured surface to a thickness of about ¼ in. (5 mm). Place on a lined baking sheet and bake for 10 minutes. Let cool completely. Break the pastry into pieces and grind to a powder in the food processor. Add the clarified butter and pulse to combine. Line the baking sheet with fresh parchment and place the baking ring on it. Press the pastry over the base and up the sides of the ring in an even layer, about ¼ in. (5 mm) thick.

PREPARING THE FILLING AND BAKING THE CHEESECAKE

Place one rack in the lower third of the oven and another rack in the center. Preheat the oven to 330°F (170°C/Gas Mark 3). Process all the filling ingredients together in the food processor for 1 minute until smooth. Pour the mixture over the crust in the ring. Place a bowl of water on the lower oven rack to create humidity and help prevent the cheesecake from cracking while it bakes. Place the cheesecake on the center rack. Bake for 40 minutes, then turn the oven off, leaving the cheesecake inside. Leave for 1 hour without opening the oven door. Let the cheesecake sit at room temperature for 1 hour, then chill.

PREPARING THE BLUEBERRY PUREE

Combine the sugar and pectin in a bowl. Heat the blueberry puree in a saucepan until the temperature reaches 104°F (40°C), then stir in the pectin and sugar until dissolved. Bring to a boil, remove from the heat, and pour directly over the top of the chilled cheesecake.

DECORATING THE CHEESECAKE

Transfer the cheesecake to a serving plate and lift off the ring. Dust the top edge of the crust with confectioners' sugar and arrange blueberries and small pieces of edible gold leaf over the blueberry puree.

CHEFS' NOTES

• This cheesecake is even better eaten the following day.

• Be careful not to let the cheesecake cool too quickly as it could sink.

• To clarify butter, melt the butter gently over low heat in a heavy saucepan. Skim off the froth, then pour the clear yellow layer of clarified butter into a jug, leaving behind the milky residue.

PANNA COTTA WITH RED CURRANTS AND CILANTRO

Groseilles et coriandre

Serves 6

Active time

1 hour 20 minutes

Drying time

12 hours

Chilling time

3–4 hours

Maturing time

12 hours

Cooking time

12 minutes

Freezing time

2–3 hours

Storage

Up to 2 days before assembling

Equipment

Food dehydrator or lined baking sheet

Food processor

Instant-read thermometer

Immersion blender

Ice cream maker

2 pastry bags

Silicone ice ball molds, ¾ in. (2 cm) in dia.

2 silicone baking mats

3 × ¾-in. (2-cm) round cookie cutters

1¼-in. (3-cm) and 1½-in. (4-cm) round cookie cutters

2 × 1⅓-in. (3.5-cm) round cookie cutters

Ingredients

Cilantro powder

⅔ oz. (20 g) cilantro sprigs

Red currant sorbet

¼ sheet (0.5 g) gold-strength gelatin, 200 Bloom

2 oz. (55 g) red currants

4 tsp (20 ml) water

5 tsp (20 g) superfine sugar

Cilantro balls

¼ sheet (0.5 g) gold-strength gelatin, 200 Bloom

1½ tbsp (25 ml) heavy cream, min. 35% fat

1¼ tsp (5 g) superfine sugar

⅕ oz. (5 g) cilantro leaves

2 tsp (10 g) mascarpone

1½ tbsp (25 ml) heavy cream, min 35% fat, well chilled

⅓ oz. (10 g) neutral glaze

Cilantro opalines

1½ oz. (40 g) white fondant

3 tbsp (2 oz./60 g) glucose syrup, DE 38

Neutral oil

Cilantro powder (see left)

Shortbread

4 tbsp (2½ oz./65 g) butter, softened

Scant ¼ cup (1 oz./30 g) confectioners' sugar

¼ tsp (2 g) salt

Scant ⅓ cup (1 oz./30 g) hazelnut flour

2 tbsp (1 oz./30 g) lightly beaten egg (about ⅔ egg)

1 cup (4 oz./120 g) all-purpose flour, divided

Red currant gel

3½ oz. (100 g) red currants

¼ tsp (1 g) pectin 325 NH 95

2 tbsp (25 g) superfine sugar

Vanilla panna cotta

1½ sheets (3.5 g) gold-strength gelatin, 200 Bloom

1⅓ cups (320 ml) heavy cream, min. 35% fat

2½ tbsp (1 oz./30 g) superfine sugar

Seeds of ½ vanilla bean

Neutral oil, for greasing

Decoration

1 oz. (30 g) red currants

Basil cress leaves

Zallotti blossom flowers

PREPARING THE CILANTRO POWDER (1 DAY AHEAD)

Remove the stems from the cilantro sprigs. Bring a saucepan of water to a boil and fill a bowl with ice water. Add the cilantro leaves to the saucepan and let boil for a few seconds. Drain with a skimmer and immediately plunge the leaves into the ice-cold water to stop them cooking. Drain and gently pat dry with paper towel. Dry them overnight in the dehydrator (if using), or spread across a lined baking sheet and place in a 115°F (45°C/Gas on lowest setting with the door propped open) oven for about 12 hours. Process to a fine powder in the food processor and store in an airtight container.

PREPARING THE RED CURRANT SORBET (1 DAY AHEAD)

Soak the gelatin in a bowl of cold water until softened. Remove the stems from the red currants, wash, and place in a bowl. Heat the water and sugar in a saucepan until the sugar dissolves. Bring to a boil, then remove from the heat. Squeeze the gelatin to remove excess water and stir into the syrup until dissolved. When the syrup has cooled to 113°F (45°C), pour it over the red currants and process to a puree using the immersion blender. Strain through a fine-mesh sieve, pressing down firmly with the back of a spoon to release as much juice as possible. Press plastic wrap over the surface and let mature in the refrigerator for 12 hours. The next day, churn in the ice cream maker. Transfer to an airtight container and freeze until assembling.

PREPARING THE CILANTRO BALLS

Soak the gelatin in a bowl of cold water until softened. Heat the first 1½ tbsp (25 ml) cream with the sugar and cilantro until the sugar dissolves. Bring to a boil, remove from the heat, and process with the immersion blender until smooth. Squeeze the gelatin to remove excess water and stir it in until dissolved. Pour over the mascarpone in a bowl and stir to blend. Add the well-chilled cream and process again with the immersion blender until smooth. Chill for at least 2–3 hours. Whip the cream until it holds its shape, spoon into one of the pastry bags, and pipe out into the cavities in the ice ball mold to fill them completely. Freeze for 2–3 hours. An hour before serving, melt the neutral glaze and dip the frozen balls into it. Chill until assembling.

PREPARING THE CILANTRO OPALINES

Heat the fondant and glucose syrup in a saucepan until the temperature reaches 320°F (160°C). Pour over one silicone mat and let cool to room temperature and harden. Preheat the oven to 400°F (200°C/Gas Mark 6) and place the other silicone mat on a baking sheet. Very lightly grease the mat with neutral oil using paper towel. When the fondant mixture has hardened, break it into small pieces and grind it to a fine powder in the food processor. Sprinkle the powder across the silicone mat, then sprinkle with the cilantro powder. Using the cookie cutters, mark twelve ¾-in. (2-cm) circles and six 1¼-in. (3-cm) circles into the mixture. Place in the oven for a few minutes until melted, remove from the oven, and let set for a few minutes before very carefully lifting the circles off the mat. Cool, then store in an airtight container until assembling.

PREPARING THE SHORTBREAD

Cream the butter, sugar, and salt together in a bowl using a flexible spatula. Stir in the hazelnut flour, followed by the egg. Stir in 3 tbsp (1 oz./30 g) of the all-purpose flour, followed by the remaining flour. Gather the dough into a ball, cover with plastic wrap, and chill for 1 hour. Preheat the oven to 340°F (170°C/Gas Mark 3). Roll out the dough on a lightly floured surface to a thickness of 1/16 in. (2 mm). Using the cookie cutters, cut out six 1½-in. (4-cm) disks, twelve 1¼-in. (3-cm) disks, and six ¾-in. (2-cm) disks. Place on the silicone mat on a baking sheet and cover with the second mat. Bake for 12 minutes, then cool on a wire rack.

PREPARING THE RED CURRANT GEL

Remove the stems from the red currants and heat in a saucepan until they soften. Combine the pectin and sugar, sprinkle over the currants, and continue to heat until the sugar and pectin dissolve. Bring to a boil. Puree using the immersion blender, then strain through a fine-mesh sieve into a bowl, pressing down with the back of a spoon to release as much juice as possible. Transfer to the second pastry bag and chill until assembling.

PREPARING THE PANNA COTTA

Soak the gelatin in a bowl of cold water until softened. Heat the cream, sugar, and vanilla seeds in a saucepan until the sugar dissolves. Bring to a boil, then remove from the heat. Squeeze the gelatin to remove excess water and stir it in until dissolved. While the panna cotta cools, lightly grease the seven cookie cutters with neutral oil and arrange them in an attractive pattern across one serving plate. When the cold panna cotta has started to thicken but is still liquid, carefully pour it around the cookie cutters. Place in the refrigerator until it is just set, then remove the cutters. If they stick, heat the insides of them slightly with a kitchen torch to release them. Repeat with the remaining serving plates.

ASSEMBLING THE DESSERT

Sprinkle the cilantro powder over the panna cotta on each plate. Place the ¾-in. (2-cm) shortbread disks in one of the ¾-in. (2-cm) holes and the 1½-in. (4-cm) disks in the 1½-in. (4-cm) hole. Fill the remaining holes with red currant gel. Arrange the two 1¼-in. (3-cm) shortbread disks on each plate so they overlap the panna cotta and the 1⅓-in. (3.5-cm) holes. Place the cilantro balls in the smallest holes and top with the opalines. Place a quenelle of red currant sorbet on top of the largest shortbread disks and pipe over swirls of red currant gel. Decorate with the red currants, cress, and Zalloti blossoms, arranging them attractively over the panna cotta. Serve immediately.

RED CURRANT AND MIXED BERRY TART

Tarte groseilles & Cie

Serves 6

Active time
1½ hours

Cooking time
20–25 minutes

Chilling time
2 hours 20 minutes

Storage
Up to 2 days
in the refrigerator

Equipment
3½ × 7½-in. (8.5 × 19-cm)
rectangular tart frame,
¾ in. (2 cm) deep

Pastry bag

Ingredients

Shortcrust pastry

⅓ cup (1½ oz./45 g)
confectioners' sugar

2½ tbsp (15 g) almond
flour

1 cup (4½ oz./125 g) all-
purpose flour

5 tbsp (2½ oz./75 g)
butter, diced, plus extra
for the tart frame

2 tbsp (1 oz./30 g) lightly
beaten egg (about
⅔ egg)

¼ tsp (1 g) salt

Seeds of ½ vanilla bean

**Almond cream
and red currant filling**

2 tbsp (25 g) butter,
softened

Generous 1 tbsp (15 g)
superfine sugar

1 tbsp plus 2 tsp
(25 g) lightly beaten
egg (½ egg), at room
temperature

¼ cup (25 g) almond flour

1 oz. (30 g) red currants

Mascarpone cream

1 sheet (2 g) gold-
strength gelatin,
200 Bloom

2 tbsp (25 g) superfine
sugar

1½ tbsp (25 ml) heavy
cream, min. 35% fat

Scant ½ cup
(3½ oz./100 g)
mascarpone

**Red currant
and berry topping**

3⅓ oz. (95 g) red
currants

4½ oz. (125 g) green
gooseberries

4½ oz. (125 g)
raspberries

4½ oz. (125 g) white
raspberries

4½ oz. (125 g)
blackberries

4½ oz. (125 g)
blueberries

PREPARING THE SHORTCRUST PASTRY

Sift the sugar, almond flour, and all-purpose flour into a bowl. Rub in the butter with your fingertips until the mixture has the texture of coarse crumbs. Mix in the egg, followed by the salt and vanilla seeds. Gather the dough into a ball, flatten it slightly, cover with plastic wrap, and chill for 2 hours. Grease the tart frame with butter and place it on a lined baking sheet. Roll the dough to a thickness of ⅛ in. (3 mm) and line the tart frame with it. Chill until filling.

PREPARING THE FILLING AND BAKING THE TART SHELL

Preheat the oven to 340°F (170°C/Gas Mark 3). Beat the butter and sugar together in a bowl, beat in the egg, and fold in the almond flour until combined. Transfer to the pastry bag and pipe into the tart shell to fill it a third full. Wash the red currants, scatter them over the cream, pressing them gently into the cream, and bake for 25–30 minutes. Let cool.

PREPARING THE MASCARPONE CREAM

Soak the gelatin in a bowl of cold water until softened. Heat the sugar and cream in a saucepan until the sugar dissolves. Squeeze the gelatin to remove excess water and stir it into the hot cream until dissolved. Gradually whisk in the mascarpone, transfer to a bowl, and let firm up in the refrigerator for about 20 minutes.

ASSEMBLING THE TART

Spread the mascarpone cream in a dome over the filling in the tart shell, then remove the frame. Wash and dry the fruits for the topping, cut some of the larger gooseberries in half, and arrange them attractively over the mascarpone cream.

NORDIC LINGONBERRY PARFAITS

Dessert Nordique aux airelles

Serves 6

Active time
1 hour

Infusing time
20 minutes

Cooking time
45 minutes

Chilling time
4 hours

Storage
Up to 2 days
before assembling

Equipment
6 heat-resistant serving
glasses

Food processor

Aerated silicone baking
mat

Pastry bag + a plain ¾-in.
(15-mm) tip

Disposable pastry bag

Ingredients
Vanilla cream
2 cups (500 ml) heavy
cream, min. 35% fat

1 vanilla bean, split
lengthwise

¼ cup (1¾ oz./50 g)
superfine sugar

1½ tsp (6 g) pectin X58

Lingonberry jelly
1½ tsp (5 g) gelatin
powder

2¼ tbsp (35 ml) cold
water

10½ oz. (300 g)
lingonberries

Water or red fruit juice
(cranberry, strawberry,
red currant), as needed

5 tsp (20 g) superfine
sugar

Vanilla chestnut paste
4 oz. (110 g) chestnut
paste

4½ oz. (130 g) chestnut
spread

Seeds of ½ vanilla bean

Marinated lingonberries
1 tsp (5 ml) chestnut
syrup

1 tsp (5 ml) lime juice

1¾ oz. (50 g)
lingonberries

Granola
1½ tbsp (1 oz./30 g)
chestnut honey

3 tbsp (1½ oz./40 g)
butter

1⅔ cups (4¾ oz./135 g)
rolled oats

¼ cup (1¼ oz./35 g)
almonds, chopped

2½ tsp (7 g) light brown
sugar

½ cup (2 oz./55 g) dried
cranberries

**Chestnut diplomat
cream**
¾ tsp (2 g) gelatin
powder

1 tbsp (15 ml) cold water

⅔ cup (150 ml) whole
milk

1½ tbsp (25 g) egg yolk
(about 1 yolk)

2½ tbsp (1 oz./30 g)
superfine sugar

4 tsp (12 g) custard
powder

⅔ cup (150 ml) heavy
cream, min. 35% fat, well
chilled

⅔ oz. (20 g) chestnut
spread

⅔ oz. (20 g) chestnut
paste

PREPARING THE VANILLA CREAM

Pour the cream into a saucepan, scrape in the vanilla seeds, and add the bean. Bring to a boil, remove from the heat, cover, and let infuse for 20 minutes. Remove the bean and return the saucepan to the heat. Combine the sugar and pectin and stir into the cream until dissolved. Bring to a boil and pour into the serving glasses. Chill until set before preparing the jelly.

PREPARING THE LINGONBERRY JELLY

Sprinkle the gelatin over the cold water in a small bowl and let soak for 10 minutes. Reduce the lingonberries to a smooth puree in the food processor. Strain through a fine-mesh sieve, pressing down on the fruit to release as much juice as possible. Measure the juice and add water or red fruit juice to make 1 cup (250 ml), as necessary. Heat the juice in a saucepan with the sugar until the sugar dissolves, remove from the heat, and stir in the gelatin until dissolved. Pour over the vanilla cream in the serving glasses, checking first to ensure the cream has completely set or the hot jelly will make a hole in it. Chill for at least 2 hours or until the jelly is completely set.

PREPARING THE VANILLA CHESTNUT PASTE

Stir the chestnut paste in a bowl to soften it. Whisk in the chestnut spread and vanilla seeds. Chill until assembling.

PREPARING THE MARINATED LINGONBERRIES

Combine the syrup and lime juice in a bowl, then gently stir in the lingonberries, taking care not to crush them. Let marinate in the refrigerator until assembling.

PREPARING THE GRANOLA

Preheat the oven to 340°F (170°C/Gas Mark 3). Melt the honey and butter together. Combine the oats, almonds, and brown sugar and stir in the honey and butter. Spread the mixture across the aerated silicone baking mat and bake for 20–30 minutes until evenly golden brown, stirring frequently. Cool before mixing in the cranberries.

PREPARING THE CHESTNUT DIPLOMAT CREAM

Sprinkle the gelatin over the cold water in a small bowl and let soak for 10 minutes. Make a pastry cream by bringing the milk to a boil in a saucepan. Meanwhile, whisk together the egg yolk, sugar, and custard powder in a bowl until pale and thick. When the milk comes to a boil, slowly pour one-third into the egg yolk mixture, whisking continuously. Return to the saucepan and bring to a boil, whisking vigorously, and let boil for 2–3 minutes, still whisking. Remove from the heat and stir in the gelatin until dissolved. Transfer the pastry cream to a bowl, press plastic wrap over the surface, and chill thoroughly until assembling. Immediately before assembling, whip the cream until it holds quite firm peaks. In a separate bowl, combine the chestnut spread and chestnut paste. Whisk the pastry cream to loosen it, then stir in the chestnut mixture until combined. Using a flexible spatula, gently fold in the whipped cream. Spoon into the pastry bag with the ¾-in. (15-mm) tip.

ASSEMBLING THE PARFAITS

Transfer the vanilla chestnut paste to the disposable pastry bag and snip off the tip to make a hole about ¾ in. (15 mm) in diameter. Pipe out approximately 1½ oz. (40 g) of the paste into each glass in a thick line on one side of the lingonberry jelly. Using a small spoon, scoop out a little of the chestnut paste to make a small hollow and fill with marinated lingonberries. Pipe out an attractive mound of diplomat cream over the chestnut paste and lingonberries. Add another spoonful of marinated lingonberries to each glass next to the mound of cream. Sprinkle the cream with a little granola and accompany with the remaining granola served in small cups on the side.

ACAI AND BLACK CURRANT ENERGY BOWLS

Bowl énergétique

Serves 6

Active time

3 hours

Cooking time

10 minutes

Chilling time

2 hours

Storage time

24 hours in the refrigerator

Equipment

Instant-read thermometer

Stand mixer + whisk

Ingredients

Acai and black currant mousse

2 tsp (9.5 g) gelatin powder

Generous ¼ cup (65 ml) cold water

12¾ oz. (360 g) acai puree

3¼ oz. (90 g) black currant puree

2½ tbsp (1 oz./30 g) superfine sugar

6½ tbsp (3 oz./90 g) egg white (about 3 whites)

¼ cup (3 oz./90 g) glucose syrup

2 generous tbsp (1½ oz./45 g) invert sugar

1⅓ cups (315 ml) heavy cream, min. 35% fat

Fruits

1 mango

3 kiwifruits

3 bananas

1 pomegranate

Decoration

Apple blossom cress

Red-veined sorrel leaves

PREPARING THE ACAI AND BLACK CURRANT MOUSSE

Sprinkle the gelatin over the cold water in a bowl and let soak for 10 minutes. Meanwhile, heat the acai puree, black currant puree, and sugar in a saucepan and bring to a boil. Remove from the heat, add the gelatin, stirring until it dissolves. Transfer to a mixing bowl and let cool until the temperature reaches 104°F (40°C). Whisk the egg whites in the stand mixer until they hold soft peaks. Heat the glucose syrup and invert sugar in a saucepan until melted, then continue heating until the temperature reaches 250°F (120°C). Whisking continuously on high speed, slowly drizzle the hot syrup into the egg whites in a thin, steady stream, without letting the syrup hit the whisk. Continue whisking until a firm, glossy meringue. When the fruit puree has cooled to 104°F (40°C), gently fold it into the meringue. In a separate bowl, whip the cream until it starts to thicken, then fold it into the mousse. Divide the mousse between six serving bowls and chill for at least 2 hours.

PREPARING THE FRUITS

Peel the mango (see technique p. 56) and, using a peeler, cut the flesh into ribbons. Peel and thinly slice the kiwifruits and bananas. Cut the pomegranate open and remove the seeds (see technique p. 62).

ASSEMBLING THE BOWLS

Arrange the fruits attractively over the mousse in each bowl. Decorate with apple blossom cress and red-veined sorrel leaves and serve well chilled.

CRANBERRY AND BEET JUICE

Jus de cranberry et betterave

Makes 4 cups (1 L)

Active time
30 minutes

Setting time
3 hours

Chilling time
2 hours

Storage
Up to 3 days
in the refrigerator

Equipment
Juicer

Ingredients

Candied rose petals
1 organic rose
1 egg white, lightly beaten
½ cup (3½ oz./100 g) granulated sugar

Cranberry and beet juice
14 oz. (400 g) raw red beets
2¼ lb. (1 kg) cranberries
3½ oz. (100 g) raspberries
½ oz. (12 g) fresh ginger
1¼ tsp (6 ml) rose water
½ cup (120 ml) cane sugar syrup
¼ cup (60 ml) water

PREPARING THE CANDIED ROSE PETALS

Carefully separate the rose into individual petals. Place the egg white in a bowl and whisk it lightly with a fork to loosen it. Place the sugar in a separate bowl. Dip the petals one by one first into the egg white and then into the sugar so they are coated on both sides. Place the petals on a sheet of parchment paper in a single layer and let set at room temperature for 3 hours.

PREPARING THE CRANBERRY AND BEET JUICE

Scrub and peel the red beets. Wash and dry the cranberries and raspberries. Pass the beets and berries through the juicer together. Peel the ginger, grate it finely, and add to the juice along with the rose water, cane sugar syrup, and water. Chill for at least 2 hours before serving.

TO SERVE

Serve the juice well chilled over ice with a few candied rose petals placed on the rim of each glass.

RHUBARB, BERRY, AND PINK PRALINE TART

Tarte boulangère à la rhubarbe, fruits rouges et pralines roses

Serves 6

Active time

4½ hours

Freezing time

10 minutes

Rising time

2 hours

Chilling time

2½ hours

Cooking time

About 1 hour

Storage

Up to 2 days in the refrigerator

Equipment

Stand mixer + dough hook

9-in. (22-cm) tart ring

Medium zip-lock freezer bags

Immersion blender

Instant-read thermometer

Pastry bag + plain ½-in. (15-mm) tip

Ingredients

Saint-Tropez crumbs

3 tbsp (1½ oz./40 g) butter, melted and cooled

3½ tbsp (1½ oz./40 g) superfine sugar

½ cup plus 1 tbsp (2½ oz./70 g) all-purpose flour

1 pinch (0.2 g) *fleur de sel*

Pink praline brioche

1 cup (4 oz./120 g) pastry flour

¼ cup (2 oz./60 g) lightly beaten egg (about 1 egg)

2½ tsp (12 ml) whole milk

1 tbsp (12 g) superfine sugar

½ tsp (2.5 g) salt

⅕ oz. (4 g) fresh yeast

1½ tbsp (25 g) crème fraîche

4 tbsp (2 oz./60 g) butter, diced and softened, plus more for the ring

1 egg, lightly beaten, for the egg wash

⅔ oz. (20 g) pink pralines

Poached rhubarb

14 oz. (400 g) fresh rhubarb

2 tbsp plus 1 tsp (35 ml) water

3 tbsp (1¼ oz./35 g) superfine sugar

⅕ oz. (5 g) raspberries

1/20 oz. (1 g) dried hibiscus petals

Rhubarb, raspberry, and hibiscus jam

10¾ oz. (305 g) fresh rhubarb

⅓ cup (2½ oz./70 g) superfine sugar

Generous ½ tsp (2.25 g) pectin NH or 325NH95

1¾ oz. (50 g) raspberries

1/10 oz. (2 g) dried hibiscus petals

Seeds of 1 vanilla bean

Diplomat cream

¾ sheet (1.5 g) gold-strength gelatin, 200 Bloom

½ cup (125 ml) whole milk

2 tbsp (25 g) superfine sugar, divided

Seeds of ½ vanilla bean

1½ tbsp (12 g) all-purpose flour

2 tbsp plus 2 tsp (1½ oz./40 g) lightly beaten egg (about 1 egg)

1 tbsp (15 g) butter, diced

⅓ cup (80 ml) heavy cream, min. 35% fat

To assemble

1 oz. (30 g) neutral glaze

2 oz. (60 g) strawberries

2 oz. (60 g) raspberries

2 oz. (60 g) red currants

Elderflowers

PREPARING THE SAINT-TROPEZ CRUMBS

Using a spatula, mix the butter, sugar, flour, and salt together in a bowl until the mixture forms small balls. Spread them across a baking sheet and let harden in the freezer for 10 minutes. Break roughly into smaller crumbs and store in an airtight container until making the brioche.

PREPARING THE PINK PRALINE BRIOCHE

Knead all the ingredients, except the butter, beaten egg, and pink pralines, in the stand mixer on low speed for 5 minutes. Increase the speed to medium and knead for 15 minutes until the dough is elastic and starts to pull away from the sides of the bowl, scraping down the sides regularly. Gradually knead in the butter for 5 minutes until the dough leaves the sides of the bowl. Cover with plastic wrap and let rise at room temperature for 30 minutes. Punch the dough down with your hand to make it stronger, cover, and let rest in the refrigerator for at least 2 hours. Lightly grease the tart ring with butter and place on a lined baking sheet. Roll the dough to a thickness of about ⅛ in. (3 mm) and cut out a 9-in. (22-cm) disk. Let rise at warm room temperature or in a very low oven (80°F/26°C) for 1½ hours. Preheat the oven to 325°F (160°C/Gas Mark 3). Brush the dough with the egg wash, scatter the pralines and Saint-Tropez crumbs over the top, and bake for 20 minutes until golden.

PREPARING THE POACHED RHUBARB

Wash the rhubarb, trim off the ends, and peel it. Cut into pieces that will just fit inside the freezer bags. Combine the water, sugar, and raspberries in a bowl, then puree using the immersion blender. Strain through a fine-mesh sieve into a saucepan, add the hibiscus petals, and bring to a simmer. Remove from the heat and let cool to about 122°F (50°C). Place the rhubarb in the freezer bags in single layers and divide the syrup between the bags. Seal, removing as much air as possible. Heat a large saucepan of water to 176°F (80°C), immerse the bags in the water, and cook for 20 minutes at 162°F (72°C). Remove the bags, lay them flat, and chill until assembling.

PREPARING THE JAM

Wash the rhubarb, trim off the ends, and peel it. Cut into approximately ¾-in. (2-cm) cubes. Combine the sugar and pectin in a bowl. Place the rhubarb in a saucepan over low heat with the raspberries, hibiscus petals, and vanilla seeds. Cut a circle of parchment paper the same diameter as your saucepan and press it over the rhubarb mixture to help the fruits release their juices. Cook until the rhubarb reduces to a compote, add the sugar and pectin mixture, and stir until dissolved. Bring to a boil, pour into a container, press plastic wrap over the surface. Chill until assembling.

PREPARING THE DIPLOMAT CREAM

To make a pastry cream, soak the gelatin in a bowl of cold water until softened. Heat the milk with one-third of the sugar in a saucepan until the sugar dissolves. Combine the remaining sugar with the vanilla seeds and flour in a bowl, then whisk in the egg. As soon as the milk comes to a boil, slowly pour half of it into the egg mixture, whisking vigorously. Return to the saucepan and bring to a boil, stirring continuously with a spatula to prevent the custard sticking to the bottom of the pan. Continue to boil, still stirring, for 1 minute. Remove from the heat and mix in the butter. Squeeze the gelatin to remove excess water and whisk it in until dissolved. Spread the pastry cream over a baking sheet, press plastic wrap over the surface, and let cool completely in the refrigerator (about 30 minutes). Transfer the pastry cream to a bowl and whisk to loosen it. Whip the cream in a separate bowl until it holds its shape, then gently whisk it into the pastry cream one-third at a time. Spoon into the pastry bag.

ASSEMBLING THE TART

Drain the poached rhubarb and cut it into diagonal slices about 2 in. (5 cm) long. Place the slices on a flat plate and brush them very lightly with the neutral glaze to make them shine. Wash, hull, and quarter the strawberries and wash and dry the raspberries and currants. Place the brioche on a serving plate and pipe out mounds of diplomat cream in a ring on top, leaving a ¾-in. (1.5-cm) border. Fill the center with the jam and arrange the rhubarb slices, strawberries, and raspberries attractively over the jam. Scatter with the red currants and elderflowers.

TROPICAL FRUITS

FROZEN PINEAPPLE SOUFFLÉS

Soufflé glacé à l'ananas

Serves 4

Active time
45 minutes

Drying time
12 hours

Cooking time
15 minutes

Freezing time
At least 1 hour

Storage
Up to 3 days

Equipment
Mandoline
Silicone baking mat
4 × 3-in. (8-cm) soufflé dishes
Food-safe acetate sheet (or parchment paper)
Food processor

Ingredients

Pineapple chips
3½ oz. (100 g) peeled and cored pineapple, preferably Victoria (see technique p. 28)

Toasted almond crumbs
Scant ⅓ cup (1 oz./30 g) almond flour

Frozen pineapple soufflé mixture
9 oz. (250 g) pineapple, preferably Victoria
¹⁄₁₀ oz. (3 g) ginger, preferably organic
Seeds of 1 vanilla bean
2 tsp (10 ml) white rum
⅓ cup (80 ml) heavy cream, min. 35% fat
¼ cup (2 oz./60 g) egg white (about 2 whites)
5 tsp (20 g) coconut sugar
Scant ⅓ cup (2 oz./60 g) white cane sugar

Candied pineapple marmalade
10 oz. (280 g) peeled and cored pineapple, preferably Victoria (see technique p. 28)
2 tbsp (1½ oz./40 g) acacia honey
2½ tsp (10 g) coconut sugar
Seeds of 1 vanilla bean
3½ tbsp (50 ml) lemon juice
Finely grated zest of ½ lime

PREPARING THE PINEAPPLE CHIPS (1 DAY AHEAD)
Preheat the oven to 115°F (45°C/Gas on lowest setting with the oven door propped open). Using the mandoline, cut the pineapple lengthwise into paper-thin slices. Spread the slices across the silicone baking mat and dry in the oven for 12 hours. Let cool, then store in an airtight container in a dry place until using.

PREPARING THE TOASTED ALMOND CRUMBS
Preheat the oven to 350°F (180°C/Gas Mark 4). Spread the almond flour across a lined baking sheet and toast in the oven for 10 minutes, watching closely and stirring often, until lightly browned. Let cool, then store in a dry place until using.

PREPARING THE FROZEN PINEAPPLE SOUFFLÉ MIXTURE
Wrap a strip of acetate sheet or parchment paper around each soufflé dish so it stands ¾ in. (2 cm) above the dish and fix in place with adhesive tape. Cut four 4-in. (10-cm) squares of acetate (or parchment paper) and roll into cylinders 1 in. (2.5 cm) in diameter, using adhesive tape to hold them together. Peel the pineapple (see technique p. 28) and cut it into pieces. Peel and grate the ginger. Place the pineapple, ginger, vanilla seeds, and rum in the food processer and process until smooth. Strain through a fine-mesh sieve into a mixing bowl. Whip the cream until it holds its shape and gently fold it into the pineapple mixture. Whisk the egg whites until they hold soft peaks, add the coconut and cane sugars, and continue whisking until the peaks are firm. Gently fold into the pineapple cream. Fill the dishes to the top of the acetate sheet or parchment paper collars and smooth with a spatula. Insert an acetate cylinder into the center of each, reaching to the bottom of the dish. Freeze for about 1 hour, then carefully remove the cylinders from the centers, leaving a hole in the middle of each soufflé. Return to the freezer until serving.

PREPARING THE CANDIED PINEAPPLE MARMALADE
Cut the pineapple into ¼-in. (5-mm) dice. Place in a saucepan with the honey, coconut sugar, and vanilla seeds. Cook over low heat for 5 minutes until the sugar dissolves, then stir in the lemon juice and lime zest. Transfer to a covered container and chill until serving.

ASSEMBLING THE SOUFFLÉS
Remove the parchment paper or acetate collars from the soufflés and dust with the toasted almond crumbs. Heat the marmalade to lukewarm and fill the centers of the soufflés with it. Top each soufflé with a pineapple chip and serve immediately.

PAPAYA AND GINGER CARPACCIO WITH CHAMPAGNE SABAYON

Carpaccio de papaye et gingembre, sabayon au champagne

Serves 4

Active time
1 hour

Drying time
24 hours

Chilling time
12 hours

Infusing time
30 minutes

Storage
Up to 24 hours
in the refrigerator

Equipment
Food processor

Silicone baking mat

Instant-read thermometer

Immersion blender

2-cup (500-ml) whipping
siphon + 1 N₂O gas
cartridge

Mandoline

Ingredients

Papaya tuiles
⅔ oz. (20 g) papaya

Papaya and chia confit
2¾ oz. (80 g) papaya
2 tsp (8 g) chia seeds

Champagne sabayon
2 sheets (4 g) gold-
strength gelatin,
200 Bloom
2½ tbsp (1½ oz./40 g)
egg yolk (about 2 yolks)
2 tbsp (25 g) superfine
sugar
½ cup (125 ml) whole milk
Seeds of ½ vanilla bean
½ cup (125 ml)
champagne

Green papaya julienne
2¾ oz. (80 g) green
papaya
⅒ oz. (2 g) fresh ginger,
preferably organic
Scant ½ cup (115 ml)
water
2 tbsp (25 g) superfine
sugar
Finely grated zest of
½ lime
1 tsp (5 ml) lime juice
1 kaffir lime leaf

Papaya jam
4 oz. (115 g) papaya
1½ tsp (7 ml) lime juice
1¾ tsp (7 g) superfine
sugar
1 tsp (1 g) mint leaves
1 kaffir lime leaf

Papaya carpaccio
¾ lb. (335 g) papaya
2½ tbsp (40 ml) olive oil
4 tsp (20 ml) lime juice
2 tsp (4 g) finely grated
lime zest

Decoration
Golden sesame seeds
Black sesame seeds

PREPARING THE PAPAYA TUILES (1 DAY AHEAD)
Preheat the oven to 140°F (60°C/Gas on lowest setting with the oven door propped open). Peel the papaya and puree in the food processor. Spread across the silicone baking mat into a thin layer and dry in the oven for 24 hours.

PREPARING THE PAPAYA AND CHIA CONFIT (1 DAY AHEAD)
Peel the papaya and puree in the food processor. Stir in the chia seeds, cover with plastic wrap, and chill for 12 hours to allow the chia seeds to swell.

PREPARING THE CHAMPAGNE SABAYON
Soak the gelatin in a bowl of cold water until softened. In a separate bowl, whisk together the egg yolks and sugar until pale and thick. Bring the milk to a simmer in a saucepan, then gradually pour it into the egg yolk mixture, whisking continuously. Return to the saucepan and cook, stirring with a spatula, until the temperature reaches 180°F (82°C). Remove from the heat, squeeze the gelatin to remove excess water, and stir it into the hot custard until dissolved. Incorporate the vanilla seeds and champagne, then process with the immersion blender until smooth. Transfer to the siphon, seal it with the cartridge, and shake to distribute the gas. Chill until assembling.

PREPARING THE GREEN PAPAYA JULIENNE
Peel the papaya and slice it thinly using the mandoline Cut the slices into julienne and place in a freezer bag. Peel and grate the ginger. In a saucepan, heat the water, sugar, ginger, lime zest, lime juice, and lime leaf until the sugar dissolves. Bring to a boil, remove from the heat, and let infuse until the syrup cools to lukewarm. Pour into the freezer bag containing the green papaya. Press out as much air as possible, seal the bag, and let infuse for 30 minutes. Drain the papaya and set aside.

PREPARING THE PAPAYA JAM
Peel the papaya and puree in the food processor. Place in a saucepan, add the remaining ingredients, and heat until the sugar dissolves. As soon as the mixture comes to a simmer, remove it from the heat. Cool and chill until serving.

PREPARING THE PAPAYA CARPACCIO
Peel the papaya and remove the seeds. Cut the fruit into 1/16-in. (2-mm) slices using the mandoline. Lay the slices flat on a plate. Combine the olive oil, lime juice, and lime zest in a bowl and brush over the papaya slices.

ASSEMBLING THE DESSERT
Arrange the carpaccio slices in a rosette around the edge of four serving bowls. Place the papaya jam in the center and top it with the papaya and chia confit. Arrange the papaya julienne like a "nest" around the jam and confit and sprinkle it with golden and black sesame seeds. Dispense mounds of champagne sabayon in the center over the nests. Serve with the papaya tuiles.

BANANA, MILK CHOCOLATE, AND SPECULAAS GÂTEAU

Entremets banane, chocolat lait et spéculoos

Serves 6

Active time

3 hours

Chilling time

1 hour

Cooking time

25 minutes

Freezing time

At least 4½ hours

Storage

Up to 3 days in the refrigerator

Equipment

Instant-read thermometer

Immersion blender

Stand mixer + paddle beater

Silicone baking mat

6-in. (15-cm) cake ring, 1½ in. (4 cm) deep

Food processor

Kitchen torch

Velvet spray gun

7-in. (18-cm) round silicone cake pan, 2 in. (5 cm) deep

2 food-safe acetate sheets

Ingredients

Banana crémeux

Scant ½ tsp (2 g) gelatin powder

2½ tsp (12 ml) cold water

3½ tbsp (1¾ oz./50 g) lightly beaten egg (1 egg)

¼ cup (1¾ oz./50 g) superfine sugar

3½ tbsp (50 ml) heavy cream, min. 35% fat

2 oz. (60 g) banana puree

Scant 1 oz. (25 g) white chocolate, 33% cacao, chopped

6 tbsp (3 oz./90 g) butter, diced

Speculaas crumbs

3 tbsp (1½ oz./40 g) butter, diced

¼ cup (1½ oz./40 g) brown sugar

⅛ tsp (0.5 g) fine salt

Scant ¼ tsp (0.5 g) ground cinnamon

Scant ¼ tsp (0.5 g) ground nutmeg

3 tsp (14 g) lightly beaten egg (about ¼ egg), at room temperature

½ cup (2 oz./55 g) all-purpose flour

¼ tsp (1 g) baking powder

Speculaas crust

2½ oz. (70 g) blond chocolate, 35% cacao (preferably Valrhona Orelys), chopped

4¾ oz. (135 g) speculaas crumbs (see left)

2½ oz. (70 g) *feuillantine* flakes (or crushed wafers)

Scant ½ cup (1¾ oz./50 g) toasted chopped pecans

⅛ tsp (0.5 g) *fleur de sel*

Banana sponge

3½ oz. (100 g) banana puree

4¼ oz. (120 g) raw almond paste, chopped

1½ tbsp (15 g) all-purpose flour

⅓ cup (3 oz./90 g) lightly beaten egg (about 2 eggs)

1¾ tsp (10 g) egg yolk (about ½ yolk)

1½ tbsp (15 g) muscovado sugar

5½ tsp (25 g) egg white (1 scant white)

1¼ tsp (5 g) superfine sugar

2 tbsp (1 oz./30 g) butter, melted and cooled

Scant 3 tbsp (20 g) chopped toasted pecans

Banana compote

2 ripe bananas

2 tbsp (25 g) butter, melted and cooled

Scant 3 tbsp (25 g) brown sugar

1¾ oz. (50 g) banana puree

Generous ½ tsp (3 ml) lemon juice

Chocolate triangle

3½ oz. (100 g) yellow cocoa butter

½ oz. (15 g) milk chocolate, chopped

Milk chocolate mousse

Scant 1 tsp (4 g) gelatin powder

1½ tbsp (25 ml) cold water

2 tbsp plus 2 tsp (1½ oz./45 g) egg yolk (about 2¼ yolks)

2½ tbsp (1 oz./30 g) superfine sugar

Generous ⅔ cup (165 ml) whole milk

5¼ oz. (150 g) milk chocolate, 46% cacao, chopped

Generous ¾ cup (210 ml) heavy cream, min. 35% fat

Neutral glaze and decoration

9 oz. (250 g) neutral glaze

2 tbsp (30 ml) water

Banana chips

PREPARING THE BANANA CRÉMEUX

Sprinkle the gelatin over the cold water in a bowl and let soak for 10 minutes. Whisk together the egg, sugar, and cream. Warm the banana puree in a saucepan, then whisk in the egg mixture. Bring to a boil, whisking continuously. Remove from the heat and whisk in the gelatin and chocolate. Let cool to 104°F (40°C), add the butter, and process with the immersion blender until smooth. Press plastic wrap over the surface and chill for 1 hour.

PREPARING THE SPECULAAS CRUMBS

Preheat the oven to 300°F (150°C/Gas Mark 2) on fan setting. Cream together the butter, brown sugar, salt, and spices in the stand mixer. Beat in the egg, sift in the flour and baking powder, and beat until combined. Press through a sieve with ¼-in. (5-mm) mesh to make large crumbs and spread across the silicone baking mat. Bake for 15 minutes.

PREPARING THE SPECULAAS CRUST

Melt the chocolate in a bowl over a bain-marie until the temperature reaches 113°F (45°C). Place the speculaas crumbs, *feuillantine* flakes, and pecans in a bowl and add the *fleur de sel*, crushed between your fingers. Pour in the melted chocolate and gently stir to combine using a flexible spatula. Place the cake ring on a lined baking sheet, add the mixture, and press it down in a layer, ⅛ in. (3 mm) thick. Remove the ring and freeze until assembling.

PREPARING THE BANANA SPONGE

Preheat the oven to 350°F (180°C/Gas Mark 4). Process the banana puree, almond paste, flour, eggs, egg yolk, and muscovado sugar together in the food processor until smooth. Transfer to a mixing bowl. In a separate bowl, whisk the egg whites until holding soft peaks, then gradually whisk in the sugar until the peaks are firm. Fold the whites into the banana mixture, followed by the melted butter and pecans. Place the cake ring on the silicone mat, pour in the batter, and bake for 10–15 minutes until a toothpick inserted into the center comes out clean. Let cool before removing the ring.

PREPARING THE BANANA COMPOTE

Preheat the oven to 325°F (160°C/Gas Mark 3). Peel and slice the bananas and place in a bowl. Add the melted butter and brown sugar and, using a flexible spatula, gently stir to combine, taking care not to crush the bananas. Spread across the silicone mat and bake for 10 minutes. Let cool, then roughly mash with a fork. Stir in the banana puree and lemon juice and chill until assembling the insert.

ASSEMBLING THE INSERT

Return the speculaas layer to the cake ring and top with the banana sponge. Spread the banana compote in an even layer over the sponge and freeze for 30 minutes. Add the crémeux

to fill the ring, smoothing it into an even layer using an offset spatula. Freeze for 1 hour. Remove the ring, heating the outside slightly with the kitchen torch, if necessary. Return to the freezer until assembling the dessert.

PREPARING THE CHOCOLATE TRIANGLE

Melt the cocoa butter in a bowl over a bain-marie until the temperature reaches 86°F (30°C). Temper the chocolate in a separate bowl by melting it over a bain-marie until the temperature reaches 113°F (45°C). Stand the bowl in a larger bowl filled with ice water, stir until the chocolate cools to 81°F–82°F (27°C–28°C), then place back over the bain-marie and raise the temperature to 84°F (29°C). Transfer the melted cocoa butter to the spray gun and spray it over the base and sides of the cake pan. Dip the tip of a paintbrush with firm bristles into the milk chocolate and scrape the bristles with a knife to splatter specks of chocolate over the cocoa butter. Roll the remaining milk chocolate into a very thin layer between the two acetate sheets, let set for a few minutes, then peel off the top sheet. Using the back of a knife and a ruler, score lines into the chocolate to make a 7-in. (18-cm) long triangle, measuring approximately 1¼ in. (3 cm) at the base and with a narrow tip. Place in the bowl of the stand mixer and let set for a few minutes in a curved shape before very carefully removing it from the acetate sheet.

PREPARING THE MILK CHOCOLATE MOUSSE

Sprinkle the gelatin over the cold water in a bowl and let soak for 10 minutes. In a separate bowl, whisk together the egg yolks and sugar until pale and thick. Warm the milk in a saucepan, then whisk in the yolks and sugar mixture. Stirring continuously, heat until the temperature reaches 181°F (83°C). Remove from the heat, whisk in the gelatin until dissolved, then pour over the chocolate in a mixing bowl. Process with the immersion blender until smooth and let cool to 84°F (29°C). In a separate bowl, whip the cream until it holds its shape, then gently fold it into the mousse.

ASSEMBLING, GLAZING, AND DECORATING THE GÂTEAU

Pour a ½-in. (1-cm) layer of the mousse into the silicone cake pan, taking care not to create air bubbles at the base. Using a spatula, coat the sides of the mold with mousse. Nestle the insert into the mousse with the speculaas layer uppermost. Smooth the edges, if necessary, then freeze for at least 3 hours to make unmolding easier. When you are ready to unmold the gâteau, stir the neutral glaze and water together using a flexible spatula. Carefully turn the gâteau out and spread the neutral glaze over it using a palette knife. Decorate with the chocolate triangle and banana chips.

PITON TROPICAL FRUIT VOLCANOES

Piton de la Fournaise

Serves 6

Active time
40 minutes

Setting time
10 minutes

Storage
Up to 24 hours
in the refrigerator

Equipment
Instant-read thermometer
1 food-safe acetate sheet
5-in. (12-cm) round cookie
cutter

Ingredients

Passion fruit jelly
2 passion fruit
1¼ lb. (600 g) passion
fruit puree
1½ tsp (3 g) agar-agar
powder

Fruit salad
1 mango
½ pineapple
1 kiwifruit
1 papaya
1 dragon fruit
10 lychees
3 passion fruit
Baby basil leaves

PREPARING THE PASSION FRUIT JELLY

Cut the passion fruit in half, scoop out the seeds, and reserve the juice for the fruit salad. Rinse the seeds in a sieve under cold water and remove any remaining flesh. Heat the passion fruit puree and agar-agar in a saucepan until the agar-agar dissolves. Bring to a boil, then let boil for 30 seconds. Remove from the heat and let the mixture cool until the temperature reaches 122°F (50°C). Pour it over the acetate sheet in a thin layer and scatter with the passion fruit seeds before the jelly sets.

PREPARING THE FRUIT SALAD

Peel the mango (see technique p. 56), pineapple (see technique p. 28), kiwifruit, papaya, dragon fruit, and lychees, removing the pits and seeds as necessary. Cut all the fruit into approximately ⅛-in. (4-mm) dice. Place in a bowl and gently stir to mix with the reserved passion fruit juice.

TO SERVE

Using the cookie cutter, cut out twelve 5-in. (12-cm) disks of passion fruit jelly. Place one disk on each serving plate and spoon a mound of fruit salad in the center. Carefully drape a second jelly disk over the fruit so it hangs in attractive folds. Using the tip of a knife, score a cross in the center of the jelly so the fruit can be seen. Decorate the plates with the remaining fruit salad and baby basil leaves.

CHEFS' NOTES

Piton de la Fournaise, on the French island of Réunion
in the Indian Ocean, is one of the most active volcanoes
in the world, its most recent eruption beginning
on December 7, 2020.

LYCHEE HARMONY

L'harmonie au litchi

Serves 6

Active time

3 hours

Maturing time

At least 4 hours

Freezing time

3 hours

Chilling time

2 hours

Cooking time

12 minutes

Storage

Up to 24 hours
in the refrigerator
before assembling

Equipment

Instant-read thermometer

Immersion blender

Ice cream maker

6 silicone ring molds,
3½-in. (8.5-cm) outer dia.,
2-in. (5-cm) inner dia.,
¾ in. (1.8 cm) deep, or a
pastry bag + plain ½-in.
(12-mm) tip

Food processor

4-in. (10-cm) square
confectionery frame

Silicone baking mat

2½-in. (6.5-cm) and 2-in.
(5-cm) round cookie
cutters

Ingredients

**Red currant and pink
champagne sorbet**

¼ cup (1¾ oz./50 g)
sugar

¹⁄₁₀ oz. (2.5 g) stabilizer

7¾ oz. (220 g) red
currant puree

Scant ⅓ cup
(3½ oz./100 g) glucose
syrup

½ cup (125 ml) pink
champagne

Lychee crémeux rings

¾ sheet (1.5 g) gold-
strength gelatin,
200 Bloom

2¼ lb. (1 kg) lychee puree

2 tsp (15 g) honey

Scant ½ cup
(3½ oz./100 g) lightly
beaten egg (2 eggs)

1 tbsp (20 g) egg yolk
(1 yolk)

3 tbsp (1¾ oz./50 g)
butter, diced

Umeboshi jelly cubes

1 sheet (2 g) gold-
strength gelatin,
200 Bloom

Generous ⅓ cup (90 ml)
water

3¼ oz. (90 g) umeboshi
(salted Japanese plums)

1½ tbsp (25 ml) lime juice

¼ teaspoon (1 g) salt

**Almond and hazelnut
shortbread rings**

½ cup (2 oz./55 g) all-
purpose flour

¼ tsp (1 g) *fleur de sel*

5 tsp (14 g) confectioners'
sugar

3½ tsp (7 g) almond
flour

3½ tsp (7 g) hazelnut
flour

2 tbsp (25 g) butter,
diced and chilled

3 tsp (15 g) lightly beaten
egg (about ⅓ egg)

Decoration

¹⁄₁₀ oz. (2.5 g) red
currants

2¼ lb. (1 kg) lychees

Red-veined sorrel leaves

PREPARING THE SORBET

Combine the sugar and stabilizer. In a saucepan, heat the red currant puree and glucose syrup to 104°F (40°C). Stir in the sugar and stabilizer and continue heating to 185°F (85°C). Remove from the heat and process with the immersion blender until smooth. Cover and let mature for at least 4 hours in the refrigerator. Add the champagne and process again. Churn in the ice cream maker and freeze until assembling.

PREPARING THE LYCHEE CRÉMEUX RINGS

Soak the gelatin in a bowl of cold water until softened. Heat the lychee puree and honey in a saucepan. Whisk together the eggs and egg yolk and whisk into the hot puree. Cook, stirring continuously, until the temperature reaches 180°F (82°C) and the custard coats the spatula. Remove from the heat, squeeze the gelatin to remove excess water, and stir it into the custard until dissolved. Let cool to 122°F (50°C), then stir in the butter. Pour the crémeux into the ring molds, if using, and freeze for 3 hours, or spoon it into the pastry bag and let set in the refrigerator.

PREPARING THE UMEBOSHI JELLY CUBES

Soak the gelatin in a bowl of cold water until softened. Bring the water to a boil in a saucepan, remove from the heat, and add the umeboshi. Let soak for 10 minutes until plump, then puree in the food processor. Return to the saucepan, stir in the lime juice and salt, and bring to a boil. Remove from the heat, squeeze the gelatin to remove excess water, and stir it in until dissolved. Place the confectionery frame on the silicone baking mat and pour the jelly into the frame. Chill for 1 hour until set. Remove the frame and cut the jelly into ½-in. (1-cm) cubes.

PREPARING THE ALMOND AND HAZELNUT SHORTBREAD

Mix all the dry ingredients together on the work surface, then rub in the butter with your fingertips until the mixture resembles coarse crumbs. Make a well in the center and add the egg. Mix it in by gathering the dough together and pushing down on it with the heel of your hand, smearing it against a work surface until smooth (*fraisage*). Gather the dough into a ball, cover with plastic wrap, and chill for 1 hour. Preheat the oven to 340°F (170°C/ Gas Mark 3). Roll the dough to a thickness of ⅛ in. (3 mm) and, using the larger cutter, cut out six 2½-in. (6.5-cm) disks. With the smaller cutter, cut out a 2-in. (5-cm) hole from the center of each to make rings. Place on the silicone baking mat and bake for 12 minutes. Let cool completely.

ASSEMBLING THE DESSERT

Wash and dry the red currants. Peel and quarter the lychees, discarding the seeds. Place or pipe out a crémeux ring on each serving plate and top with a shortbread ring. Add three quenelles of sorbet and some lychees. Decorate with the umeboshi jelly cubes, red currants, and sorrel leaves.

MANGO WITH COCONUT RINGS FROM THE LEVANT

Mangue au pays du Levant

Serves 6

Active time
1 hour

Maturing time
12 hours

Freezing time
30 minutes

Cooking time
35 minutes

Storage
Up to 1 day in the refrigerator

Equipment
Immersion blender

Ice cream maker

1½-in. (4-cm), 1¼-in. (3-cm), and 2½-in. (6-cm) round cookie cutters

Ingredients

Mango sorbet

Generous ¼ tsp (1.5 g) gelatin powder

2 tsp (10 ml) plus scant ½ cup (115 ml) water

Scant ½ cup (3¼ oz./90 g) superfine sugar

2½ tsp (12 ml) lemon juice

5¼ oz. (150 g) mango puree

Coconut tapioca rings

Scant 2½ cups (600 ml) coconut milk

Scant 2½ cups (600 ml) water

Scant ½ cup (2 oz./60 g) small pearl tapioca

Generous ¾ cup (200 ml) heavy cream, min. 35% fat

Seeds of 1 vanilla bean

Mango confit

14 oz. (400 g) mangos (see technique p. 56)

3½ tbsp (1½ oz./40 g) superfine sugar

¾ tsp (3 g) pectin NH

Decoration

2 mangos

1½ oz. (40 g) fresh calendula petals

Small pieces of edible gold leaf

PREPARING THE MANGO SORBET (1 DAY AHEAD)

Sprinkle the gelatin over the 2 tsp (10 ml) water in a bowl and let soak for 10 minutes. Heat the scant ½ cup (115 ml) water and sugar in a saucepan until the sugar dissolves. Bring to a boil, remove from the heat, and add the lemon juice and gelatin, stirring until the gelatin dissolves. Let cool. Add the mango puree and process with the immersion blender until smooth. Transfer to a covered container and let mature in the refrigerator for 12 hours. The next day, churn in the ice cream maker. Spread the sorbet evenly over a lined baking sheet into a ½-in. (1-cm) layer and freeze for 30 minutes. Cut out six disks using the 1½-in. (4-cm) cookie cutter and another six using the 1¼-in. (3-cm) cutter. Return to the freezer on the baking sheet until assembling.

PREPARING THE COCONUT TAPIOCA RINGS

Bring the coconut milk and water to a boil in a saucepan. Stir in the tapioca, reduce the heat to low, and simmer for 35 minutes until the tapioca is tender. Strain through a fine-mesh sieve and let cool in the refrigerator. Whip the cream with the vanilla seeds until it starts to thicken, then fold it into the tapioca using a spatula. Place the 1¼-in. (3-cm) cookie cutter in the center of the 2½-in. (6-cm) cutter on a lined second baking sheet and fill the space between the two cutters with the tapioca mixture to make a ring about ¾ in. (2 cm) thick. Carefully remove the cutters, rinse, and dry them. Repeat to make six tapioca rings. Freeze until firm. Transfer to the refrigerator 20 minutes before serving.

PREPARING THE MANGO CONFIT

Peel and cut the mango flesh (see technique p. 56) into 1/16-in. (2-mm) dice (*brunoise*) and warm it with half the sugar in a saucepan. Combine the remaining sugar with the pectin and add to the pan. Heat until the sugar and pectin dissolve, then bring to a boil. Cool and chill in a covered container.

ASSEMBLING THE DESSERT

Cut the mango flesh into 1/16-in. (2-mm) slices and the trimmings into fine dice. Process the mango confit with the immersion blender until smooth and divide it between six serving bowls. Place the larger sorbet disks on top, followed by the coconut tapioca rings. Gently fold the mango slices in half and tuck them around the rings, overlapping them slightly so they resemble the petals of a flower. Place a small sorbet disk in the center of each ring and top with the finely diced mango. Decorate with the calendula petals and a small piece of edible gold leaf. Serve immediately.

COCONUT SQUARES INFUSED WITH LEMONGRASS

Carré tout coco, infusion citronnelle

Serves 16

Active time

2½ hours

Chilling time

6 hours

Freezing time

2 hours

Infusing time

12 hours

Maturing time

12 hours

Cooking time

15 minutes

Storage

Best served immediately but can be stored for up to 2 days

Equipment

16 × 2-in. (5-cm) square stainless steel confectionery frames, ¾ in. (1.8 cm) deep

¾-in. (2-cm) round cookie cutter

Instant-read thermometer

Ice cream maker

Immersion blender

6-in. (16-cm) square confectionery frame

Velvet spray gun (optional)

Ingredients

Coconut whipped cream squares

1 tsp (4 g) gelatin powder

2 tbsp (30 ml) cold water

¾ cup (7 oz./200 g) coconut cream

1 cup (250 ml) heavy cream, min. 35% fat, divided

2 tbsp (25 g) sugar

Seeds of 1 vanilla bean

Coconut and lemongrass gel

½ cup (125 ml) coconut milk

¼ stalk lemongrass, thinly sliced

1 tsp finely chopped fresh ginger

Zest of ¼ lime

2½ tsp (10 g) superfine sugar

Generous ¼ tsp (1.25 g) pectin 325 NH 95

Generous ¼ tsp (1.25 g) cornstarch

1 tsp (5 ml) lime juice

Coconut sorbet squares

¼ cup (2½ oz./75 g) egg yolk (about 4 yolks)

Scant ½ cup (3¼ oz./90 g) superfine sugar

⅒ oz. (2 g) ice cream stabilizer (optional)

1¼ cups (300 ml) coconut milk

⅔ cup (150 ml) heavy cream, minimum 35% fat

Whipped coconut ganache

¼ tsp (0.75 g) gelatin powder

1¼ tsp (5.25 ml) cold water

1 oz. (25 g) white couverture chocolate, 35% cacao (preferably Valrhona Ivoire), chopped

⅒ oz. (2 g) cocoa butter

6 tbsp (90 ml) heavy cream, min. 35% fat, divided

1 oz. (30 g) coconut puree

Coconut shortbread crumbs

3 tbsp (1 oz./30 g) all-purpose flour

1½ tbsp (22 g) butter

3 tbsp (15 g) unsweetened shredded coconut

1 tbsp (10 g) brown sugar

¼ tsp (1 g) baking powder

Finely grated zest of ¼ lime

Scant 1 tsp (5 g) egg yolk (about ¼ yolk)

Coconut sponge

2 tbsp plus 2 tsp (1½ oz./40 g) lightly beaten egg (about 1 egg)

2¾ tsp (15 g) egg yolk (about 1 yolk)

5 tbsp (2 oz./60 g) superfine sugar, divided

⅛ tsp (0.5 g) fine salt

2½ tbsp (15 g) almond flour

⅔ cup (1¾ oz./50 g) unsweetened shredded coconut

1½ tbsp (15 g) all-purpose flour

¼ tsp (1 g) baking powder

2 tbsp (1¼ oz./35 g) butter

2 tbsp (1 oz./30 g) egg white (1 white)

White chocolate velvet spray

3½ oz. (100 g) white couverture chocolate, 35% cacao (preferably Valrhona Ivoire), chopped

2 oz. (60 g) cocoa butter, chopped

Neutral glaze and coconut coating

¾ cup (5 oz./150 g) superfine sugar, divided

1¼ tsp (5 g) pectin NH

⅔ cup (150 ml) water

1¾ tsp (12 g) glucose syrup, 38 DE

½ tsp (2.5 ml) lemon juice

1⅓ cups (3½ oz./100 g) unsweetened shredded coconut, plus extra for decoration

White glaze

1 sheet (2 g) gold-strength gelatin, 200 Bloom

½ tsp (2 g) pectin 325 NH 95

2½ tsp (10 g) superfine sugar

¾ cup (180 ml) whole milk

3½ tbsp (50 ml) heavy cream, min. 35% fat

COCONUT CREAM SQUARES (1 day ahead) Sprinkle the gelatin over the cold water and let soak for 10 minutes. Heat the coconut cream, a scant ⅓ cup (70 ml) of the heavy cream, sugar, and vanilla seeds until the sugar dissolves. Bring to a simmer, remove from the heat, and stir in the gelatin until dissolved. Stir in the remaining cream, press plastic wrap over the surface, and chill for 4 hours. Whip until the mixture holds its shape. Place the 2-in. (5-cm) square frames on a lined baking sheet and spoon in the mixture. Freeze for 1 hour. Using the cookie cutter, cut a ¾-in. (2-cm) hole out of the center of each square, then return to the freezer. When frozen solid, remove the frames. Store in the freezer until serving.

COCONUT AND LEMONGRASS GEL (1 day ahead) Heat the coconut milk with the lemongrass and ginger. Add the lime zest, transfer to a bowl, cover with plastic wrap, and let infuse overnight in the refrigerator. The next day, combine the sugar, pectin, and cornstarch. Strain the infused coconut milk through a fine-mesh sieve, add the lime juice, and heat until warm. Stir in the pectin mixture and bring to a boil, stirring continuously. Pour into a bowl, cover with plastic wrap, and let cool completely in the refrigerator.

SORBET SQUARES (1 day ahead) Whisk together the egg yolks, sugar, and stabilizer, if using, until pale and thick. Heat the coconut milk and cream to 113°F (45°C), whisk a little into the yolks, then pour the mixture into the saucepan. Cook until the custard coats the back of a spoon (180°F/82°C), stirring continuously. Pour into a bowl, press plastic wrap over the surface, and let mature in the refrigerator for 12 hours. The next day, churn in the ice cream maker. Place the 2-in. (5-cm) frames on a lined baking sheet and fill with the sorbet. Freeze for at least 45 minutes until the squares are solid.

COCONUT GANACHE (1 day ahead) Sprinkle the gelatin over the cold water and let soak for 10 minutes. Place the chocolate and cocoa butter in a heat-resistant bowl. Bring 2 tbsp (30 ml) of the cream and the coconut puree to a simmer, remove from the heat, add the gelatin, and stir until dissolved. Pour over the chocolate and cocoa butter, and stir until melted. Add the remaining cream and process with the immersion blender until smooth. Press plastic wrap over the surface and chill for at least 6 hours.

COCONUT SHORTBREAD CRUMBS Preheat the oven to 325°F (160°C/Gas Mark 3). Rub the flour and butter together until it resembles coarse crumbs. Using your hands, mix in the shredded coconut, brown sugar, baking powder, and lime zest, followed by the egg yolk. Place the 6-in. (16-cm) square frame on a lined baking sheet, crumble the mixture into it, and bake for 5 minutes. Let cool in the frame.

COCONUT SPONGE Preheat the oven to 350°F (180°C/Gas Mark 4). Whisk the egg and egg yolk together, then whisk in 3 tbsp (1¼ oz./35 g) of the sugar, salt, almond flour, and shredded coconut, followed by the all-purpose flour and baking powder. Melt the butter and add to the mixture. Whisk the egg white with the remaining sugar until it holds soft peaks, then fold into the batter. Pour over the coconut shortbread in the frame and bake for 10 minutes. Let cool before removing the frame.

WHITE CHOCOLATE SPRAY Melt the chocolate and cocoa butter over a bain-marie, then pour into the spray gun. Take the sorbet squares out of the freezer, remove the frames, and spray them. Alternatively, coat with a store-bought white velvet spray. Return to the freezer until serving.

SHORTBREAD AND SPONGE LAYERS Whisk the coconut ganache, then spread an even layer about ⅛ in. (3 mm) thick over a lined baking sheet. Set the 2-in. (5-cm) square frames on the ganache and place in the freezer for 20 minutes. Spread some of the remaining ganache around the inside of each frame in an even layer using a small palette knife. Cut the shortbread sponge into sixteen 1½-in. (4-cm) squares, about ¾ in. (1.5 cm) thick, and place a square with the shortbread side uppermost on the ganache, in the center of each frame. Cover with the remaining ganache and smooth the surface so it is flush with the tops of the frames. Freeze for about 30 minutes, or until the ganache is solid.

NEUTRAL GLAZE AND COCONUT COATING Combine 2 tbsp of the sugar with the pectin. Heat the water, glucose syrup, and remaining sugar until the sugar dissolves. Stir in the sugar and pectin, and bring to a boil. Let boil for 1 minute, then stir in the lemon juice. Return to a boil, pour into a bowl, press plastic wrap over the surface, and let cool to room temperature. When ready to use, heat the glaze to 140°F (60°C); if using a spray gun, add 25% of its volume in water before heating it. Take the frozen shortbread and sponge layers from the freezer, remove the frames, and place on a wire rack. Pour the neutral glaze over the squares to evenly coat with a thin layer, or use the spray gun. Coat the tops and sides with shredded coconut. Chill until serving.

WHITE GLAZE Soak the gelatin in cold water until softened. Combine the pectin and sugar. Warm the milk and cream, stir in the pectin and sugar until dissolved, and bring to a boil. Remove from the heat. Squeeze the gelatin to remove excess water, add to the hot mixture, and process with the immersion blender until smooth.

ASSEMBLING THE SQUARES Heat the white glaze to 122°F (50°C). Remove the coconut cream squares from the freezer, place on a wire rack, and pour over the glaze to evenly coat with a thin layer, or use the spray gun. Chill for 30 minutes to allow the centers to thaw. Just before serving, sprinkle a little shredded coconut over each serving plate. Place a shortbread and sponge square on each plate, then a coconut sorbet square on top, at a 45° angle. Place a coconut cream square on top, at a 45° angle, and fill the centers with the coconut and lemongrass gel. Serve immediately.

DRAGON FRUIT GÂTEAU

Gâteau pitaya

Serves 6

Active time
2 hours

Infusing time
16 minutes

Freezing time
3 hours

Cooking time
10 minutes

Chilling time
4 hours

Storage
Up to 2 days
in the refrigerator

Equipment
Instant-read thermometer

6-in. (16-cm) tart ring,
(4.5 cm) deep

Food-safe acetate strip,
(4.5 cm) wide

Juicer

Immersion blender

5½-in. (14-cm) tart ring

Ingredients

Swiss meringue
(see Chefs' Notes)

Scant ¼ cup
(1¾ oz./50 g) egg white
(about 1⅔ whites)

½ cup (3½ oz./100 g)
superfine sugar

**Tea jelly and dragon
fruit layer**

2 sheets (4 g) gold-
strength gelatin,
200 Bloom

½ cup (125 ml) water

1 tsp (2 g) loose-leaf
white tea

Scant ¾ tsp (5 g) honey

1 red dragon fruit

1 white dragon fruit

Dragon fruit mousse

2½ sheets (5 g)
gold-strength gelatin,
200 Bloom

⅔ cup (165 ml) red
dragon fruit juice

1½ oz. (40 g) Swiss
meringue (see left)

Generous ½ cup
(130 ml) heavy cream,
min. 35% fat

White tea crémeux

Scant ½ cup (110 ml)
heavy cream, min.
35% fat

5 tsp (10 g) loose-leaf
white tea

1 sheet (2 g) gold-
strength gelatin,
200 Bloom

1 tbsp plus 2 tsp
(1 oz./30 g) egg yolk
(about 1½ yolks)

3½ tbsp (1¾ oz./50 g)
lightly beaten egg (1 egg)

2½ tbsp (1 oz./30 g)
superfine sugar

3 tbsp (1½ oz./45 g)
butter

Joconde sponge

⅓ cup (1¾ oz./50 g)
confectioners' sugar

½ cup (1¾ oz./50 g)
almond flour

½ cup (4 oz./120 g)
lightly beaten egg
(about 2½ eggs)

¼ cup (2 oz./55 g) egg
white (about 2 whites)

2½ tsp (10 g) superfine
sugar

⅔ oz. (20 g) red dragon
fruit seeds and pulp
leftover from juicing

1 tbsp (20 g) butter,
melted and cooled

3 tbsp (1 oz./30 g)
all-purpose flour, sifted

Decoration

3½ oz. (100 g) peeled
fresh dragon fruit,
cut into small dice

PREPARING THE SWISS MERINGUE

Place the egg white in a bowl over a bain-marie, add the sugar, and whisking continuously to prevent the egg white cooking, heat until the temperature reaches 113°F–122°F (45°C–50°C). Remove the bowl to the work surface and continue whisking on high speed until the meringue holds firm peaks.

PREPARING THE TEA JELLY AND DRAGON FRUIT LAYER

Soak the gelatin in a bowl of cold water until softened. Line the 6-in. (16-cm) tart ring with the acetate strip and place on a lined baking sheet. Freeze until assembling.

In a saucepan, heat the water until the temperature reaches 185°F (85°C), remove from the heat, add the white tea, and let infuse for 6 minutes. Strain through a fine-mesh sieve and return to the saucepan. Add the honey and reheat. Squeeze the gelatin to remove excess water and stir it in until dissolved. Cool to 68°F (20°C). Peel the dragon fruits, cut them into slices about ½ in. (1 cm) thick, and cut the slices into random geometric shapes (such as rectangles or triangles). When the jelly cools to 68°F (20°C), pour a very thin layer into the tart ring. Let set, then arrange the dragon fruit slices attractively over the jelly, filling any spaces with jelly. This layer should be no more than ½ in. (1 cm) thick. Let set in the refrigerator before assembling. Pass the dragon fruit trimmings through the juicer to obtain the ⅔ cup (165 ml) juice for preparing the mousse. Reserve ⅔ oz. (20 g) of the seeds and pulp for the sponge.

PREPARING THE DRAGON FRUIT MOUSSE

Soak the gelatin in a bowl of cold water until softened. Heat 3½ tbsp (50 ml) of the dragon fruit juice, squeeze the gelatin to remove excess water, and stir it in until dissolved. Stir in the remaining juice, then fold in the meringue. Let the mixture cool to 68°F (20°C). Whip the cream until it holds its shape and fold in. Chill until assembling.

PREPARING THE CRÉMEUX LAYER

Heat the cream in a saucepan, remove from the heat, and stir in the white tea. Let infuse for 10 minutes. Soak the gelatin in a bowl of cold water until softened. Strain the cream through a fine-mesh sieve, adding a little more cream if necessary so you still have a scant ½ cup (110 ml). Whisk the egg yolks, egg, and sugar together until pale and thick. Bring the cream to a boil, whisk a little into the yolk mixture, and return to the saucepan. Cook, stirring continuously with a spatula, until the custard coats the spatula and the temperature reaches 180°F

(82°C). Squeeze the gelatin to remove excess water and stir it into the hot custard until dissolved. Let cool to 104°F (40°C). Add the butter and process with the immersion blender until smooth. Place the 5½-in. (14-cm) tart ring on a lined baking sheet. Weigh out 5¼ oz. (150 g) of the crémeux and pour it into the ring. Freeze for 2 hours before assembling.

PREPARING THE JOCONDE SPONGE

Preheat the oven to 350°F (180°C/Gas Mark 4). Whisk together the confectioners' sugar, almond flour, and lightly beaten eggs on medium speed until thick and creamy. In a separate bowl, whisk the egg whites with the sugar until holding firm peaks. Gently fold the whites into the batter, followed by the dragon fruit seeds and pulp, melted butter, and sifted flour. Spread across a lined baking sheet and bake for 8–10 minutes. Let cool.

ASSEMBLING THE GÂTEAU

Cut out a 5½-in. (14-cm) disk of sponge and a strip of sponge 1⅓ in. (3.5 cm) wide and the length of the circumference of the 6-in. (16-cm) tart ring. Line the sides of the ring containing the tea jelly and dragon fruit with the sponge strip, add half the mousse, and spread it into an even layer. Remove the ring from the crémeux and set it over the mousse. Cover the crémeux with the remaining mousse and scatter with the diced dragon fruit. Finish with the sponge disk. Chill the gâteau for at least 2 hours in the refrigerator until set, then invert it onto a serving plate and remove the ring.

CHEFS' NOTES

• It is difficult to prepare a smaller quantity of Swiss meringue so use what is leftover to make meringue kisses to serve with coffee. Pipe out small mounds onto a lined baking sheet and bake for 2 hours in a 160°F (70°C/ Gas on lowest setting) oven.

• This gâteau pairs well with white tea from the Columbian Andes.

CHOCOLATE AND PRICKLY PEAR BONBONS

Bonbons chocolat figue de barbarie

Makes 56

Active time
1½ hours

Setting time
40 minutes

Storage
Up to 1 week
in an airtight container

Equipment
Instant-read thermometer

2 silicone half-sphere
molds, 1¼ in. (3 cm) in dia.

Pastry bag

Scraper

Juicer

Piston funnel

2 food-safe acetate
sheets

Ingredients

Chocolate shells

1¾ oz. (50 g) green-
colored cocoa butter

1 lb. 2 oz. (500 g) dark
couverture chocolate,
66% cacao, chopped

Prickly pear filling

10½ oz. (300 g) prickly
pears (Barbary figs)

Scant 1 cup (6 oz./175 g)
superfine sugar

Scant ½ cup (100 ml)
tequila

PREPARING THE CHOCOLATE SHELLS

In a saucepan over low heat, melt the cocoa butter until the temperature reaches 86°F (30°C). Using a small paintbrush, paint the cocoa butter into attractive designs over the inside of the molds. Let set while you temper the chocolate (see p. 140). Transfer the chocolate to the pastry bag and pipe it into the molds filling them completely. Invert the molds to allow excess chocolate to drain out, saving the excess for sealing the bonbons. Using the scraper, scrape the tops of the molds so the edges are clean. Stand the molds upright and let the chocolate set for at least 20 minutes at room temperature.

PREPARING THE PRICKLY PEAR FILLING

Wearing thick gloves to protect your hands from thorns, peel the prickly pears and pass them through the juicer. Measure out 4 tsp (20 ml) of the juice and set aside. Measure out ⅓ cup (80 ml) of the juice and place in a saucepan with the sugar. Heat until the sugar dissolves and the temperature of the syrup reaches 265°F (130°C). Remove from the heat, add the tequila and the 4 tsp (20 ml) juice to stop the cooking. Carefully pour the syrup back and forth between two bowls to cool it down. Let cool to about 68°F (20°C) before using.

ASSEMBLING THE BONBONS

Transfer the prickly pear filling (at 68°F (20°C) to the piston funnel and fill the chocolate shells two-thirds full. Re-temper the chocolate leftover from making the shells, if necessary. Using an offset spatula, divide the chocolate between the acetate sheets, spreading it in a thin layer. Invert the sheets over the chocolate molds to seal the bonbons, running the scraper over the acetate sheets to smooth out the chocolate. Let set for about 20 minutes before removing the sheets and carefully turning the molds upside down to remove the bonbons.

TEA-POACHED TAMARILLOS WITH MATCHA CREAM

Tamarillo poché au thé et crème matcha

Serves 4

Active time
15 minutes

Chilling time
At least 3 hours

Infusing time
5 minutes

Cooking time
12–15 minutes

Storage
Up to 2 days
in the refrigerator

Equipment
Immersion blender
Food-safe cheesecloth

Ingredients

Matcha whipped cream

⅔ sheet (1.25 g) gold-strength gelatin, 200 Bloom

½ cup (120 ml) heavy cream, min. 35% fat, divided

1 cup (7 oz./200 g) sugar

¾ tsp (1.5 g) matcha powder

2 tbsp (1 oz./30 g) mascarpone

Tea-poached tamarillos

4 cups (1 L) water

1 cup (7 oz./200 g) superfine sugar

⅔ oz. (20 g) fresh ginger, preferably organic

½ oz. (12 g) kaffir lime leaves

2 vanilla beans

1 star anise pod

4 black tea bags

4 tamarillos (tree tomatoes)

Decoration

Matcha powder for dusting

PREPARING THE MATCHA WHIPPED CREAM

Soak the gelatin in a bowl of cold water until softened. In a saucepan, heat ¼ cup (60 ml) of the cream with the sugar and matcha powder until the sugar dissolves. Bring to a boil and remove from the heat. Squeeze the gelatin to remove excess water and stir it into the hot cream mixture until dissolved. Pour over the mascarpone in a bowl and process with the immersion blender until smooth. Add the remaining cream and process again until smooth. Chill for at least 3 hours. Whip the matcha cream until it holds its shape and chill until serving.

PREPARING THE TEA-POACHED TAMARILLOS

Combine all the ingredients except the tea bags and tamarillos in a saucepan. Heat until the sugar dissolves, then bring to a boil. Remove from the heat, add the tea bags, and let infuse for 5 minutes. Strain through a fine-mesh sieve, return to the saucepan, and set over low heat. Wash the tamarillos and score a cross on the base of each. Place in the tea-infused syrup and poach over low heat for 12–15 minutes. Remove from the heat, drain the tamarillos, and carefully peel them, leaving the stems on. Strain the syrup through cheesecloth into a bowl. Chill the fruit and syrup separately until serving.

ASSEMBLING THE DESSERT

Place a little matcha whipped cream in the bottom of each serving dish. Using a small fine-mesh sieve, dust a little matcha powder over one half of each dish and carefully place a tamarillo in the center. Drizzle with a little of the poaching syrup.

SRI LANKAN HONEYMOON WITH MANGOSTEEN

Mangoustan, lune de miel au Sri Lanka

Serves 6

Active time

1½ hours

Maturing and marinating time

12 hours

Infusing time

25 minutes

Chilling time

12 hours

Cooking time

1 hour

Storage

Up to 2 days
before assembling

Equipment

Immersion blender

Ice cream maker

Instant-read
thermometer

4-in. (10-cm) square
confectionery frame

Mini baba mold with ¾-
in. (2-cm) dia. cavities

1¼-in. (3-cm) round
cookie cutter

2 aerated silicone baking
mats

Food processor

Pastry bag

Stencil with a ginko (or
another) leaf design

Ingredients

Mangosteen sorbet

11½ sheets (23 g)
gold-strength gelatin,
200 Bloom

Scant 1 cup (230 ml)
water

Scant 1 cup (6 oz./175 g)
superfine sugar

1½ tbsp (25 ml) lemon
juice

1¼ cups (300 ml)
mangosteen juice

Coconut sorbet

½ cup (125 ml) coconut
milk

⅔ oz. (20 g) invert sugar

5 tsp (20 g) superfine
sugar

1¼ tsp (4 g) dextrose
powder

1 pinch (2 g) super
neutrose

9 oz. (250 g) coconut
puree

**Marinated
mangosteens**

⅔ cup (150 ml) water

⅔ cup (4½ oz./130 g)
superfine sugar

Seeds of 1 vanilla bean

14 oz. (400 g) fresh
mangosteens

Black tea jelly

3½ sheets (7 g)
gold-strength gelatin,
200 Bloom

2 tbsp (10 g) loose-leaf
black tea

Scant ½ cup (100 ml)
hot water (about
176°F/80°C)

Scant ½ tsp (1.5 g) agar-
agar powder

1 tsp (4 g) superfine
sugar

Vanilla crémeux

1½ cups (375 ml) heavy
cream, min. 35% fat

Seeds of ½ vanilla bean

¼ cup (20 g) loose-leaf
black tea

21 sheets (1½ oz./42 g)
gold-strength gelatin,
200 Bloom

⅓ cup (3 oz./90 g) egg
yolk (about 4½ yolks)

⅓ cup (2¾ oz./75 g)
superfine sugar

Mangosteen fruit jellies

Generous ¾ cup
(205 ml) mangosteen
juice

Scant 1 cup (6 oz./175 g)
superfine sugar

Scant 1 tsp (3.5 g) yellow
pectin

1 generous tbsp (25 g)
glucose syrup

¾ tsp (4 ml) lemon juice

**Black tea and mace
shortbread**

2 tbsp (1 oz./30 g) butter

2½ tbsp (20 g)
confectioners' sugar

¼ tsp (1 g) salt

2 tsp (10 g) lightly beaten
egg (about ⅕ egg)

5 tsp (10 g) almond flour

½ cup minus 1 tbsp
(1¾ oz./50 g) all-purpose
flour

2 tsp (5 g) ground
mace

1 tsp loose-leaf black
tea

Cashew praline paste

1½ cups (5¾ oz./165 g)
cashews

1 cup plus 1 tbsp
(4 oz./115 g) sugar

Vanilla powder

2 dried vanilla beans

Decoration

Cashews

Red-veined sorrel leaves

Nutmeg (mace) flowers

PREPARING THE MANGOSTEEN SORBET (1 DAY AHEAD)

Soak the gelatin in a bowl of cold water until softened. Heat the water and sugar in a saucepan until the sugar dissolves. Bring to a boil, remove from the heat, and stir in the lemon juice. Squeeze the gelatin to remove excess water and stir it in until dissolved. Cool in the refrigerator. Add the mangosteen juice and process with the immersion blender until smooth. Let mature in a covered container for 12 hours in the refrigerator. The next day, churn in the ice cream maker and freeze in an airtight container until assembling.

PREPARING THE COCONUT SORBET (1 DAY AHEAD)

Heat the coconut milk and invert sugar in a saucepan. Meanwhile, combine the sugar, dextrose powder, and super neutrose in a bowl. When the temperature of the coconut milk reaches 104°F (40°C), stir in the sugar mixture until dissolved. Bring to a boil, then stir in the coconut puree. Let mature in a covered container for 12 hours in the refrigerator. The next day, churn in the ice cream maker and freeze in an airtight container until assembling.

PREPARING THE MARINATED MANGOSTEENS (1 DAY AHEAD)

Heat the water, sugar, and vanilla seeds in a saucepan until the sugar dissolves. Bring to a boil, remove from the heat, and let cool completely. Cut open the mangosteens, carefully remove the pulp, and immerse it in the cooled syrup. Cover and marinate in the refrigerator for about 12 hours.

PREPARING THE BLACK TEA JELLY

Soak the gelatin in a bowl of cold water until softened. Stir the tea leaves into the hot water and let infuse for 10 minutes. Strain through a fine-mesh sieve into a saucepan and begin heating. Combine the agar-agar and sugar in a bowl and stir into the hot tea until dissolved. Bring to a boil, then remove from the heat. Squeeze the gelatin to remove excess water and stir it into the hot tea until dissolved. Place the confectionery frame on a lined baking sheet, pour the jelly into it, and chill for at least 3 hours until set. Remove the frame and cut the jelly into ½ in. (1-cm) cubes.

PREPARING THE VANILLA TEA CRÉMEUX

Heat the cream in a saucepan with the vanilla seeds and tea. Remove from the heat, cover, and let infuse for 15 minutes. Meanwhile, soak the gelatin in a bowl of cold water until softened. Strain the cream through a fine-mesh sieve, return it to the saucepan, and bring to a boil. Meanwhile, whisk the egg yolks and sugar in a bowl until thick and creamy. When the cream comes to a boil, whisk a little into the yolk mixture, return to the saucepan, and cook, stirring continuously until the temperature reaches 185°F (85°C). Remove from the heat, squeeze the gelatin to remove excess water, and stir it into the hot custard until dissolved. Transfer to a bowl, press plastic wrap over the surface, and chill for at least 1 hour before assembling.

PREPARING THE MANGOSTEEN FRUIT JELLIES

Heat the mangosteen juice with half the sugar in a saucepan until the sugar dissolves. Combine the remaining sugar in a bowl with the pectin and stir into the juice. Bring to a boil, stir in the glucose syrup, and heat to 221.9°F (105.5°C). Remove from the heat, stir in the lemon juice, and immediately pour into the mini baba molds. Let set for about 30 minutes in the refrigerator or until the jellies are easy to unmold.

PREPARING THE SHORTBREAD

Preheat the oven to 340°F (170°C/Gas Mark 3). Mix the butter and confectioners' sugar together until evenly combined. Add the salt and mix in the egg. Add the almond flour, all-purpose flour, and mace and mix to make a dough. Shape it into a ball, flatten a little, and cover with plastic wrap. Chill for 30 minutes. Roll the dough to a thickness of ¾ in. (1.5 cm) on a lightly floured surface and, using the cookie cutter, cut out eighteen 1¼-in. (3-cm) rounds. Lightly sprinkle the rounds with the tea leaves, place on a silicone baking mat, and cover with the second mat. Bake for 7 minutes, remove the top mat, and let cool.

PREPARING THE CASHEW PRALINE PASTE

Preheat the oven to 285°F (140°C/Gas Mark 1). Spread the cashews across a lined baking sheet and roast them in the oven for 30 minutes. Heat the sugar in a heavy saucepan, without adding any water, until it melts and cooks to a rich brown caramel. Pour over the roasted cashews on the baking sheet and let cool completely. Break the nut brittle into pieces and place in the bowl of the food processor. Process to a smooth paste (see technique p. 116). Spoon into the pastry bag.

PREPARING THE VANILLA POWDER

Grind the vanilla beans to a powder in a food processor.

ASSEMBLING THE DESSERT

Place the leaf stencil on a serving plate and dust with the vanilla powder. Repeat with the remaining plates. Arrange the different elements of the dessert attractively on each plate, adding a few cashews and piping out dots of the cashew paste. Add a quenelle of mangosteen sorbet and two small quenelles of coconut sorbet to each serving. Decorate with red-veined sorrel leaves and nutmeg flowers and serve immediately.

MINI ROLLED GUAVA CAKES

Petits gâteaux roulés à la goyave

Makes 6

Active time

1 hour

Cooking time

1½ hours

Freezing time

2 hours

Infusing time

10 minutes

Chilling time

1¾ hours

Setting time

15 minutes

Storage

Up to 2 days
in the refrigerator

Equipment

Silicone half-sphere mold,
1½ in. (3.5 cm) in dia.,
⅔ in. (1.75 cm) deep

Stand mixer + whisk

Instant-read thermometer

Pastry bag

Silikomart Goutte 55
(water drop-shaped)
silicone mold, 2¼ in.
(5.4 cm) in dia., 1½ in.
(4.1 cm) deep

2 silicone baking mats

2-in. (5-cm) round cookie
cutter

2 food-safe acetate sheets

Immersion blender

Ingredients

Guava inserts

3½ oz. (100 g) fresh guava

2½ tbsp (1 oz./30 g)
superfine sugar, divided

3½ oz. (100 g) guava
puree

½ tsp (2 g) pectin NH

**Tea-infused guava
Bavarian cream**

1 tsp (5 g) gelatin powder

2 tbsp (30 ml) cold water

8 oz. (225 g) guava puree

Generous 1 tbsp (15 g)
superfine sugar

1¾ oz. (50 g) loose-leaf
black tea

⅔ cup (155 ml) heavy
cream, min. 35% fat

3 tbsp plus 1 tsp
(1½ oz./45 g) egg white
(about 1½ whites)

Generous 2 tbsp
(1½ oz./45 g) glucose
syrup

¾ oz. (22 g) invert sugar

Joconde sponge

1 cup (4¾ oz./135 g)
confectioners' sugar

Scant 1½ cups
(4¾ oz./135 g) almond
flour

¾ cup (6¼ oz./180 g)
lightly beaten egg (about
3½ eggs)

¼ cup (1¼ oz./35 g)
all-purpose flour

½ cup (4 oz./120 g) egg
white (4 whites)

1½ tbsp (18 g) superfine
sugar

2 tbsp (28 g) butter,
melted and cooled

Mango confit

3½ oz. (100 g) pitted
fresh mango

3½ oz. (100 g) mango
puree

2 tbsp (1 oz./25 g)
superfine sugar, divided

½ tsp (2 g) pectin NH

**Toasted hazelnut
sweet shortcrust pastry**

½ cup plus 1 tbsp (2½ oz./
70 g) all-purpose flour

5½ tsp (15 g)
confectioners' sugar

Generous 1 tbsp (15 g)
superfine sugar

3 tbsp (15 g) ground
toasted hazelnuts

3 tbsp (2½ oz./45 g)
butter, diced

2½ tsp (12 g) lightly
beaten egg (about ¼ egg)

Chocolate disks

3½ oz. (100 g) ivory white
couverture chocolate

Guava glaze

1 lb. 2 oz. (500 g) guava
puree

Scant ⅓ cup (2 oz./60 g)
superfine sugar

2½ tsp (10 g) pectin
325 NH 95

Scant ⅓ cup
(3½ oz./100 g) glucose
syrup

2 sheets edible gold
leaf

Pink coating

7 oz. (200 g) cocoa
butter, chopped

7 oz. (200 g) white
chocolate, chopped

1 small pinch red food
coloring

Decoration

1 tsp kasha (toasted
buckwheat groats)

PREPARING THE GUAVA INSERTS

Peel the guava, cut it into small pieces, and place in a heat-resistant bowl. Stir in 1¼ tsp (5 g) of the sugar, cover the bowl with plastic wrap, and let cook over a bain-marie for 1 hour. Strain through a fine-mesh sieve into a saucepan and stir in the guava puree and 1 generous tbsp (15 g) of the sugar. Combine the remaining sugar with the pectin in a bowl. Heat the guava mixture until the sugar dissolves, stir in the pectin and sugar, and bring to a boil. Pour into 6 cavities in the half-sphere mold and freeze for at least 1 hour.

PREPARING THE TEA-INFUSED GUAVA BAVARIAN CREAM

Sprinkle the gelatin over the cold water in a bowl and let soak for 10 minutes. Heat the guava puree and superfine sugar in a saucepan until the sugar dissolves. Bring to a boil, stir in the gelatin until dissolved, then chill. Stir the tea into the cream and let infuse for 10 minutes. Strain through a fine-mesh sieve, then whip to soft peaks. Whisk the egg whites in the stand mixer until holding soft peaks. Meanwhile, heat the glucose syrup and invert sugar in a saucepan until the temperature reaches 250°F (120°C). With the mixer running, slowly pour the hot syrup over the whites and whisk continuously until you have a firm meringue. When the temperature of the meringue has cooled to 104°F (40°C), fold in the guava puree, followed by the tea-infused cream, making sure all three mixtures are about the same temperature. Transfer to a pastry bag and pipe a little into 6 cavities of the water drop-shaped mold, making sure there are no air bubbles at the tip. Place a guava insert in the center of each drop, flat side uppermost, and cover with Bavarian cream, smoothing it over with an offset spatula. Freeze for at least 1 hour to make unmolding easier.

PREPARING THE JOCONDE SPONGE

Preheat the oven to 410°F (210°C/Gas Mark 6). Whisk the confectioners' sugar, almond flour, eggs, and sifted all-purpose flour until thick and creamy. In a separate bowl, whisk the egg whites with the superfine sugar until holding firm peaks. Using a flexible spatula, gently fold the whites into the batter, followed by the melted butter. Spread the batter across a silicone baking mat to a thickness of ¼ in (5 mm) and bake for 10 minutes.

PREPARING THE MANGO CONFIT

Peel and cut the mango (see technique p. 56) into 1/16-in. (2-mm) dice (*brunoise*). Heat in a saucepan with the mango puree and 1 generous tablespoon (15 g) of the sugar until the sugar dissolves.

Combine the remaining sugar with the pectin in a bowl and stir in until dissolved. Bring to a boil, transfer to a bowl, and chill until assembling.

PREPARING THE TOASTED HAZELNUT PASTRY

Combine the flour, confectioners' sugar, superfine sugar, and ground hazelnuts and work in the butter with your fingertips until the mixture resembles coarse crumbs. Add the egg and mix in by gathering the dough together, pushing down on it with the heel of your hand, and smearing it against the work surface until smooth (*fraisage*). Gather into a ball, cover with plastic wrap, and chill for about 20 minutes. Preheat the oven to 340°F (170°C/Gas Mark 3). Roll the dough on a lightly floured surface to a thickness of 1/16 in. (2 mm) and, using the cookie cutter, cut out six 2-in. (5-cm) disks. Place on a silicone baking mat and cover with the second mat. Bake for 6 minutes. Remove the top mat and let cool.

PREPARING THE CHOCOLATE DISKS

Temper the white chocolate (see p. 131) and spread it into a thin layer between the two acetate sheets. Let set slightly (about 5 minutes), then carefully peel off the top sheet. Cut out six white chocolate disks using the cookie cutter and chill for 15 minutes until set.

PREPARING THE GUAVA GLAZE

Heat the guava puree, sugar, pectin, and glucose syrup in a saucepan until the sugar and pectin dissolve. Bring to a boil, remove from the heat, add the gold leaf, and process briefly with the immersion blender, taking care not to create air bubbles. Let cool to 95°F (35°C), unmold the Bavarian creams, place on a rack, and pour the glaze over them to coat.

PREPARING THE PINK COATING

Melt the cocoa butter and chocolate together in a bowl over a bain-marie. Stir in the food coloring until evenly tinted. Let cool to 86°F (30°C) before using.

ASSEMBLING THE CAKES

Spread the mango confit over the sponge and starting at one short side, roll it up tightly. Cut the roll into 1¼-in. (3-cm) slices and dip them into the pink coating, leaving a ¼-in. (5-mm) strip uncoated at the top. Press the kasha over the coating and place the rolls on the pastry bases coated side down. Top with the chocolate disks and place a Bavarian cream on each disk.

RAMBUTAN MOCHI

Mochi au ramboutan

Makes 6

Active time
1½ hours

Maturing time
12 hours

Cooking time
30 minutes

Storage
Up to 3 months
in the freezer

Equipment
Immersion blender
Ice cream maker
Cookie dough scoop
Steamer

Ingredients

Rambutan sorbet
1 sheet (2 g) gold-
strength gelatin,
200 Bloom
Scant ⅔ cup (140 ml)
water
Scant ½ cup (3 oz./85 g)
sugar
10½ oz. (300 g)
rambutans

Toasted rice flour
Scant 1 cup
(3½ oz./100 g) glutinous
rice flour

Mochi dough
Scant ½ cup (2 oz./55 g)
glutinous rice flour
1½ tbsp (15 g) cornstarch
2½ tbsp (20 g)
confectioners' sugar
Generous ⅓ cup (90 ml)
whole milk
1 tbsp (15 g) butter, at
room temperature

Decoration
1 tsp freeze-dried
raspberry powder (optional)

PREPARING THE RAMBUTAN SORBET (1 DAY AHEAD)
Soak the gelatin in a bowl of cold water until softened. Heat the water and sugar in a saucepan until the sugar dissolves. Bring to a boil and remove from the heat. Peel and remove the seeds from sufficient rambutans to give 5¾ oz. (160 g) of fruit (reserve the remainder). Place the fruit in a bowl, pour the syrup over it, and reduce to a puree with the immersion blender. Transfer to an airtight container and let mature for 12 hours in the refrigerator. The next day, process again with the immersion blender until smooth, then churn in the ice cream maker. Peel the remaining rambutans and remove the seeds to give 1 oz. (25 g) of fruit. Cut the fruit into ½-in. (1-cm) dice and mix into the sorbet. Scoop out six balls of sorbet, place on a lined baking sheet, and freeze until very firm before assembling.

PREPARING THE TOASTED RICE FLOUR
Preheat the oven to 325°F (160°C/Gas Mark 3). Spread the rice flour across a lined baking sheet and toast in the oven for 10 minutes. Let cool.

PREPARING THE MOCHI DOUGH
Place the rice flour, cornstarch, confectioners' sugar, and milk in a bowl. Knead until the mixture comes together in a smooth dough. Shape into a ball and steam for 30 minutes. While the dough is still warm, work in the butter with your hands. Cover with a damp towel and use quickly before it dries out.

ASSEMBLING THE MOCHI
Divide the dough into six pieces, each weighing about 1 oz. (25 g), and shape into balls. Dust a work surface with the toasted rice flour. Roll out the mochi balls over the rice flour into thick, flat disks, approximately 4 in. (10 cm) in diameter. Place a scoop of sorbet in the center of each and, using your fingers, stretch the dough up and around the sorbet to enclose it completely. Pinch the edges together to seal well and trim off any excess with kitchen scissors. You can serve the mochi right away or freeze them in an airtight container. To serve, arrange the mochi on a serving plate, seam-side down, and dust with freeze-dried raspberry powder, if desired.

CHEFS' NOTES

You can prepare the recipe using any flavor of ice cream or sorbet. To prevent the ice cream from melting too quickly, be sure to scoop out the balls in advance and freeze them until quite firm before assembling the mochi.

CAPE GOOSEBERRY SALSA VERDE WITH YELLOWTAIL GRAVLAX

Salsa verde aux physalis, gravlax de yellowtail

Serves 4

Active time

1½ hours

Chilling time

Overnight + 1½ hours

Curing time

2 hours

Cooking time

About 45 minutes

Infusing time

1 hour

Storage

Up to 1 day in the refrigerator before assembling

Equipment

Food processor

Food-safe cheesecloth

Pipette

Food-safe ultra-fine-mesh cheesecloth

Pastry bag

Conical cheesecloth sieve

Kitchen torch

Ingredients

Shiso wasabi pearls

Generous ¾ cup (200 ml) grape-seed oil

½ sheet (1 g) gold-strength gelatin, 200 Bloom

⅕ oz. (5 g) green shiso leaves

2½ tbsp (40 ml) coconut milk

1 tsp (5 ml) yuzu juice

2 tsp (10 ml) sake

1 tsp (5 g) wasabi

1 tsp (5 ml) water

¾ tsp (3 g) superfine sugar

¼ tsp (0.5 g) agar-agar powder

Small pinch (0.02 g) xanthan gum

Yellowtail gravlax

1¼ cups (10½ oz./300 g) kosher salt

¾ cup (5 oz./150 g) superfine sugar

Zest of 1 lime

7¾ oz. (220 g) trimmed yellowtail fillet

4 tsp (20 ml) mirin

1 tsp (5 ml) soy sauce

Spiced cucumber jus

9 oz. (250 g) cucumber

1 oz. (30 g) shallot

¼ cup (1¾ oz./50 g) superfine sugar

½ cup (125 ml) unseasoned rice vinegar

¼ bunch dill, chopped

¼ bunch chervil, chopped

1 tbsp coriander seeds

1 tbsp mustard seeds

1 tsp white peppercorns

1 clove

1 bay leaf

1 sprig thyme

1 tbsp (15 ml) nuoc mam

A few drops lime juice and a little finely grated zest

1 small pinch xanthan gum

3 drops toasted sesame oil

1 tsp dill oil

Cape gooseberry salsa verde

5 oz. (150 g) cape gooseberries

1½ oz. (40 g) white onion

1 tsp (5 g) eucalyptus honey

4 tsp (20 ml) unseasoned rice vinegar

1 drop Tabasco

Tangy vinaigrette

5 oz. (150 g) cape gooseberries

1½ oz. (45 g) white onion

1 tbsp (15 ml) olive oil

1 tsp (3 g) crushed garlic

1¾ tsp (8 ml) unseasoned rice vinegar

Generous ½ tsp (4 g) eucalyptus honey

Decoration

1 tsp chopped cilantro

1 tsp thinly sliced scallion

Baby cress leaves

PREPARING THE SHISO WASABI PEARLS (1 DAY AHEAD)

Pour the grape-seed oil into a tall, narrow container and chill overnight. The next day, soak the gelatin in a bowl of cold water until softened. Wash and coarsely chop the shiso leaves. Pulse the coconut milk, yuzu juice, sake, and wasabi in the food processor. Add the shiso leaves and process to a puree. In a saucepan, heat the water, sugar, agar-agar, and xanthan gum until the sugar dissolves. Bring to a boil, then remove from the heat. Squeeze the gelatin to remove excess water and stir it into the hot syrup until dissolved. Add to the food processor and process until smooth. Strain through cheesecloth and transfer to the pipette. Let cool to room temperature, then release drop by drop into the cold oil to form pearls. Rinse the pearls gently under cold water to remove the oil. Spread them across a lined baking sheet, letting them touch as little as possible, and freeze.

PREPARING THE YELLOWTAIL GRAVLAX

Combine the salt, sugar, and lime zest in a bowl and spread half across a lined baking sheet. Place the yellowtail fillet on top and cover with the remaining salt mixture. Let cure in the refrigerator for 2 hours. Rinse the salt mixture off the fish and pat it dry with paper towel. Make a marinade by stirring the mirin and soy sauce together and brushing some over the fish. Chill the fish and the remaining marinade separately until serving.

PREPARING THE SPICED CUCUMBER JUS

Process the unpeeled cucumber to a puree. Strain through the ultra-fine-mesh cheesecloth into a bowl, pressing down on the pulp to extract as much liquid as possible. Set the liquid aside, scoop the pulp into the pastry bag, and chill until using. Chop the shallot and cook in a skillet with the sugar and rice vinegar for 5 minutes, until softened. Add the dill and chervil and cover. In a separate, dry skillet, toast the coriander and mustard seeds, peppercorns, and clove until fragrant. Add to the shallot mixture with the bay leaf and thyme and remove from the heat. Cover and let infuse for 1 hour. Stir the cucumber liquid into the spiced shallot mixture and strain through the conical cheesecloth sieve into a bowl. Stir in the nuoc mam, lime juice, and zest. Add the xanthan gum to thicken the sauce. Add the sesame and dill oils and stir to blend without emulsifying the mixture. Chill until serving.

PREPARING THE CAPE GOOSEBERRY SALSA VERDE

Remove their papery husks and cut the cape gooseberries in half. Finely chop the onion. Warm the honey and rice vinegar in a saucepan until the honey liquefies, then add the onion and cape gooseberries. Cut a circle of parchment paper the same diameter as the saucepan with a small hole cut in the center. Press directly over the mixture in the saucepan and simmer until the mixture is thick and has the consistency of jam. Season with Tabasco and salt to taste, then chill until serving.

PREPARING THE TANGY VINAIGRETTE

Remove their papery husks and cut the cape gooseberries in half. Finely chop the onion and sauté in the olive oil until softened and lightly browned. Reduce the heat to low, add the cape gooseberries and garlic, cover, and cook for 10 minutes, until softened. Transfer to the food processor and process until smooth, then add the rice vinegar and honey. Season with salt and pepper, strain through cheesecloth, and chill until serving.

ASSEMBLING THE DISH

Brush the yellowtail with another layer of the mirin and soy sauce marinade, then sear it with the kitchen torch. Cut the fillet into ¾-in. (1.5-cm) slices. Divide the salsa verde between four soup plates and arrange the yellowtail on top. Add dots of tangy vinaigrette and pipe out dots of cucumber pulp around the fish. Drizzle with the cucumber jus and scatter over the shiso wasabi pearls. Sprinkle with the cilantro, scallion, and baby cress leaves and serve immediately.

POACHED OYSTERS
WITH POMEGRANATE SAUCE VIERGE

Fines de claire juste pochées, vierge de grenade

Serves 5

Active time
30 minutes

Marinating time
2 hours

Cooking time
2 minutes

Storage
Up to 12 hours
in the refrigerator

Equipment
Instant-read
thermometer

Ingredients

**Pomegranate
sauce vierge**
1¼ oz. (35 g) Granny
Smith apple

3½ oz. (100 g) Muscat
grapes

1 pomegranate

1 tbsp (10 g) goji berries

4 tsp (20 ml) lime juice

Generous ¼ cup (65 ml)
pomegranate juice

2½ tsp (12 ml) pumpkin
seed oil

2½ tsp (12 ml) olive oil

Scant ½ tsp (2 g) fine salt

½ tsp (1 g) ground black
Sarawak pepper

Oysters
5 oysters, preferably
Fine de Claire

To serve
2½ tbsp (10 g) thinly
sliced scallion

Coarse sea salt

Olive oil

Persinette cress and
red-veined sorrel leaves

PREPARING THE POMEGRANATE SAUCE VIERGE

Peel the apple, cut it into ¹⁄₁₆-in. (2-mm) dice (*brunoise*), and place in a large bowl. Peel the grapes, remove the seeds, and cut each into eight pieces. Add to the apple. Peel the pomegranate, remove the seeds (see technique p. 62), and add 2¾ oz. (75 g) to the apple and grapes. Add the remaining sauce vierge ingredients and stir to combine. Taste and adjust the seasoning, as necessary. Cover and let marinate for at least 2 hours in the refrigerator.

PREPARING THE OYSTERS

Preheat the oven to 200°F (100°C/Gas Mark ¼) on steam setting, if available. Place the oysters on a baking sheet and bake until their shells open (about 1¾ minutes). If you do not have a steam oven, open them using an oyster knife (see Chefs' Notes). As soon as the oysters are open, remove them from their shells and place in a saucepan with their liquor. Save the five rounded bottom shells, discarding the flat top shells. Warm the liquor to about 149°F (65°C) so the oysters poach. As soon as their edges begin to curl, remove the oysters from the heat. Let cool in their liquor, then chill until serving.

TO SERVE

Wash the bottom oyster shells in hot water and dry them thoroughly. Stir the scallion into the pomegranate sauce vierge and spoon a little into each shell. Drain the oysters and place on the sauce. Make a mound of coarse salt on each serving plate and nestle the oyster shells into it. Drizzle with a little olive oil and garnish with cress and sorrel leaves.

CHEFS' NOTES

To open oysters in the traditional way, wrap a dish towel over one hand for protection. Place an oyster, rounded shell down, on a board, and press down firmly to hold the oyster in place. Using an oyster shucking knife, which has a short, thick, pointed blade that will not break under pressure, place the tip of the knife at the base of the "hinge." Twist the tip of the knife firmly to work it between the two shells, then lever the blade upwards or twist it to break open the "hinge." Slide the knife under the top shell to remove it and release the oyster.

NUTS AND DRIED FRUITS

HAZELNUT SPHERES
WITH MOLTEN PRALINE CENTERS

Sphère noisette, ganache montée et praliné coulant

Makes 10

Active time

50 minutes

Cooking time

1 hour

Infusing time

24 hours

Chilling time

6 hours

Freezing time

2 hours + more as needed

Storage

Up to 2 days in the refrigerator

Equipment

Immersion blender

Instant-read thermometer

Food processor

3 pastry bags

Silicone ice ball molds, ¾ in. (2 cm), 1½ in. (4 cm), and 2¼ in. (5.8 cm) in dia.

2 sheets food-safe acetate

2½-in. (6-cm) round cookie cutter

Ingredients

Whipped hazelnut ganache

Generous ¼ cup (1½ oz./40 g) whole hazelnuts

¾ cup (175 ml) whole milk

½ tsp (2.5 g) gelatin powder

1 tbsp plus ½ tsp (17.5 ml) cold water

1¾ oz. (50 g) white chocolate, 35% cacao (preferably Valrhona Ivoire), chopped

Scant 1 cup (220 ml) heavy cream, min. 35% fat

Scant 3 tbsp (1½ oz./40 g) hazelnut butter

1¾ oz. (50 g) hazelnut praline paste

Praline marbles

1 cup (5 oz./140 g) whole hazelnuts

2½ tbsp (1 oz./30 g) superfine sugar

Seeds of ¼ vanilla bean

¾ tsp (3 g) *fleur de sel*

3½ oz. (100 g) cocoa butter, chopped

Praline crémeux

½ sheet (1 g) gold-strength gelatin, 200 Bloom

⅓ cup (80 ml) whole milk

1 tbsp (20 g) egg yolk (1 yolk)

3¾ tsp (15 g) superfine sugar

2½ tsp (8 g) cornstarch

2 tbsp (1 oz./30 g) butter, diced

1¾ oz. (50 g) hazelnut praline paste

Chocolate streusel disks

½ cup (1¾ oz./50 g) hazelnut flour

⅓ cup (1½ oz./40 g) buckwheat flour

¼ cup (1½ oz./40 g) light brown sugar

3 tbsp (1½ oz./40 g) butter, at room temperature and diced

1 oz. (25 g) dark chocolate, 66% cacao (preferably Valrhona Caraïbes), chopped

1¼ oz. (35 g) *feuillantine* flakes (or use crushed wafers)

To assemble

2 tbsp (20 g) whole hazelnuts

1 oz. (25 g) cocoa butter, chopped

1 oz. (25 g) milk chocolate, 40% cacao (preferably Valrhona Jivara), chopped

1¾ oz. (50 g) neutral glaze

PREPARING THE HAZELNUT GANACHE (1 DAY AHEAD)

Preheat the oven to 300°F (150°C/Gas Mark 2). Spread the hazelnuts out over a lined baking sheet and roast them in the oven for 20 minutes. Transfer to a saucepan, add the milk, and bring to a simmer. Remove from the heat and process with the immersion blender. Let infuse for 24 hours in the refrigerator. The next day, sprinkle the gelatin over the cold water in a bowl and let soak for 10 minutes. Place the chocolate in a bowl. Strain the blended hazelnuts through a fine-mesh sieve and measure out ½ cup (125 ml) of the milk. Place in a saucepan and heat until the temperature reaches 185°F (85°C), then stir in the gelatin until dissolved. Pour over the chocolate one-third at a time, process with the immersion blender until smooth, then add the cream. In a separate bowl, combine the hazelnut butter and praline paste, then add to the ganache. Process with the immersion blender until smooth, cover with plastic wrap, and chill for at least 4 hours.

PREPARING THE PRALINE MARBLES

Preheat the oven to 300°F (150°C/Gas Mark 2). Spread the hazelnuts out over a lined baking sheet and roast them in the oven for 20 minutes. Heat the sugar with the vanilla seeds in a saucepan without adding any water, until the sugar dissolves to form a syrup. Boil until the syrup becomes a golden caramel. Pour over the hazelnuts and let cool until the caramel hardens. Break roughly into pieces, place in the food processor with the *fleur de sel*, and process to a smooth paste. Spoon into one of the pastry bags and pipe into the smallest ice ball mold to form ten small spheres ¾ in. (2 cm) in diameter. Let set in the freezer for about 2 hours. When set, melt the cocoa butter in a bowl over a bain-marie. Remove the spheres from the mold, spear each one with a toothpick, and briefly dip them once in the cocoa butter. Let set for a few seconds, place on a baking sheet, and remove the toothpicks. Return to the freezer until assembling.

PREPARING THE PRALINE CRÉMEUX

Soak the gelatin in a bowl of cold water until softened. In a saucepan, bring the milk to a boil. Whisk together the egg yolk, sugar, and cornstarch in a bowl until pale and thick. When the milk comes to a boil, pour over the egg yolk mixture, whisking continuously. Pour the mixture into the saucepan and whisk until it comes to a simmer. Remove from the heat, squeeze the gelatin to remove excess water, and stir it in until dissolved. Let cool to 104°F (40°C), then whisk in the butter. Add the praline paste and process with the immersion blender until smooth. Press plastic wrap over the surface and chill for 2 hours.

PREPARING THE CHOCOLATE STREUSEL DISKS

Preheat the oven to 340°F (170°C/Gas Mark 3). Combine the hazelnut flour, buckwheat flour, and brown sugar in a bowl and rub in the butter with your fingertips until the mixture has the texture of coarse crumbs. Spread out over a prepared baking sheet and bake for 10 minutes. Melt the chocolate in a bowl over a bain-marie. Weigh out 6¼ oz. (180 g) of the streusel mixture. Coarsely grind in the food processor, add the *feuillantine* flakes and chocolate, and process to combine. Roll the mixture out between the two acetate sheets to a thickness of ¼ in. (7 mm) and chill for a few minutes to firm it up a little. Cut out ten 2½-in. (6-cm) disks using the cookie cutter.

ASSEMBLING THE SPHERES

Whisk the ganache until it just holds its shape. Spoon into a pastry bag and chill until using. Spoon the crémeux into another pastry bag and pipe into 10 cavities of the 1½-in. (4-cm) ice ball mold, filling them two-thirds full. Place a praline marble in each one and cover with more crémeux, filling the cavities completely. Freeze until the spheres can be easily removed from the mold. Fill 10 cavities of the 2¼-in. (5.8-cm) mold two-thirds full with the ganache, nestle the crémeux spheres inside, and cover with more ganache, filling the cavities completely. Freeze until the spheres can be easily removed from the mold. Using a fine grater, shave the hazelnuts into flakes. When the assembled spheres are firm enough to unmold, melt the cocoa butter and chocolate over a bain-marie until the temperature reaches 113°F (45°C). Spear the spheres with toothpicks and dip them into the melted chocolate. Let set on a lined baking sheet for 5 minutes. Coat them with a thin layer of neutral glaze and cover with the hazelnut shavings. Place the spheres on the streusel disks and decorate with small pieces of hazelnut skin.

PISTACHIO, PRALINE, AND CHOCOLATE BONBONS

Bonbons à la pâte pistache et d'amandes, praliné, ganache

Makes 130

Active time
2 hours

Cooking time
20 minutes

Resting time
4 hours

Storage
Up to 3 days
in the refrigerator
in an airtight container

Equipment
Stand mixer + paddle
beater

14½-in. (37-cm) square
confectionery frame,
½ in. (1 cm) deep

Food processor

Instant-read thermometer

Immersion blender

2 food-safe acetate
sheets

Ingredients

Pistachio and almond paste

14 oz. (400 g) almond
paste, 50% almonds

2¾ oz. (80 g) pistachio
paste

Pistachio praline layer

3 tbsp (1¼ oz./35 g)
whole raw almonds

2¼ cups (4¾ oz./135 g)
shelled pistachios

½ cup plus 1 tbsp
(4 oz./110 g) sugar

Scant 2 tsp (10 g) milk
powder

½ tsp (2 g) *fleur de sel*

1 oz. (30 g) milk
couverture chocolate,
chopped

1 oz. (30 g) cocoa butter,
chopped

Chocolate and pistachio ganache

12½ oz. (355 g) dark
couverture chocolate,
66% cacao, chopped

1⅓ cups (310 ml) heavy
cream, min. 35% fat

2½ tbsp (2 oz./55 g)
invert sugar

1 oz. (25 g) pistachio and
almond paste (see above)

4 tsp (20 g) sorbitol
liquid

5 tbsp (3 oz./80 g) butter,
diced

Chocolate squares

1¼ lb. (600 g) dark
couverture chocolate,
66% cacao, chopped

Decoration

Pistachio halves, shelled
and skinned

PREPARING THE PISTACHIO AND ALMOND PASTE

Beat the almond and pistachio pastes together in the stand mixer until smooth. Roll between two sheets of parchment paper to a thickness of ⅛ in. (3 mm), peel off the top sheet, and trim the edges of the paste into a neat square the same size as the confectionery frame. Set the frame on a lined baking sheet and place the paste in it. Weigh out 1 oz. (25 g) of the trimmings and set aside for the chocolate ganache.

PREPARING THE PISTACHIO PRALINE LAYER

Preheat the oven to 325°F (160°C/Gas Mark 3). Blanch the almonds (see technique p. 30), spread them out over a lined baking sheet, and toast in the oven for 10 minutes. Remove from the oven, add the pistachios, and toss to distribute the nuts evenly. Heat the sugar in a saucepan without adding any water, until it dissolves to form a syrup. Boil until the syrup becomes a golden caramel. Immediately pour the caramel over the nuts and let them cool completely. Break roughly into large pieces and process in the food processor to obtain a smooth paste. Add the milk powder and *fleur de sel* and pulse briefly until combined. Transfer to a mixing bowl. Melt the chocolate and cocoa butter in a bowl over a bain-marie until the temperature reaches 86°F (30°C). Stir into the praline using a flexible spatula. Pour the praline over the pistachio and almond paste in the confectionery frame, spreading it into an even layer ⅛ in. (3 mm) thick, using an offset spatula.

PREPARING THE CHOCOLATE AND PISTACHIO GANACHE

Melt the chocolate in a bowl over a bain-marie until the temperature reaches 95°F (35°C), stirring until smooth. In a saucepan, heat the cream and invert sugar until the temperature reaches 95°F (35°C). Stir the pistachio and almond paste trimmings into the melted chocolate until combined, followed by the hot cream. Add the sorbitol and butter and process with the immersion blender until smooth. Pour over the pistachio praline layer in the frame and spread it into an even layer using an offset spatula. Let rest for 4 hours.

PREPARING THE CHOCOLATE SQUARES

Temper the chocolate (see p. 140). Spread it into a ¹⁄₁₆ in. (2 mm) layer between the two acetate sheets and let set slightly (about 5 minutes). Peel off the top sheet and cut the chocolate into ⅛-in. (3-cm) squares.

ASSEMBLING THE BONBONS

Remove the confectionery frame and cut the layers into ⅛-in. (3-cm) square bonbons. Top each one with a chocolate square and decorate with a halved pistachio.

CALISSONS

Makes about 20

Active time
1 hour

Cooking time
10 minutes

Resting time
72 hours

Storage
Up to 1 week
in an airtight container

Equipment
Food processor

Ingredients

Calisson base

¾ cup (3½ oz./100 g) confectioners' sugar

1⅓ cups (4½ oz./125 g) almond flour

2 tsp (10 ml) orange blossom water

2 oz. (60 g) candied orange

½ oz. (15 g) candied lemon

2 oz. (60 g) candied melon

8-in. (20-cm) square of rice paper

Royal icing

3¼ tsp (15 g) egg white (about ½ white)

Generous 1 cup (5¼ oz./150 g) confectioners' sugar, plus more as needed

Scant ½ tsp (2 ml) lemon juice

Decoration

Small pieces of edible silver leaf

PREPARING THE BASE (3 DAYS AHEAD)

Place the confectioners' sugar, almond flour, and orange blossom water in a saucepan. Cook over low heat for 10 minutes, stirring to make a paste. Transfer to the food processor and add the candied orange, lemon, and melon. Process on high speed until the mixture is smooth and sticky. Pour over the rice paper and roll into a ½-in. (1-cm) layer—grease your rolling pin with a little neutral oil, if necessary, to prevent sticking. Let rest in a dry place at room temperature for 72 hours.

PREPARING THE ROYAL ICING

Lightly whisk the egg white in a bowl until frothy. Sift in the confectioners' sugar and whisk until smooth, then whisk in the lemon juice. The icing should be creamy with a spreadable but not runny consistency. If necessary, whisk in a little more confectioners' sugar. Use immediately or press plastic wrap over the surface of the icing to prevent crusting.

ICING AND DECORATING THE CALISSONS

Using an offset spatula, spread a thin layer of royal icing over the base and let set for 1–2 minutes (but no longer, as the icing dries quickly and it will harden too much for it to be cut without cracking). Using a chef's knife dipped in hot water, cut into diamond shapes with 1¼-in. (3-cm) sides. The base will be sticky in the center, so wipe the knife clean and re-dip it between each cut. Top each diamond with a small piece of silver leaf.

CHEFS' NOTES

As the base mixture is very sticky, lightly oiling
your rolling pin makes it easier to roll it into an even layer.

WALNUT TARTLETS

Tartelettes aux noix

Makes 6

Active time

1 hour

Chilling time

7 hours

Infusing time

15 minutes

Freezing time

3 hours

Cooking time

30 minutes

Thawing time

1 hour

Storage

Up to 2 days in the refrigerator

Equipment

Immersion blender

Instant-read thermometer

Stand mixer + paddle beater

Silkomart Klassik tart ring kit with 6 × 2¾-in. (7-cm) rings, ¾ in. (2 cm) deep, and a mold with 6 × 2¾-in. (7-cm) round cavities, ¾ in. (1.5 cm) deep

3-in. (8-cm) round cookie cutter

Food processor

Silicone mat

Ingredients

Coffee glaze

Scant ½ cup (5 oz./150 g) glucose syrup

¼ cup (60 ml) water

Seeds of ½ vanilla bean

¾ cup (5 oz./150 g) superfine sugar

5¼ oz. (150 g) blond chocolate, chopped

Scant ½ cup (3½ oz./100 g)

unsweetened condensed milk

1 tsp (5 ml) liquid coffee extract

Coffee mousse

7 sheets (14 g) gold-strength gelatin, 200 Bloom

Scant 2 tbsp (8 g) coffee beans

¼ cup (60 ml) whole milk

1 tbsp (20 g) egg yolk (1 yolk)

Scant ½ tsp (2 ml) liquid coffee extract

2 tbsp (1 oz./30 g) egg white (1 white)

1 tbsp (12 g) superfine sugar

1 tbsp (20 g) glucose syrup

Scant ½ cup (115 ml) heavy cream, min. 35% fat

Coffee and walnut shortbread

5 tbsp (2½ oz./75 g) butter

⅓ cup (1½ oz./40 g) confectioners' sugar

2 tbsp (1 oz./30 g) lightly beaten egg (about ⅔ egg)

¼ tsp (1.5 g) salt

Scant ¼ cup (20 g) almond flour

Scant ¼ cup (20 g) walnut flour

1 cup plus 2 tbsp (5¼ oz./150 g) all-purpose flour, divided

Scant ¼ cup (20 g) ground coffee

Walnut financier

3 tbsp (1½ oz./40 g) butter, softened

1½ oz. (40 g) walnut paste

½ cup (1¾ oz./50 g) almond flour

⅓ cup (1¾ oz./50 g) confectioners' sugar

3 tbsp plus 1 tsp (1½ oz./45 g) egg white (about 1½ whites)

10 walnut halves

2½ tbsp (25 g) all-purpose flour

Walnut oil

Coffee and walnut praline

Scant ¼ cup (1¼ oz./35 g) blanched almonds (see technique p. 30)

1 cup (4¾ oz./135 g) walnut halves

¼ cup plus 2 tbsp (1 oz./30 g) coffee beans

5 tsp (20 g) superfine sugar

1¼ tsp (5 g) *fleur de sel*

Walnut tuiles

¼ cup (2 oz./55 g) egg white (about 2 whites)

⅓ cup (1½ oz./45 g) confectioners' sugar

2½ tbsp (25 g) all-purpose flour

Scant 1 cup (240 ml) water

1½ tbsp (22 g) butter

Scant ½ tsp (2 g) salt

A few walnut pieces

PREPARING THE COFFEE GLAZE

Combine the glucose syrup, water, and vanilla seeds in a saucepan and bring to a boil. In a separate saucepan, heat the sugar without adding any water until it dissolves to form a syrup. Boil until the syrup becomes a golden caramel. Carefully pour the hot vanilla syrup into the caramel, stirring with a spatula. Weigh the mixture and add enough hot water to make 12¾ oz. (360 g). Melt the chocolate in a bowl over a bain-marie. Pour the caramel mixture over the condensed milk and add the melted chocolate, followed by the coffee extract. Process with the immersion blender until smooth. Press plastic wrap over the surface and chill for 6 hours before using.

PREPARING THE COFFEE MOUSSE

Soak the gelatin in a bowl of cold water until softened. Roughly chop the coffee beans. Bring the milk to a simmer in a saucepan, then remove from the heat. Add the coffee beans, cover, and let infuse for 15 minutes. Strain through a fine-mesh sieve, return the milk to the saucepan, and bring to a boil. Whisk the egg yolk in a bowl and, when the milk comes to a boil, whisk a little into the yolk. Pour the mixture into the saucepan and cook until the temperature reaches 185°F (85°C), stirring continuously. Remove from the heat. Squeeze the gelatin to remove excess water and stir it in until dissolved. Stir in the coffee extract and let the custard cool in the refrigerator for 20 minutes. Heat the egg white and sugar in a bowl over a bain-marie until the temperature reaches 113°F (45°C), whisking often. Whisk in the glucose, remove from the heat, and continue whisking until a stiff, shiny meringue is obtained. In a separate bowl, whip the cream until it just holds its shape and gently fold it into the meringue, followed by the coffee custard. Immediately fill the Silkomart mold with the mousse and freeze for 3 hours.

PREPARING THE COFFEE AND WALNUT SHORTBREAD

Cream the butter and confectioners' sugar in the stand mixer. Beat in the eggs and salt, then the almond flour, walnut flour, and ⅓ cup (1½ oz./40 g) of the all-purpose flour. Beat in the remaining flour and ground coffee. Gather into a ball, cover with plastic wrap, and chill for 30 minutes. Place the tart rings on a lined baking sheet. Preheat the oven to 350°F (180°C/Gas Mark 4). Roll the dough on a lightly floured surface to a thickness of about ¹⁄₁₀ in. (2.5 mm) and cut out six disks using the cookie cutter. Place in the tart rings and blind-bake for 6 minutes. Keep the oven switched on at the same temperature for the financier.

PREPARING THE WALNUT FINANCIER

Beat the butter and walnut paste together in the stand mixer. Sift the almond flour and confectioners' sugar together into the mixer bowl and beat to combine. In a separate bowl, whisk the egg whites until they hold quite firm peaks. Gradually whisk them into the batter, then finish by stirring them in with a flexible spatula until combined. Finely chop the walnuts, then fold them in to the mixture with the all-purpose flour. Pour into the rings over the shortbread to a thickness of ½ in. (1 cm). Bake for 15 minutes. Remove from the oven and brush lightly with walnut oil.

PREPARING THE COFFEE AND WALNUT PRALINE

Preheat the oven to 300°F (150°C/Gas Mark 2). Spread the almonds and walnuts out over a lined baking sheet and roast them in the oven for 10 minutes. Remove and add the coffee beans to the nuts. Heat the sugar in a saucepan without adding any water until it dissolves to form a syrup. Boil until the syrup becomes a rich brown caramel. Immediately pour it over the nuts and coffee beans and let cool to room temperature. Break into large pieces, place in the food processor with the *fleur de sel*, and process to a smooth paste.

PREPARING THE WALNUT TUILES

Preheat the oven to 340°F (170°C/Gas Mark 3). Whisk together the egg whites, confectioners' sugar, and flour in a bowl. Heat the water, butter, and salt in a saucepan and bring to a boil. Whisk in the egg white mixture and bring to a boil, whisking continuously. Pour over a lined baking sheet, spreading it into a thin, even layer using an offset spatula. Scatter over the walnut pieces and bake for 10 minutes. Remove from the oven and let cool for a few minutes, then break into pieces.

ASSEMBLING THE TARTLETS

Top the financier with the praline mixture, filling the tart rings completely. Remove the rings. Heat the glaze until the temperature reaches 86°F (30°C). Turn the frozen coffee mousse out of the mold, spear the top of each mousse in the center with a toothpick, and dip it into the glaze to coat. Scrape the excess glaze off the base using a spatula and place upright over the tartlet bases. Gently twist the toothpicks to remove them. Place a walnut tuile over each tartlet. Let thaw for 1 hour in the refrigerator before serving.

CARAMEL PECAN BROWNIES

Brownie aux noix de pécan et caramel tendre

Serves 6

Active time
20 minutes

Setting time
15 minutes

Cooking time
35–40 minutes

Storage
Up to 2 days
in an airtight container

Equipment
Immersion blender

Pastry bag

6-in. (16-cm) square cake
frame

Silicone baking mat

Instant-read thermometer

Ingredients

Soft caramel

Generous 1 tbsp (25 g)
glucose syrup, DE 38

2 tbsp (25 g) superfine
sugar

3 tbsp (45 ml) heavy
cream, min. 35% fat

2 tsp (10 g) butter

⅛ tsp (0.5 g) *fleur de sel*

Caramelized pecans

⅔ cup (2¾ oz./80 g)
pecan halves

1 tbsp (15 ml) water

¼ cup (1¾ oz./50 g)
superfine sugar

A few drops neutral oil

Brownies

3 oz. (85 g) dark
chocolate, 65% cacao
(preferably Valrhona
Caraïbes), chopped and
divided

4 tbsp (2½ oz./65 g)
butter, diced

2 tsp (10 ml) walnut oil

⅓ cup (2½ oz./75 g)
lightly beaten egg
(about 1½ eggs)

2 tbsp (25 g) superfine
sugar

2 tbsp (25 g) rapadura
sugar

2½ tbsp (25 g) all-
purpose flour

2 tsp (5 g) unsweetened
cocoa powder

Scant ½ tsp (1.5 g)
baking powder

⅓ cup (1¼ oz./35 g)
almond flour

¼ tsp (1 g) salt

Scant ½ cup
(1¾ oz./50 g) chopped
caramelized pecans, plus
more for decoration

PREPARING THE SOFT CARAMEL

Heat the glucose syrup and sugar in a saucepan until the sugar dissolves to form a syrup. Boil until the syrup becomes a golden-brown caramel. While the syrup is boiling, bring the cream to a simmer in a separate saucepan. Carefully pour the hot cream into the caramel, a little at a time, stirring continuously. Let boil for 1 minute, remove from the heat, and add the butter and *fleur de sel*. Process with the immersion blender until smooth. Let the caramel set at room temperature for about 15 minutes, then transfer to the pastry bag.

PREPARING THE CARAMELIZED PECANS

Preheat the oven to 325°F (160°C/Gas Mark 3). Spread the pecans out over a lined baking sheet and toast in the oven for 15 minutes. Meanwhile, heat the water and sugar in a saucepan until the sugar dissolves. Bring to a boil and let boil for 1 minute. Add the pecans and cook, stirring with a spatula, until the sugar crystallizes and has a sandy appearance (see technique p. 116). Increase the heat slightly and continue stirring until the sugar dissolves, coats the nuts, and turns a golden caramel color. Add a few drops of neutral oil, stir to blend, and spread the nuts out over the baking sheet (lining it with fresh parchment paper, if necessary), leaving space between them. Let cool completely. Weigh out a scant ½ cup (1¾ oz./50 g) of the pecans and chop them roughly for the brownie batter. Leave the rest for decorating the tops of the brownies.

PREPARING THE BROWNIES

Preheat the oven to 325°F (160°C/Gas Mark 3). Place the cake frame on the silicone baking mat. Melt 2¼ oz. (65 g) of the chocolate with the butter and walnut oil in a bowl over a bain-marie and continue heating until the temperature reaches 122°F (50°C), stirring until smooth. Whisk together the eggs, superfine sugar, and rapadura sugar until thick and creamy. Sift the all-purpose flour, cocoa powder, and baking powder together into a separate bowl and add the almond flour and salt. Stir the melted chocolate into the whisked mixture, sprinkle over the dry ingredients, and fold in until just combined. Add the scant ½ cup (1¾ oz./50 g) caramelized pecans and the remaining chopped chocolate. Pour the batter into the cake frame and scatter a mix of whole and chopped caramelized pecans over the top. Bake for 20–25 minutes until a toothpick pushed into the center comes out with just a few crumbs sticking to it. Remove the frame and let the brownies cool at room temperature. Pipe out diagonal lines of caramel over the brownies and cut into bars or squares.

MACADAMIA NOUGAT

Nougat aux noix de macadamia

Makes 32 bars

Active time

30 minutes

Cooking time

15 minutes

Resting time

24 hours

Storage

Up to 2 months
in an airtight container

Equipment

Instant-read thermometer

Stand mixer + whisk and
paddle beater

2 × 6-in. (16-cm) square
confectionery frames,
1½ in. (4 cm) deep

Ingredients

3⅓ cups
(1 lb. 2 oz./500 g)
macadamia nuts

½ cup plus 2 tsp (135 ml)
water

2 cups (14 oz./400 g)
superfine sugar

Generous ½ cup
(7 oz./200 g) glucose
syrup

1½ cups
(1 lb. 2 oz./500 g)
honey

⅓ cup (2½ oz./70 g) egg
white (about 2 whites)

4 sheets rice paper

Preheat the oven to 340°F (170°C/Gas Mark 3). Spread the macadamia nuts out over a lined baking sheet and toast them for 7 minutes. When they are cool enough to handle, carefully cut them in half. Do not let them cool completely as they need to be warm when added to the nougat mixture.

Heat the water, sugar, and glucose syrup in a saucepan until the sugar dissolves. Boil until the temperature reaches 293°F (145°C). In a separate saucepan, heat the honey to 265°F (130°C). Meanwhile, whisk the egg whites in the bowl of the stand mixer until they hold soft peaks.

When the temperature of the honey reaches 265°F (130°C), slowly pour it into the whites in a thin stream, whisking continuously and taking care not to let the syrup touch the whisk. Gradually whisk in the sugar and glucose syrup mixture. Continue whisking for about 5 minutes, or until the mixture has cooled to 160°F (70°C). When you can roll a small piece of it into a ball between your fingers, it is the correct consistency.

Replace the stand mixer whisk with the paddle beater and beat the mixture until it has cooled to 140°F (60°C). Add the warm macadamia nuts. Take care not to overmix as the nuts could break up.

Place 2 sheets of rice paper side by side on a board or baking sheet and set a confectionery frame on each one. Immediately pour the nougat mixture into the frame and press the remaining sheets of rice paper over the top.

Place a sheet of parchment paper over the two frames and flatten the surface of the nougat with a rolling pin. Neaten the edges of the rice paper by trimming away any excess.

Let rest for 24 hours in a cool, dry place. Unmold by sliding the blade of a knife between the nougat and the sides of the frames. Using a serrated knife, cut the nougat into ½-in. (1-cm) bars.

BRAZIL NUT BARS

Barre aux noix du Brésil

Makes 10–12

Active time
1½ hours

Cooking time
1 hour–1 hour 10 minutes

Chilling time
Overnight

Setting time
10 minutes

Storage
Up to 3 days
in an airtight container

Equipment
8-in. (20-cm) square cake
frame, 1½ in. (4 cm) deep
Stand mixer + paddle
beater
Instant-read thermometer
Immersion blender
Food processor
Pastry bag + a plain ½-in.
(10-mm) tip
Melon baller

Ingredients

Brazil nut shortbread
Generous ¼ cup
(1½ oz./40 g) Brazil nuts
¼ cup (1¾ oz./50 g)
superfine sugar
1 cup plus 2 tbsp
(5¼ oz./150 g) all-
purpose flour
7 tbsp (3½ oz./100 g)
butter, diced
1¼ tsp (5 g) *fleur de sel*

Soft caramel
4 tsp (20 ml) water
½ cup (3⅓ oz./95 g)
superfine sugar
3½ tbsp (2½ oz./75 g)
glucose syrup
Scant ½ cup (115 ml)
heavy cream, min. 35%
fat, lukewarm
¼ cup (2 oz./55 g)
unsweetened condensed
milk
Seeds of 1 vanilla bean

1 stick plus 2 tbsp
(5¼ oz./150 g) butter,
diced
¼ tsp (1 g) *fleur de sel*

Brazil nut praline paste
Scant ¾ cup
(3½ oz./100 g) Brazil
nuts
⅓ cup (1¾ oz./50 g)
whole almonds
1½ tbsp (25 ml) water
2½ tsp (10 g) sugar

**Whipped praline
ganache**
½ sheet (1 g) gold-
strength gelatin,
200 Bloom
2 oz. (55 g) milk
couverture chocolate,
40% cacao (preferably
Valrhona Jivara), chopped
1½ oz. (45 g) Brazil nut
praline paste (see above)
¾ cup (175 ml) heavy
cream, min. 35% fat

Chocolate coating
1 lb. 2 oz. (500 g) dark
couverture chocolate,
55% cacao (preferably
Valrhona Équatoriale
Noir), chopped
1 tsp (5 ml) neutral oil

Decoration
Small pieces of edible
gold leaf

PREPARING THE BRAZIL NUT SHORTBREAD

Preheat the oven to 325°F (160°C/Gas Mark 3). Roughly chop the Brazil nuts, spread them out over a lined baking sheet, and toast them in the oven for 10 minutes. Let cool completely. Once cooled, preheat the oven to 340°F (170°C/Gas Mark 3). Place the cake frame on a lined baking sheet. Beat the sugar, flour, butter, and *fleur de sel* in the stand mixer until the ingredients bind together. Mix in the toasted Brazil nuts. Using your fingers, press the dough into an even layer in the baking frame. Bake for 30–40 minutes until lightly golden. Let cool completely in the frame.

PREPARING THE SOFT CARAMEL

Heat the water, sugar, and glucose syrup in a saucepan until the sugar dissolves. Bring to a boil and continue cooking until the temperature reaches 365°F (185°C) and the syrup becomes a light golden caramel. Remove from the heat and slowly pour in the warm cream, whisking continuously until evenly combined. Bring to a boil, remove from the heat, and add the condensed milk, vanilla seeds, butter, and *fleur de sel*. Process with the immersion blender until smooth, then pour over the shortbread in the frame. Cover and chill overnight.

PREPARING THE BRAZIL NUT PRALINE PASTE

Preheat the oven to 325°F (160°C/Gas Mark 3). Spread the Brazil nuts and almonds out over a lined baking sheet and toast in the oven for 10 minutes. Meanwhile, heat the water and sugar in a large saucepan until the sugar has dissolved and the temperature of the syrup reaches 230°F (110°C). Add the hot nuts and cook until the sugar crystallizes and has a sandy appearance, then caramelizes again, stirring constantly. Transfer the nuts back onto the baking sheet and let cool completely. When cool, break them into large chunks and grind to a smooth paste in the food processor.

PREPARING THE WHIPPED PRALINE GANACHE

Soak the gelatin in a bowl of cold water until softened. Place the chocolate in a mixing bowl with the praline paste. In a saucepan, bring the cream to a simmer. Squeeze the gelatin to remove excess water, then stir it into the hot cream until dissolved. Pour over the chocolate and praline paste and blend until smooth using the immersion blender. Cover and chill overnight.

PREPARING THE CHOCOLATE COATING

Temper the chocolate (see p. 140). Stir in the oil and remove from the heat.

ASSEMBLING THE BARS

Cut the shortbread into 1¼ × 4-in. (3 × 10-cm) bars while the caramel is still very cold. Remove the cake frame and spear each bar at either end using two toothpicks, then dip into the chocolate until evenly coated on all sides. Place on a lined baking sheet and let set for about 10 minutes. Whip the ganache (do this lightly so it does not split) and transfer to the pastry bag. Pipe small mounds of ganache over the chocolate bars. Using the cupped side of the melon baller, press down the centers of some of the mounds, and fill the hollows with a little praline paste. Place small pieces of gold leaf on top of the bars.

CHEFS' NOTES

Do not process the praline paste for too long, as the oil may separate out. If it does begin to separate, chill the paste for several minutes before continuing.

CASHEW NUT MENDIANTS

Mendiants aux noix de cajou

Makes 6

Active time
15 minutes

Cooking time
10 minutes

Setting time
At least 2 hours

Storage
Up to 4 days
in an airtight container

Equipment
Instant-read
thermometer
Pastry bag
6 × 2¾-in. (7-cm)
baking rings

Ingredients

Caramelized cashews
¼ cup (2 oz./50 g)
superfine sugar
3½ tbsp (50 ml) water
Seeds of ½ vanilla bean
Generous ½ cup
(2¼ oz./65 g) cashews

Chocolate coating
3½ oz. (100 g) dark
couverture chocolate,
64% cacao (preferably
Valrhona Manari),
chopped

PREPARING THE CARAMELIZED CASHEWS
Place the sugar, water, vanilla seeds, and cashews in a saucepan. Heat until the sugar dissolves and the temperature of the syrup reaches 270°F (130°C). Lower the heat and cook until the syrup crystallizes and has a sandy appearance, stirring continuously with a spatula. Immediately turn out onto a sheet of parchment paper. Working in two batches for even cooking, return the cashews to the saucepan and cook until the sugar dissolves, coats the nuts, and turns a golden caramel color. Turn out onto a clean sheet of parchment paper, leaving space between the nuts, and let cool completely.

PREPARING THE CHOCOLATE COATING
Temper the chocolate (see p. 140). Transfer to the pastry bag.

ASSEMBLING THE MENDIANTS
Place the baking rings on a lined baking sheet and pipe a thin layer of chocolate, about ⅛ in. (3–4 mm) thick, into each ring. Cover the chocolate with the caramelized cashews. Let set for at least 2 hours before removing the rings.

PEANUT CHICKEN

Cuisse de poulet aux cacahuètes

Serves 8

Active time
30 minutes

Marinating time
Overnight

Cooking time
45 minutes

Resting time
30 minutes

Storage
Up to 2 days
in the refrigerator

Equipment
Thin bamboo skewers
Oven-safe skillet

Ingredients

Marinade
2 lb. (900 g) chicken thighs, skin on

3½ tbsp (1½ oz./40 g) superfine sugar

4 tsp (20 ml) soy sauce

⅔ cup (150 ml) oyster sauce

Scant ⅓ cup (70 ml) water

1 tbsp (15 ml) sesame oil

⅕ oz. (5 g) fresh ginger, preferably organic, peeled and finely chopped

To assemble
1 banana leaf

Neutral oil

1½ tsp (5 g) white sesame seeds (optional)

¼ cup (1½ oz./40 g) raw peanuts

3½ oz. (100 g) snow peas

1 tbsp (15 ml) sesame oil

A few Zallotti blossom flowers (optional)

Freshly ground white pepper

MARINATING THE CHICKEN (1 DAY AHEAD)

Remove the bones from the chicken thighs, retaining their shape as much as possible. Combine all the marinade ingredients together in a bowl, add the chicken, and toss until coated. Cover and let marinate overnight in the refrigerator.

ASSEMBLING THE DISH

The next day, shape the banana leaf into a basket, using thin bamboo skewers to hold it together (see photograph). Preheat the oven to 350°F (180°C/Gas Mark 4). Take the chicken thighs out of the marinade, scrape off as much of it as possible back into the bowl, and reserve.

Heat a drizzle of neutral oil in the skillet, add the chicken thighs, skin side down, and lightly brown. Transfer the skillet to the oven and bake the chicken for about 10 minutes, or until cooked. Place on a rack and let rest for 30 minutes. If using the sesame seeds, lower the oven temperature to 300°F (150°C/Gas Mark 2). Spread the sesame seeds out over a lined baking sheet and toast them in the oven for 15 minutes. Roughly chop the peanuts and toast them over medium heat in a dry skillet until lightly golden. Fill a bowl with ice water. Wash the snow peas and cook them in a saucepan of boiling salted water for 3–4 minutes, until just cooked but still crisp. Remove with a skimmer and plunge immediately into the ice water to stop the cooking. Using the skimmer, transfer the peas to paper towel to drain. When ready to serve, cut the chicken into ¾-in. (2-cm) cubes and reheat in a skillet with 1 tbsp (15 ml) sesame oil. Pour in the reserved marinade and cook until the chicken is glazed, stirring continuously. Thread 3–4 cubes of chicken onto small skewers, if desired. Place the chicken and snow peas in the banana leaf basket, then sprinkle over the peanuts and the toasted sesame seeds and Zallotti blossoms, if using. Add a few grinds of white pepper and serve immediately.

MONT BLANC PYRAMIDS

Mont Blanc en pyramide

Makes 3 pyramids, each serving 2

Active time

2½ hours

Cooking time

2 hours 10 minutes

Chilling time

8 hours

Storage time

Up to 2 days
in the refrigerator

Equipment

Immersion blender

Silicone baking mat

Instant-read thermometer

6-in. (15-cm) square cake frame

2 pastry bags

9 triangles cut from food grade (cake board) cardboard with 5½-in. (14-cm) sides

Velvet spray gun

Ingredients

Whipped cream

1 sheet (2 g) gold-strength gelatin, 200 Bloom

⅔ cup (160 ml) heavy cream, min. 35% fat, divided

1¼ tsp (6 g) superfine sugar

Seeds of 1 vanilla bean

Reduced-sugar meringue

2 tbsp (1 oz./30 g) egg white (1 white)

5 tsp (20 g) superfine sugar

2 tsp (10 g) glucose syrup DE 38

2½ tbsp (20 g) confectioners' sugar

Chestnut sponge

3½ oz. (100 g) chestnut spread

3 tbsp (1¾ oz./50 g) butter, melted and cooled

1 tbsp (20 g) egg yolk (1 yolk)

½ cup (1¾ oz./50 g) chestnut flour

1¾ tsp (7 g) baking powder

¼ teaspoon (1 g) fine salt

2 tbsp (1 oz./30 g) egg white (1 white)

5 tsp (20 g) superfine sugar

Chestnut mousse

¼ tsp (1.3 g) gelatin powder

Scant 2 tsp (9 ml) cold water

Scant ¾ cup (170 ml) heavy cream, min. 35% fat

1¼ oz. (35 g) chestnut spread

2¾ oz. (75 g) chestnut paste

2 tsp (10 ml) warm water

Black currant confit

½ tsp (2 g) pectin NH

1¼ tsp (6 g) superfine sugar

2¾ oz. (75 g) black currant puree

4 tsp (20 ml) lemon juice

Chestnut shortbread

Scant ⅓ cup (1 oz./30 g) chestnut flour

1¾ tsp (3.5 g) almond flour

2 tsp (5 g) confectioners' sugar

⅛ tsp (0.5 g) salt

Scant 1 tbsp (17 g) butter

1¼ tsp (6 g) lightly beaten egg (about ⅛ egg)

To assemble

2¾ oz. (75 g) white chocolate

10 candied chestnuts (see technique p. 89), roughly chopped

Chocolate velvet finish

2¾ oz. (75 g) milk couverture chocolate, 40% cacao (preferably Valrhona Jivara), chopped

1¼ oz. (35 g) cocoa butter, chopped

To serve

2 tsp (10 g) glucose syrup

Small pieces of edible silver

PREPARING THE WHIPPED CREAM

Soak the gelatin in a bowl of cold water until softened. Heat a scant ¼ cup (55 ml) of the cream in a saucepan with the sugar and vanilla seeds until the sugar dissolves. Remove from the heat, squeeze the gelatin to remove excess water, and stir it into the hot cream until dissolved. Add the remaining cream and process with the immersion blender until smooth. Cover and chill for at least 6 hours. Whip the cream until it holds its shape.

PREPARING THE MERINGUE

Preheat the oven to 175°F (80°C/Gas on lowest setting). Grease the silicone baking mat with a little oil. Place the egg white, superfine sugar, and glucose syrup in a bowl over a bain-marie and heat until the temperature reaches 131°F (55°C). Remove from the bain-marie and place on the work surface, then whisk on high speed until the egg white holds soft peaks. Add the confectioners' sugar and continue whisking until the peaks are firm. Spread over the silicone mat in an even ¼-in. (5-mm) layer. Bake for 1½ hours until dry. Let cool, then carefully cut into three triangles with 5-in. (13-cm) sides, using a sharp knife. Store in a dry place.

PREPARING THE CHESTNUT SPONGE

Preheat the oven to 330°F (165°C/Gas Mark 3). Place the cake frame on a lined baking sheet. Stir together the chestnut spread and butter until combined. Stir in the egg yolk, followed by the chestnut flour, baking powder, and salt. Whisk the egg white until it holds soft peaks, then whisk in the sugar until the peaks are firm. Gently fold the egg white into the batter. Pour into the cake frame and bake for 25 minutes. Let cool completely before removing the frame. Cut the sponge in half using a serrated knife, then cut into three triangles with 5-in. (13-cm) sides and three with 2-in. (5-cm) sides.

PREPARING THE CHESTNUT MOUSSE

Sprinkle the gelatin over the cold water in a bowl and let soak for 10 minutes. Whip the cream until it starts to thicken and keep chilled. Work the chestnut spread and paste together in a bowl using a flexible spatula until softened and combined. Add the warm water to the gelatin to dissolve it, then stir into the chestnut mixture. Fold in the whipped cream, one-third at a time. Spoon the mousse into one of the pastry bags and chill until assembling.

PREPARING THE BLACK CURRANT CONFIT

Combine the pectin and sugar in a bowl. In a saucepan, heat the black currant puree and lemon juice until the temperature reaches 113°F (45°C). Stir in the pectin and sugar until dissolved, then bring to a boil. Remove from the heat and let cool. Process with the immersion blender until smooth, or strain through a fine-mesh sieve. Transfer to the second pastry bag.

PREPARING THE CHESTNUT SHORTBREAD

Preheat the oven to 325°F (160°C/Gas Mark 3). Combine the chestnut flour, almond flour, confectioners' sugar, and salt in a bowl. Rub in the butter with your fingertips until the mixture has the texture of coarse crumbs. Add the egg and gently mix in. Break up the dough into small pieces and scatter them over the silicone baking mat. Bake for 15 minutes.

PREPARING AND ASSEMBLING THE PYRAMIDS

Make three pyramid molds by taping three food grade cardboard triangles together with adhesive tape for each mold. Temper the white chocolate (see p. 131) and brush it over the inside of the molds in a thin, even layer. Working with one mold at a time, hold the pyramid upside-down, so the tip points downward, and pipe a ½-in. (1-cm) layer of chestnut mousse into the tip. Scatter a few shortbread crumbs and candied chestnut pieces over the mousse, then add a ½-in. (1-cm) layer of whipped cream, followed by a thin layer of black currant confit. Top the confit with a second layer of chestnut mousse and place the smaller chestnut sponge triangles over the mousse. Add the meringue layer, cover with a second layer of whipped cream and black currant confit, and scatter with a few more chestnut pieces, reserving the rest for decoration. Pipe in a final layer of mousse and finish with the larger chestnut sponge triangles. Place the pyramids upright and chill for at least 2 hours.

PREPARING THE VELVET FINISH AND SERVING

Melt the milk chocolate and cocoa butter together in a bowl over a bain-marie until the temperature reaches 113°F (45°C). Let cool to 90°F (32°C), then pour into the spray gun. Carefully remove the food grade cardboard from the pyramids and spray the white chocolate sides to give them a velvety finish. Decorate each pyramid with chestnut pieces and pieces of gold leaf fixed in place with dots of glucose syrup.

ORANGE BLOSSOM AND DATE MACARONS

Macarons à la fleur d'oranger et datte

**Makes about 25
(50 macaron shells)**

Active time

2 hours

Chilling time

Overnight + 2 hours

Cooking time

15 minutes

Resting time

30 minutes

Storage

Up to 3 days
in the refrigerator

Equipment

Instant-read thermometer

Immersion blender

Stand mixer + whisk

Food processor

2 silicone baking mats

2 pastry bags + ½-in.
(10-mm) and ¼-in. (6-mm)
plain tips

Stencil or sponge for
decorating the macarons

Ingredients

Orange blossom filling

½ oz. (12 g) ivory
chocolate, chopped

¾ cup (175 ml) heavy
cream, min. 35% fat,
divided

⅓ cup (2¼ oz./65 g)
superfine sugar

3 tbsp (45 ml) orange
blossom water

2 drops liquid green food
coloring

2 tbsp (20 g) cornstarch

1 stick plus 1 tbsp
(4¾ oz./135 g) butter,
diced

Macaron shells

3½ tbsp (50 ml) water

1 cup (7 oz./200 g)
superfine sugar

⅔ cup (5 oz./150 g) egg
white (about 5 whites),
divided

2 cups (7 oz./200 g)
almond flour

1½ cups (7 oz./200 g)
confectioners' sugar

1¾ oz. (50 g) activated
charcoal

¾ tsp (4 ml) colorless
alcohol, 40° (such as rum
or kirsch)

Date paste

7 oz. (200 g) dried dates

2½ tbsp (40 ml) orange
juice

Scant ¼ cup (20 g)
slivered almonds

PREPARING THE ORANGE BLOSSOM FILLING (1 DAY AHEAD)

Place the chocolate in a mixing bowl. Heat a generous ½ cup (130 ml) of the cream in a saucepan with the sugar, orange blossom water, and food coloring until the sugar dissolves. Cook until the temperature reaches 122°F (50°C). Meanwhile, combine the remaining cream with the cornstarch in a small bowl. Stir into the hot cream mixture and bring to a boil, stirring continuously. Pour over the chocolate and stir well to form a smooth ganache. Let cool to 104°F (40°C), then add the butter and process with the immersion blender until smooth. Press plastic wrap over the surface and refrigerate overnight.

PREPARING THE MACARON SHELLS

Make an Italian meringue by heating the water and sugar in a saucepan until the sugar dissolves, then boil until the temperature reaches 243°F (117°C). Meanwhile, place ⅓ cup (2½ oz./75 g) of the egg whites in the stand mixer and begin beating on high speed. When the syrup reaches 243°F (117°C), reduce to medium speed and carefully drizzle the syrup over the egg whites in a thin, steady stream, taking care not to let the syrup touch the whisk. Increase the speed to high and whisk for 2 minutes. Reduce the speed again and beat until the meringue cools to 122°F (50°C). In a separate bowl, combine the almond flour and confectioners' sugar. Transfer to the food processor and pulse to a flour-like consistency, being careful not to over-work and heat the ingredients. Using a bowl scraper, fold in the remaining egg whites, then fold in the Italian meringue one third at a time. Continue folding until the meringue has deflated slightly, is smooth, and it falls off the scraper in thick ribbons. Line baking sheets with the silicone mats. Spoon the batter into a pastry bag fitted with the ½-in. (10-mm) tip and pipe shells approximately 1½ in. (4 cm) in diameter onto the mats. Carefully lift up the baking sheets and gently drop them back onto the work surface to make the tops of the macarons smooth. Let rest at room temperature for about 30 minutes until a thin crust forms on top of each shell. Preheat the oven to 300°F (150°C/Gas Mark 2), then bake the shells for 15 minutes. Dissolve the charcoal in the alcohol. As soon as the shells come out of the oven, use a stencil or sponge to mark a design on top of them with the charcoal. Let cool before removing from the baking mats.

PREPARING THE DATE PASTE

Remove the pits from the dates and place in a bowl with the orange juice. Mash to a paste using a fork (see Chefs' Notes). Stir in the almonds.

ASSEMBLING THE MACARONS

Spoon the orange blossom filling into a pastry bag fitted with the ¼-in. (6-mm) tip. Pipe a ring of filling over the flat side of half the shells and fill the centers with a mound of date paste. Gently place the rest of the shells on top, with the charcoal pattern visible. Chill for at least 2 hours before serving.

CHEFS' NOTES

It is best to mash the dates by hand
rather than use a food processor
or electric mixer, which could make
the paste turn white.

RAISIN SWIRLS

Pain aux raisins secs

Makes 12

Active time
3 hours

Rising time
2½ hours

Chilling time
3½ hours

Freezing time
30 minutes

Cooking time
15 minutes

Storage
Up to 24 hours

Equipment
Food processor
Stand mixer + dough hook

Ingredients

Raisin pastry cream

Heaping ⅔ cup
(3½ oz./100 g) black
raisins

Generous ¾ cup
(200 ml) water

1¾ cups (450 ml) milk,
divided

⅓ cup (3½ oz./100 g)
egg yolk (5 yolks)

⅓ cup (2½ oz./70 g)
sugar

¼ cup (1½ oz./40 g)
cornstarch

4 tsp (20 ml) rum

Croissant dough

Scant ⅔ cup (145 ml)
whole milk, lukewarm

4 tbsp (2 oz./60 g) butter,
melted

½ oz. (12 g) fresh yeast

1¼ tsp (6 g) salt

3 tbsp (1¼ oz./35 g)
sugar

1 cup plus 2 tbsp
(5¼ oz./150 g) all-
purpose flour

1 cup plus 2 tbsp
(5¼ oz./150 g) white
bread flour

1 stick plus 2 tbsp
(5¼ oz./150 g) butter,
preferably 84% fat

Simple syrup

Scant ½ cup (100 ml)
water

½ cup (3½ oz./100 g)
superfine sugar

CHEFS' NOTES

You can sprinkle rum-soaked raisins
over the swirls after baking
and before brushing them with
the syrup glaze.

PREPARING THE RAISIN PASTRY CREAM

Place the raisins and water in a saucepan and bring to a boil. Remove from the heat and let soak until the raisins are plump. Drain and blend to a rough paste in the food processor with 3½ tbsp (50 ml) of the milk. Pour the remaining milk into the saucepan, stir in the raisin paste, and bring to a boil. Meanwhile, whisk together the egg yolks, sugar, and cornstarch until pale and thick. When the milk and raisin paste come to a boil, whisk a little into the egg yolk mixture, pour it back into the saucepan, and, whisking continuously, return to a boil over medium heat. Let boil for 1 minute, whisking constantly. Remove from the heat and whisk in the rum. Transfer to a bowl, press plastic wrap over the surface, and cool quickly in the refrigerator.

PREPARING THE CROISSANT DOUGH

Combine the warm milk and melted butter in a bowl, crumble in the yeast, and stir to dissolve. Place the salt, sugar, all-purpose flour, and bread flour in the stand mixer. Add the yeast mixture and knead on low speed for 7–8 minutes, until the dough is smooth and slightly elastic. Shape into a ball, cover the bowl with plastic wrap, and let rise at room temperature for 30 minutes. Transfer the dough to a lightly floured surface, flatten it to burst any air bubbles trapped inside, and roll into a 6 × 8-in. (15 × 20-cm) rectangle. Cover with plastic wrap and chill for 1 hour. Using a rolling pin, flatten the 84% fat butter into a 4 × 6-in. (10 × 15-cm) rectangle. Place the butter on the dough and fold it over to enclose the butter, sealing the edges well. Roll the dough into a 6 × 16-in. (15 × 40-cm) rectangle and, with one short side facing you, fold it into three. Rotate it 90° clockwise to make a single turn. Cover the dough with plastic wrap and chill for 1 hour. Roll the dough again into a rectangle. Fold the shorter sides of the dough toward the center, one-third of the way down from the top and two-thirds up from the bottom so the two edges meet. Fold the dough in half like a book, to make a double turn. Cover with plastic wrap and chill for 1 hour. Roll the dough into a 16-in. (40-cm) square with a thickness of ¼ in. (5 mm), cover it with plastic wrap, and chill for 30 minutes.

ASSEMBLING AND BAKING THE RAISIN SWIRLS

Weigh out 9 oz. (250 g) of the raisin pastry cream and spread it in an even layer across the dough, leaving a ¾-in. (2-cm) border at the top. Carefully roll up the dough from bottom to top, brush the border lightly with water, and press the dough edges together to seal them. Freeze the roll for 30 minutes. Cut the roll into 1½-in. (3.5-cm) slices and place them flat on a lined baking sheet. Let rise in a steam oven (or in a conventional oven that is switched off, with a container of boiling water inside) for about 2 hours. Preheat the oven to 325°F (160°C/Gas Mark 3). Bake for 15 minutes, or until puffed and golden. Meanwhile, prepare the simple syrup by heating the water and sugar in a saucepan until the sugar dissolves, then bringing it to a boil. Remove from the heat and brush over the swirls as soon as they come out of the oven.

MONKFISH TAGINE WITH PRUNES AND BLOOD ORANGE BROTH

Tajine de lotte aux pruneaux, bouillon d'orange sanguine

Serves 4

Active time
20 minutes

Cooking time
2 hours 20 minutes

Storage
Up to 2 days
in the refrigerator

Equipment
Oven-safe sauté pan
Tagine dish

Ingredients
5 oz. (140 g) carrots
7¾ oz. (220 g) waxy potatoes
6 baby carrots
6 baby turnips
2½ oz. (70 g) fennel
⅕ oz. (5 g) garlic (about 1 large clove)
2½ oz. (70 g) white onions
1 tbsp (15 ml) olive oil
¾ teaspoon (2 g) ground ginger
½ tsp (1 g) green anise seeds
Scant ½ tsp (1 g) ground cinnamon
Scant ¼ tsp (0.5 g) Sichuan peppercorns
Generous ½ tsp (1.5 g) turmeric
Scant ½ tsp (1 g) ground cumin
Scant 3 cups (700 ml) blood orange juice
14 oz. (400 g) monkfish fillet, skinned and cut into pieces
4¼ oz. (120 g) pitted prunes

To serve
Sliced almonds
Cilantro leaves
Angel hair (Chinese long chilies, dried and finely shredded)

PREPARING THE VEGETABLES AND MONKFISH
Wash the vegetables. Peel the carrots and cut them into approximately 2-in. (5-cm) lengths. Halve or quarter them lengthwise, depending on the size. Peel and quarter the potatoes. Turn each quarter using a paring knife to trim off a little of the outer flesh; work from top to bottom and turn the potato as you do so, until an elongated oval shape is obtained.

Scrub the baby carrots and turnips and cut the fennel into 1-in. (2-cm) wedges. Peel and halve the garlic and remove the germ. Peel the onion and chop it finely.

Sweat the onion in the sauté pan with the olive oil. Add the garlic, followed by the ginger, anise seeds, cinnamon, peppercorns, turmeric, and cumin. Cook briefly until fragrant. Add the orange juice and bring to a boil. Reduce the heat, then let simmer for 1 hour. Taste and adjust the seasoning if necessary. Add the remaining vegetables, cover the pan, and cook over low heat for 1 hour until the vegetables can be easily pierced with the tip of a knife.

When the vegetables are nearly tender, preheat the oven to 200°F (100°C/Gas Mark ¼) on steam setting, if available. Remove the sauté pan from the heat and, using a skimmer, drain the vegetables from the broth. Place them on a tray, cover with plastic wrap, and set aside at room temperature until serving.

Add the monkfish and prunes to the hot broth and place the sauté pan in the oven. If you are using a steam oven, let the fish cook uncovered for 8 minutes. If not, cover the pan and cook the fish for 10 minutes. Immediately remove the fish from the broth to avoid overcooking it. Keep the oven switched on for the next step.

TO SERVE
Arrange the vegetables attractively in the base of the tagine dish. Add the monkfish and prunes and pour in the broth. Put the cover on the dish and place in the oven for 8 minutes. Immediately before serving, sprinkle the tagine with the sliced almonds, cilantro, and angel hair chilies.

DRIED FIG SHORTBREAD COOKIES

Sablés de randonnée à la figue séchée

Makes 6

Active time
1 hour

Chilling time
30 minutes

Cooking time
22 minutes

Storage
Up to 5 days
in an airtight container

Equipment
Stand mixer + paddle beater

6 × 2½-in. (6-cm) baking rings, ¾ in. (1.5 cm) deep

Silicone baking mat

Instant-read thermometer

Food processor

2 pastry bags

Ingredients

Breton shortbread

2 sticks (9 oz./250 g) butter, softened

1 cup plus 1 tbsp (7½ oz./210 g) superfine sugar

1 tbsp (20 g) date syrup

Scant ½ cup (4½ oz./125 g) egg yolk (about 6 yolks)

3 cups (12 oz./350 g) all-purpose flour

3¾ tsp (14 g) baking powder

¾ tsp (3 g) *fleur de sel*

¼ oz. (8 g) finely grated lemon zest

1 oz. (30 g) candied lemon, cut into 1/16-in. (2-mm) dice

Scant ¼ cup (1 oz./30 g) pumpkin seeds

5 oz. (150 g) dried figs, cut into thin strips

Almond and pumpkin seed praline paste

¼ cup (1¼ oz./35 g) blanched almonds (see technique p. 30)

1 cup (4¾ oz./135 g) pumpkin seeds

½ cup plus 1 tbsp (4 oz./110 g) superfine sugar

Seeds of 1 vanilla bean

¾ tsp (3 g) *fleur de sel*

Fig caramel

¼ cup (60 ml) heavy cream, min. 35% fat

1¾ oz. (50 g) fig puree

⅓ cup (2½ oz./70 g) superfine sugar

3 tbsp plus scant 1 tsp (2½ oz./70 g) glucose syrup

2 tbsp (1 oz./30 g) butter

½ tsp (2 g) *fleur de sel*

Decoration

Dried figs, cut into thin strips

PREPARING THE BRETON SHORTBREAD

Preheat the oven to 340°F (170°C/Gas Mark 3). Cream the butter, sugar, and date syrup together in the bowl of the stand mixer. Beat in the egg yolks, then add the flour, baking powder, *fleur de sel*, and lemon zest until just combined. Add the candied lemon, pumpkin seeds, and dried figs, and mix on medium-low speed. Gather the dough into a disk with your hands, cover in plastic wrap, and chill for 30 minutes. Place the baking rings on the silicone baking mat, divide the dough into six equal pieces, and lightly press each piece into a baking ring in an even layer with a thickness of ¾ in. (1.5 cm), using your fingertips. Bake for 12 minutes until lightly golden. Let cool completely in the rings.

PREPARING THE PRALINE PASTE

Preheat the oven to 300°F (150°C/Gas Mark 2). Spread the almonds and pumpkin seeds out over a lined baking sheet and toast them in the oven for 10 minutes. Make a dry caramel by heating the sugar in a heavy-bottomed saucepan over low heat, without adding water, until the sugar dissolves to form a syrup. Boil until the syrup becomes a golden-brown caramel and the temperature reaches a maximum of 340°F (170°C). Pour the caramel over the toasted almonds and pumpkin seeds on the baking sheet and let cool. Remove from the sheet, break into pieces, and grind to a smooth paste in the food processor. Add the vanilla seeds and *fleur de sel* and pulse to blend. Transfer to one of the pastry bags.

PREPARING THE FIG CARAMEL

In a saucepan, bring the cream and fig puree to a boil. Meanwhile, heat the sugar and glucose syrup in a separate saucepan until they dissolve, then cook to a golden-brown caramel. Stir in the butter until melted. Carefully stir in the cream and fig puree, followed by the *fleur de sel*. Cook until the temperature reaches 228°F (109°C). Transfer to a bowl and press plastic wrap over the surface. Let cool, then chill until using.

ASSEMBLING THE COOKIES

Place the fig caramel in the second pastry bag. Remove the baking rings from the shortbread and pipe small mounds of almond and pumpkin seed praline paste and fig caramel attractively over each one. Arrange the strips of dried fig over the top.

DRIED APRICOT LOAF CAKE

Cake aux abricots secs

Serves 6

Active time
1 hour

Chilling time
10–20 minutes

Cooking time
40 minutes

Storage
Up to 5 days in a dry place, well covered in plastic wrap, or up to 3 months in the freezer

Equipment
Food processor

2 pastry bags + plain ½ in. (12-mm) and ⅓-in. (10-mm) tips

6 × 3-in. (16 × 8-cm) loaf pan

Ingredients

Dried apricot jam

3½ tbsp (50 ml) water

1½ oz. (45 g) dried apricots

2½ oz. (70 g) apricot puree

Cake batter

Generous ½ cup (4¾ oz./135 g) lightly beaten egg (about 2¾ eggs)

¾ cup (4¾ oz./135 g) superfine sugar

1 stick plus 1 tbsp (4¾ oz./135 g) butter, diced and softened

½ cup minus 1 tbsp (1¾ oz./50 g) all-purpose flour

Generous 2 tbsp (22 g) custard powder

½ tsp (2 g) baking powder

Scant 1 cup (3 oz./90 g) almond flour

2 oz. (55 g) dried apricot jam (see above)

1½ oz. (40 g) dried apricots, finely chopped

Almond dacquoise

Scant ½ cup (3½ oz./100 g) egg white (about 3 whites)

Scant ⅓ cup (2 oz./60 g) superfine sugar

1 cup (3½ oz./100 g) almond flour

¼ cup (1¼ oz./35 g) confectioners' sugar

2 tbsp (20 g) all-purpose flour

To assemble

Butter for the pan

Scant ¼ cup (20 g) sliced almonds

Decoration

2 tbsp (1 oz./30 g) apricot glaze, warmed

Dried apricot jam

A few candied apricots, cut lengthwise into strips

PREPARING THE DRIED APRICOT JAM

Place the water and dried apricots in a bowl and microwave on high for 1 minute until the apricots have softened. Drain, place in the food processor with the apricot puree, and reduce to a coarse puree. Chill until assembling.

PREPARING THE CAKE BATTER

Whisk together the eggs and sugar in a mixing bowl until pale and thick. Gradually whisk in the butter until combined. In a separate bowl, mix together the all-purpose flour, custard powder, baking powder, and almond flour. Gradually fold into the whisked mixture until just combined. Finally, fold in the dried apricot jam and dried apricots. Chill the batter until baking.

PREPARING THE ALMOND DACQUOISE

Whisk the egg whites until they hold soft peaks. Gradually whisk in the superfine sugar until the peaks are firm and glossy. Sift the almond flour, confectioners' sugar, and all-purpose flour together. Gradually sprinkle over the meringue, folding in each addition using a flexible spatula before adding the next. When combined, spoon the batter into a pastry bag with the ½-in. (12-mm) tip.

ASSEMBLING AND BAKING THE CAKE

Preheat the oven to 340°F (170°C/Gas Mark 3). Grease the loaf pan with butter and cover the base and sides with the sliced almonds, lining them up end to end in neat rows. Freeze for 10 minutes or refrigerate for 20 minutes, so the butter firms up and holds the almonds in place. Pipe the dacquoise batter over the base and up the sides of the pan to cover the almonds. Pour the cake batter into the center. Bake for 4 minutes, then reduce the oven temperature to 325°F (160°C), cover the cake with a sheet of parchment paper and a wire rack, and continue to bake for an additional 30 minutes, or until a knife inserted into the cake comes out clean. Turn the cake out onto a wire rack and let cool completely.

DECORATING THE CAKE

When the cake has cooled to room temperature, trim the ends. Brush the warm apricot glaze over the top and sides of the cake. Spoon some of the remaining dried apricot jam into a pastry bag with the ⅓-in. (10-mm) tip and pipe a line down one side of the top of the cake. Arrange the candied apricot strips attractively over the jam.

CRÉMET D'ANJOU AND GOJI BERRY BOWLS

Crémet d'Anjou aux baies de goji

Serves 4

Active time
30 minutes

Soaking time
Overnight

Chilling time
At least 3 hours

Storage
Up to 2 days
in the refrigerator
before assembling

Equipment
Food-safe cheesecloth

4 perforated 2½-in.
(6-cm) half-sphere molds
or 4 small soft cheese
strainers (*pots à faisselle*)

Ingredients

Goji berries

Scant ½ cup
(2½ oz./70 g) goji berries

Generous ⅓ cup (90 ml)
fresh orange juice, plus
more as needed

Crémet d'Anjou

Scant ½ cup (100 ml)
heavy cream, min. 35%
fat

2 tsp (8 g) superfine
sugar

Seeds of 1 vanilla bean

1½ tbsp (20 g) egg white
(about 1 small white)

⅛ tsp (0.5 g) fine salt

Decoration

2 tbsp (20 g) toasted
sesame seeds

Baby garden cress leaves

SOAKING THE GOJI BERRIES (1 DAY AHEAD)

Place the goji berries and orange juice in a bowl. Cover and let soak overnight in the refrigerator. The berries need to be moist and plump; if they look dry, add more orange juice as needed.

PREPARING THE CRÉMET D'ANJOU

Whip the cream with the sugar and vanilla seeds until it holds its shape. In a separate bowl, whisk the egg white with the salt until it holds firm peaks. Fold the white into the whipped cream. Line the molds with cheesecloth, leaving enough overhang to fold over the mousse mixture. Fill each mold with the mousse and cover completely with the overhanging cheesecloth. Stand the molds in a shallow dish, place in the refrigerator, and let drain for at least 3 hours.

ASSEMBLING THE BOWLS

Divide the goji berries between four serving bowls, placing about 3 tablespoons in each one. Remove the cheesecloth from the top of each crémet and lift the crémet carefully out of its mold. Place it upside down over the berries and peel away the cheesecloth. Sprinkle each crémet with the sesame seeds and decorate with a few leaves of garden cress.

CHEFS' NOTES

If you do not have suitable perforated molds,
use empty yogurt containers with small holes punched
at regular intervals in the sides and over the base.

APPENDIXES

GENERAL ADVICE

Bain-marie

A way of gently heating delicate mixtures such as chocolate or egg-based creams and sauces that can separate or burn easily. A stovetop bain-marie consists of a heatproof bowl set over a saucepan of barely simmering water, with the bottom of the bowl not touching the water. A double boiler can be used instead. A bain-marie used in the oven for baking flans and custards prevents the eggs from curdling and the tops from drying out and cracking by surrounding them with an even, gentle heat.

Butter

Unless the ingredients for a recipe state otherwise, use unsalted butter, preferably with a butterfat content of least 82%. The higher its fat content, the less water the butter contains, which equates to richer, more flavorful creams, sauces, ganaches, and flakier crusts. A high butterfat content is particularly important when making laminated doughs such as puff pastries, which benefit from butter with a minimum 84% butterfat content being used. When a recipe calls for softened butter, remove the butter from the refrigerator at least 30 minutes before starting.

Cream

Unless stated otherwise, use cream with a minimum of 35% fat. Higher fat creams can be whipped and are less likely to curdle when added to hot mixtures. In the US, look for products labeled "heavy cream" or "heavy whipping cream"; in the UK, use double or whipping cream.

Degrees Brix and refractometers

Degrees Brix (°Brix), a measure of the sweetness or sugar content in a liquid, is determined with a refractometer. While not essential, refractometers are useful in preparing fruit-based recipes such as jams, jellies, syrups, ice creams, and sorbets. Knowing the exact sugar content in your preparations helps ensure consistently good results. When making jam, for instance, a final sugar content of 60–65% (including natural and added sugars) is ideal. This prevents most harmful microorganisms from growing, it improves the storage time, and the preserve is not overly sweet. One degree Brix is equivalent to 1% sugar in a liquid, so if the refractometer measures 10 degrees, it means the liquid contains 10% sugar. For making the recipes in this book, look for a refractometer with a Brix scale range of 0–80%, and use according to the manufacturer's instructions.

Eggs

Hens' eggs are used in these recipes with their quantities mainly given by weight and volume, as well as the approximate number of whole eggs, egg white, or egg yolk. Unless otherwise specified, the number given is based on a standard "large" egg in the US and Canada and "medium" egg in the UK, with an average in-shell weight of about 2 oz. (55 g). Remove eggs from the refrigerator about 30 minutes before you intend to use them so they have time to come to room temperature and are the same temperature as your other ingredients.

Fresh yeast

Fresh yeast can be found in the refrigerated sections of larger supermarkets, purchased online or possibly from your local bakery or pizzeria. If you cannot find it, substitute 50% of the weight of fresh yeast with active dry yeast, or 40% with instant yeast, following the instructions on the package.

Gelatin

Gelatin is available in sheet and powder form, and can often be used interchangeably. Both types must first be hydrated in water and then fully dissolved in a warm liquid (no hotter than 158°F/70°C). To rehydrate sheet gelatin, soak the sheets in a bowl of cold water (it will only absorb the amount it needs so the quantity of water does not need to be measured) for about 5 minutes or until the sheets soften. Once soft, squeeze the sheets to remove excess water and add them immediately to your mixture, which must be hot but not boiling, as this will adversely affect the gelatin's setting properties. Stir until the sheets dissolve and are evenly incorporated into the mixture. Gold-strength gelatin sheets, which have a setting power of 200 Bloom and generally weigh $\frac{1}{10}$ oz. (2 g) each, are recommended for the recipes in this book. To rehydrate powdered gelatin, sprinkle it over the quantity of cold water specified in the recipe and let soak for about 10 minutes until the granules have swollen and absorbed the water. Stir it into a hot liquid until the gelatin is dissolved and evenly incorporated. Plant-based alternatives to gelatin are available and include agar-agar, carrageen, and vegan jel.

Measurements

For successful results, it is always advisable to weigh your ingredients using a digital scale, preferably using metric weights. The volume and imperial measures included throughout this book have been rounded up or down to avoid awkward or unmeasurable amounts. When using cups and spoons, they must be level unless stated otherwise.

INDEX

Acknowledgments

We would like to thank
Marine Mora and the **Matfer Bourgeat** group
as well as the **Mora store** for the utensils and equipment.

www.matferbourgeat.com
www.mora.fr